LOVELAND PUBLIC LIBRARY

000522369

12/23/13
$26.99
B&T
A S
Large
Type
14 days

1114

The Trident

Withdrawn

The Forging and Reforging of a Navy SEAL Leader

Jason Redman
with John R. Bruning

HARPER LUXE

An Imprint of HarperCollinsPublishers

This is a work of nonfiction. The events and experiences depicted in this book are all true and have been faithfully rendered as the author remembered them, to the best of his ability. Some names and identities have been changed, however, in order to protect the anonymity or security of the various individuals involved.

THE TRIDENT. Copyright © 2013 by Jason Redman. All rights reserved. Printed in the United States of America. No part of this book may be used or reproduced in any manner whatsoever without written permission except in the case of brief quotations embodied in critical articles and reviews. For information address HarperCollins Publishers, 10 East 53rd Street, New York, NY 10022.

HarperCollins books may be purchased for educational, business, or sales promotional use. For information, please e-mail the Special Markets Department at SPsales@harpercollins.com.

FIRST HARPERLUXE EDITION

HarperLuxe™ is a trademark of HarperCollins Publishers

Library of Congress Cataloging-in-Publication Data is available upon request.

ISBN: 978-0-06-227843-2

13 14 ID/RRD 10 9 8 7 6 5 4 3 2 1

The US Navy SEAL Trident appears on the front cover of this book with the permission of the Department of the Navy. Although the Department of the Navy has reviewed this book for security purposes, all views presented are those of the author and do not necessarily represent the views of the Department of the Navy, the Department of Defense, the United States Government, or any components thereof.

This book is dedicated to my wife and kids.
Their love brought me home.

This book is also dedicated to the warriors, those men and women who are willing to go beyond the city walls and slay dragons . . . who are willing to go into the lion's den again and again . . . and who sometimes don't come back out. Specifically, it is for my Naval Special Warfare brothers who answered the call after 9/11 and never made it back home.

Ensign (SEAL) Jerry "Buck" Pope—Yemen—2002
HMC (SEAL) Matthew J. Bourgeois—Afghanistan—2002
ABH1 (SEAL) Neil C. Roberts—Afghanistan—2002
CDR (SEAL) Peter G. Oswald—El Salvador—2002
PH1 (SEAL) David M. Tapper—Afghanistan—2003
IT2 (SEAL) Mario Maestas—Training—2003
IC1 (SEAL) Thomas E. Retzer—Afghanistan—2003
BM1 (SEAL) Brian Ouellette—Afghanistan—2004
BM1 (SWCC) Robert P. Vetter—Training—2004
HMCS (SEAL) Theodore D. Fitzhenry—Training—2004
LT (SEAL) Michael P. Murphy—Afghanistan—2005
GM2 (SEAL) Danny P. Dietz—Afghanistan—2005
STG2 (SEAL) Matthew G. Axelson—Afghanistan—2005

ITCS (SEAL) Daniel R. Healy—Afghanistan—2005

QM2 (SEAL) James Suh—Afghanistan—2005

MM2 (SEAL) Shane Patton—Afghanistan—2005

LCDR (SEAL) Erik S. Kristensen—Afghanistan—2005

LT (SEAL) Michael M. McGreevy Jr.—Afghanistan—2005

FCC (SEAL) Jacques J. Fontan—Afghanistan—2005

HM1 (SEAL) Jeffrey S. Taylor—Afghanistan—2005

ET1 (SEAL) Jeffrey A. Lucas—Afghanistan—2005

AO2 (SEAL) Marc A. Lee—Iraq—2006

MA2 (SEAL) Michael A. Monsoor—Iraq—2006

SN Freddie Porter—Training—2007

SO2 Joseph C. Schwedler—Iraq—2007

SO1 Jason D. Lewis—Iraq—2007

MC1 Robert R. McRill—Iraq—2007

CTT1 Steven P. Daugherty—Iraq—2007

SOC Mark T. Carter—Iraq—2007

SOC Jason R. Freiwald—Afghanistan—2008

SOCS John W. Marcum—Afghanistan—2008

SO1 Joshua T. Harris—Afghanistan—2008

SOCS Thomas J. Valentine—Training—2008

SOC Lance M. Vaccaro—Training—2008

SO2 Shapoor "Alex" Ghane—Training—2008

EOD1 Luis Souffront—Iraq—2008

SOC Michael Koch—Iraq—2008

SOC Nathan Hardy—Iraq—2008

PR1 Andrew J. Lightner—Training—2009

SOC Eric F. Shellenberger—Training—2009

SO2 Ryan Job—Wounded Iraq 2006—United States—2009

EOD2 Tyler J. Trahan—Iraq—2009

LT Brendan J. Looney—Afghanistan—2010

CTRCS David B. McClendon—Afghanistan—2010

SO2 Adam O. Smith—Afghanistan—2010

SO3 Denis C. Miranda—Afghanistan—2010

SOC Adam Brown—Afghanistan—2010

SO1 Tyler Stimson—United States—2010

SO2 Ronald Woodle—Training—2010

SOC Collin Thomas—Afghanistan—2010

SO1 Caleb A. Nelson—Afghanistan—2011

LCDR (SEAL) Jonas Kelsall—Afghanistan—2011

SOCM Louis Langlais—Afghanistan—2011

SOCS Thomas Ratzlaff—Afghanistan—2011

SOCS Robert Reeves—Afghanistan—2011

SOCS Heath Robinson—Afghanistan—2011

EODCS Kraig Vickers—Afghanistan—2011

SOC Brian Bill—Afghanistan—2011

SO1 Aaron Vaughn—Afghanistan—2011

SO1 Christopher Campbell—Afghanistan—2011

SO1 Darrik Benson—Afghanistan—2011

IT1 Jared Day—Afghanistan—2011

SO1 Jason Workman—Afghanistan—2011

SO1 Jesse Pittman—Afghanistan—2011

MA1 John Douangdara—Afghanistan—2011

SOC John Faas—Afghanistan—2011

SO1 Jon Tumilson—Afghanistan—2011

SOC Kevin Houston—Afghanistan—2011

SOC Matthew Mason—Afghanistan—2011

CTR1 Michael Strange—Afghanistan—2011

EODC Nicholas Null—Afghanistan—2011

SO2 Nicholas Spehar—Afghanistan—2011

SOC Stephen Mills—Afghanistan—2011

LT Thomas C. Fouke—Training—2012

SO1 Patrick D. Feeks—Afghanistan—2012

SO1 David J. Warsen—Afghanistan—2012

GM2 Dion R. Roberts—Afghanistan—2012

SO1 Mathew G. Kantor—Afghanistan—2012

SO1 Kevin R. Ebbert—Afghanistan—2012

SO1 Nicolas D. Checque—Afghanistan—2012

CDR (SEAL) Job Price—Afghanistan—2012

SO1 Matthew Leathers—Training—2013

CTTC Christian M. Pike—Afghanistan—2013

SOC Chris Kyle—United States—2013

SOC Brett Shadle—Training—2013

SO3 Jonathan H. Kaloust—Training—2013

The mark of a man is not found in his past,
but how he overcomes adversity and builds his future.
Quitting is not an option.
Regardless of the overwhelming odds or obstacles in
   your path,
you always have an opportunity to overcome.
It is your attitude that will determine the outcome.

JCR

Foreword

I first met Lieutenant Jay Redman at Bethesda Naval Hospital where he was recuperating from his many wounds. He had posted a sign on his door that, for me, spoke for so many of our wounded in its message of courage, resolve, and optimism. I was deeply moved and later would welcome Jay and his family to my office. As the wars in Iraq and Afghanistan raged on, he and his story would continue to inspire me.

This book is about Lieutenant Redman's journey serving his country. It is an admirably honest account of a young man going through the toughest physical training imaginable only to discover along the way that physical toughness, tactical proficiency, and bravado are not the principal attributes of a successful warrior leader; that even more important on the battlefield are self-discipline, character, and the ability to earn the trust and confidence of one's comrades, superiors, and subordinates. And embracing personal accountability and responsibility for one's actions. This book is about that journey of discovery before and after Jay's near-fatal wounding, a journey that ended in success due in large part, as he writes, to the steadfast support and love of his equally courageous and resolute wife.

His story of healing, like combat, is the story of a team: his wife and family, doctors and nurses, his friends and fellow warriors, all of whom helped restore him. In this story, he is representative of all who have been wounded in these wars and their long road to recovery. This, too, is a story of courage and heroism.

One of my senior military assistants, Vice Admiral Joe Kernan, is a SEAL and commanded SEALs in combat, and eventually commanded all SEALs. We talked a lot about Jay Redman, and Joe once told me that the quality most needed to become a SEAL was not physical but mental toughness. This was driven home for me one Friday morning in Coronado, California, when I stood in front of a wet, cold, and exhausted SEAL training class and informed them their Hell Week was over. It was clear that only their minds were keeping them on their feet after six days of near continuous, exhausting physical exertion. But I believe Redman's mental toughness went beyond even this and is reflected in his candor describing his flaws and deficiencies, and his humble account of the people and circumstances that helped him overcome them.

There already are many books on the wars in Iraq and Afghanistan. There will be more, including by those who experienced the fire of combat. This story, though, is not just about a SEAL on the Iraqi battlefield, but a SEAL at war with himself, and his ultimate victory. I believe his story will inspire the reader, just as it did me.

Robert M. Gates
SECRETARY OF DEFENSE, 2006–2011

Author's Note

The US Navy SEAL Teams have received unprec-edented exposure over the last several years. A small segment of the community welcome the exposure while the vast majority wish all the attention would go away, adhering to the original humble roots of the SEAL Teams, which hold on to the tenet "The deed is all, not the glory." Every man who has decided to talk has his reasons to do so. I originally chose not to, but as I began to speak to friends and leaders about the ups and downs of my personal journey, they encouraged me to share my story.

Over the last six years, I have had ample time to reflect on my twenty-year career in the SEAL Teams. I served in Iraq, Afghanistan, and various hot spots in South and Central America during deployments both pre- and post-9/11. I took pride in my accomplishments, but I also forced myself to face difficult truths about who I was when I was a younger man. I thought about those lessons from my own experience as I spent long weeks in hospital beds around the United States. I wish I'd paused and been so contemplative earlier in my life. I wrote this book to be both a signpost toward a successful future and a cautionary tale of hubris.

I grew up in a community of warriors, but I possessed an immaturity that lingered far too long. Hard lessons showed me the right path, and with help from admirable and respected friends, I found myself taking it. In time, I learned the true meaning of leadership, and the responsibility required to lead men into battle. Today, I look back and feel supremely honored to have been with men far better than me on missions bigger than all of us.

Many of the SEAL narratives written over the years have portrayed us as infallible machines. We are not. We are humans, driven to achieve and be the best at what we do—but still humans complete with all the frailties built into our species. How we manage those frailties is one of the reasons for our success. My story sheds some light on that reality and how I overcame my own shortcomings.

Being a SEAL took me to the edge and beyond. It shaped me into who I am today. When I look back, I liken my path to that of an ancient sword being made into an effective combat weapon. I was selected and hardened, hammered and sharpened, until I was finally used in battle. But the rigors of combat revealed my flaws, and I was broken at one point. A second chance reforged me into a better leader and allowed me the honor of fighting alongside some of the greatest warriors this nation has ever produced.

This is my journey.

JCR

Prologue

Colombia, South America
1997

I stood in the middle of Mother Nature's dumping ground for her most sadistic creations and smiled. This was the place to be. Beneath the triple canopy rain forest lurked jaguars, caiman, panthers, and the fer-de-lance viper that can kill a grown man in minutes with its deadly venom. At times, the jungle floor would be carpeted by hundreds of thousands of red ants, moving like a Roman legion as they devoured anything in their path. Vampire bats lurked in the darkness after sundown. Even the caterpillars here in the jungle could poison you.

I remember when I volunteered for this deployment, one of our old salts warned me, "Don't forget, never sleep on the ground because everything in the jungle wants to kill you."

I could live with the snakes and the caiman and the piranhas lurking in the eddies and pools that skirted the Guaviare River. I drew the line at the microscopic fish called the candiru that the locals told us liked to swim into a man's urethra and jab its spiked dorsal fin into the soft tissue there. I was a dedicated patriot and SEAL, but that was a boundary I didn't want to cross. I steered clear of the river whenever I could—I wouldn't even take a leak near it, lest those little demon fish could swim upstream.

The small outpost we had been assigned to was the South American jungle version of a Foreign Legion fortress. Forty miles from the nearest settlement, it sat astride the Guaviare River surrounded by virgin rain forest. If the things living in the river sparked alarm, the water itself wasn't much better. It moved with sludge-like speed, an ocher-colored mess of mud and jungle debris that was a nightmare for our boats to navigate. During the days, the temperature hit almost a hundred degrees before noon. The humidity made us sweat like we were running marathons even while hunkered down in the shade with water, not that there was any ice to cool it. After our first day in-country, I gave up trying to stay clean. The minute you stepped out of the shower to dry off, you'd start sweating again. By the time you dressed, your uniform was already stained from perspiration.

Despite the natural and man-made dangers and heat, I loved every minute of it. Colombia was my first real deployment after I joined my first SEAL platoon. We were based out of Panama at the time, a place I also remember fondly. We had a great platoon made up mostly of new guys, and after we finished training for the day, we'd hit the bars. We partied and trained and became brothers in that tropical paradise.

One night a few months before I found myself on my Colombian vacation, we were getting particularly festive in a Panamanian American neighborhood in the Canal Zone. A fire broke out not far from us, and a fire truck came roaring through our soiree. The party had spread to the house across the street, and by the time the fire trucks arrived at least four hundred people stood in the yards and in the middle of the street between the two houses. I was on one side of the street practicing my Spanish and a buddy of mine, Bill Jensen, was on the other. When the fire trucks, sirens blaring, horns blasting, finally managed to part the crowd like the Red Sea, I found myself within reach of the platform on the back of the truck so I did what any young hell-raiser would do: I jumped onto the back of the fire truck. Suddenly clear of the throng of people, the fire truck gunned it and I found myself hanging on for dear life. I looked over to my right and there was Bill hanging on and yelling like we were on a roller coaster. Who knew that two young drunken idiot friends could have the same good bad idea? We rode it almost all the way to the fire, whooping and hollering and having the time of our lives. Then we realized we'd have to jump off while the rig was still moving if we were going to get back to the party. That landing in the ditch next to the road still elicits a wince when I think about it. We hiked back to the party, grabbed another beer, and carried on with the rest of the night.

The camaraderie and friendships I built during those months in Panama lasted the rest of my life. I will always cherish those memories. I was young— barely twenty-two years old—and through hard work, luck, and a lot of mental toughness, I'd joined a warrior fraternity filled with men I admired, whose skill and professionalism were unsurpassed in the field of arms. So was their ability to party during our downtime. Life at full speed in the service of our nation—I embraced every second of it.

But I wanted more. I was a fresh-faced junior new guy—an E-4 intelligence specialist who'd never been tested under fire. During the '90s there were very few hot spots around the world where you could go as a Naval Special Warfare operator and see combat. With the drug war waging, Colombia was one of those places that you had a remote chance, and in those pre-9/11 days, combat experience was the Holy Grail. Few had it. The hardest chargers coveted it.

When a chance to deploy to Colombia for a month came up, I jumped at it. I packed my bags and got on the bird and found myself in the middle of a jungle hell-hole so sparse and run-down that our fellow Americans would have condemned the place.

We lived in corrugated tin Quonset huts left over from the Second World War. The place functioned as a training facility for the Colombian Army. Those Colombians were a motley group, and teaching them to fight had its moments. Though my primary duty was as an aspiring intel expert, all of us served as tactical instructors to teach some of the basic shooting and fire and movement drills on the rifle range. We used to run alongside the conscripts when they moved from station to station and took aim and fired at targets, just to make sure they didn't do something stupid. They frequently did. Once, I was pacing a teenage farmer conscript with all of about six weeks in uniform. At one point, his rusty Belgian-made FAL rifle jammed. Instead of taking a minute to clear it properly, he grabbed the weapon by the barrel and tried to peer inside. I saw the muzzle come up toward his eye and snatched it right out of his hands before he could make a canoe out of his skull.

I couldn't get too mad at him. Many of the conscripts couldn't read or write and had no life experience or knowledge of firearms. Most had lived on the fringes of the modern world their entire lives. Television was a novelty for the majority of them.

It was our job to train, motivate, and professionalize the Colombian Army as it struggled to win a war against the Hydra-like drug cartels that flooded America's streets with cheap cocaine. I relished the work and found some of their soldiers earnestly interested in improving themselves and their country. Those were guys I respected, and I gave them all I had. I enjoyed their culture and thoroughly enjoyed working with them. At the same time, I knew we couldn't get too carried away. A lot of those soldiers were double agents and worked for the Fuerzas Armadas Revolucionarias de Colombia, or FARC, as many in the small nation affectionately called them. They were the twenty-thousand-strong insurgent army that worked to destabilize the Colombian government and protected Colombia's coke lords.

When we helped plan raids on drug warehouses, or manufacture sites, we had to be very careful about who gained knowledge of the operation and when. We learned the hard way that operational security, or OPSEC, was essential in this jungle. Eyes and ears were always in our midst. Thanks to the easy money flowing from the drug trade, spies in uniform abounded.

We did conduct a few joint missions with the Colombians outside the wire. Most were surveillance-related with little chance for contact with a hostile force. Not to say they were not dangerous, though. One night, we'd been sent to recover some of our sensors that we had placed in the jungle a few days earlier. One of the Colombian officers with us warned, "The rebels like to booby-trap such things."

Our detachment's senior chief, Rex Digby, turned to me and said, "Okay, FNG . . . go get 'em."

I stepped forward with my mind racing. I was so paranoid that everything around the sensor site looked like a possible booby trap. But I circled it anyway, searching for any tangible sign of a trip wire or half-buried explosive device. It was the first moment of my life where I thought I might be facing death, yet I was slightly less concerned about being blown up than I was about getting yelled at for doing something stupid. So I studied the area intently until I was absolutely convinced the rebels hadn't messed with our sensor. I was right, and I learned that night to trust my gut while doing dangerous things carefully.

One summer afternoon a few weeks later, I was sweltering away inside our Quonset hut writing an intel report when a single gunshot rang out. A moment later, one of the Colombians came running over and said, "We've got a wounded man. Can you help?"

Our senior chief, Rex, also functioned as our detachment's corpsman. He grabbed his medical bag and assured the Colombians, "We'll do what we can."

As he headed for the door, he turned to me and said, "Hey, New Guy, let's go."

I'd always been fascinated by medicine and had been thinking about becoming a corpsman after this deployment as the next step in my career progression, so I jumped at the opportunity. Together, the two of us ran through the stifling heat until we found the Colombians' wounded man. He lay sprawled on his back, a ragged hole in his face.

Rex set his gear down and knelt before the man. I did the same, helping out whenever Rex asked me to do something. A quick exam told us most of what we needed to know. The Colombian had taken a bullet in the left cheek just below his eye. The round most likely had lodged in his brain. No exit wound pointed to that.

"What happened?" Rex asked.

A Colombian officer stepped forward and said in Spanish that the rebels had fired harassing shots from the jungle, and this soldier caught one of them while on duty.

Rex and I exchanged glances. That would have been a million-to-one shot. Those things happen at times, but both of us saw the officer's pistol on his hip, the holster flap unbuckled, and wondered if there may have been a different version of events.

Rex checked the man's pulse. Very shallow and erratic. Given the nature of the wound, I was surprised at how little blood he'd lost.

Rex said, "Get the J-hook into his mouth and open the airway."

I reached into Rex's bag and found the instrument. Inserting it into the Colombian's mouth, I moved it into his jaw and rotated it to open his airway. No air escaped so it was possible the bullet had bounced around and done damage to his airway.

"Jay, we need to do a cricothyroidotomy."

"Roger. What do you need from me?"

Rex produced a scalpel and handed it to me. In a low voice he said, "Look, this guy's pretty much dead, and there is nothing we can really do to save him, but we have to act like it to save face with our Colombian counterparts, okay?"

I nodded as I learned my first lesson in international relations.

"Make the incision."

I'd never cut into anything alive before, but after all the training I'd been through I knew that I had the capacity to learn almost anything. Rex talked me through it. I felt down the man's neck to the divot by his Adam's apple. I found the spot and put the blade to skin. But I didn't push hard enough, and as I made the incision, I didn't get through the cartilage to open his airway.

Rex took the scalpel and showed me how to do it. I watched carefully, making mental notes. I hated to make the same mistake twice—it was a source of professional pride with me that I could learn most things after only being shown once. Next time I was in this situation, I wouldn't be so gentle.

"We gotta start CPR," Rex told me.

I shifted and began compressing the Colombian's chest as I had been taught in our trauma medical training. Rex continued to work on him. We bagged him and got him on a stretcher.

"We need to get him to a hospital," Rex told the Colombian officer, still hovering nearby as he watched us work.

The nearest medical facility was an hour away downstream. We rushed him to the dock, where our special boat team deployed with us had a riverine patrol boat waiting. With a hard plastic hull and a powerful engine, it could reach speeds of over forty miles an hour. If the rebels messed with us, we had three machine guns with which to defend ourselves.

We piled aboard and cast off. For an hour, the crew bobbed and weaved around floating debris and obstacles as Rex and I continued CPR. We kept the soldier alive—but only as a vegetable. Finally, we reached the nearest settlement and carried the wounded soldier to the local medical clinic. The place looked like a horror movie set—rusty instruments, moldy walls, sheets that were filthy and bloodstained. Many of the overhead lights had burned out, giving the rooms a dark and dismal ambience.

We turned our patient over to the local docs, but he died a short time later. His brain had been almost totally destroyed by that bullet, and it was a miracle he hadn't succumbed earlier. That we'd tried everything we could to save him earned us a lot of respect from the Colombians, though they never did fess up to what had really happened. Rex and I talked about it later, and it seemed much more likely the officer had lost his temper and shot the soldier in a heated moment. This was my first encounter with a gunshot wound and someone I worked with dying.

Not long after the Colombian died, we received an intel report warning us that four hundred armed rebels were moving through the jungle toward our little outpost. We had less than a quarter of that force, with no prospects of American reinforcements. Each night, the intel reports grew more dire as the large force closed the distance to us. They'd been known to test the outpost's defenses with hit-and-run attacks, but never had they assembled the size of force that moved our way.

The night before we expected them to arrive, the machine guns guarding our perimeter suddenly lit up the darkness. On every corner of the perimeter of the camp, Colombians had an M-60 machine gun and a 40mm grenade launcher, and as I lay in my bunk, I was suddenly and violently awakened by the sound of all four corners going cyclic on their machine guns. Amid the automatic fire I could hear the *Crump! Crump! Crump!* of 40mm shells exploding somewhere in the jungle beyond the wire.

I quickly rolled over and looked out the window next to my bunk. I could see muzzle flashes, flares shooting skyward, and the red-orange blossom of grenade blasts. Just in case the rebels attacked us earlier than we anticipated, I'd gone to bed that night still dressed in my battle uniform. I jumped off the bunk onto our weapons box, pulled my boots on, and grabbed my rifle hanging from the end of my bed. Rex dashed in just as another long burst of machine-gun fire echoed through the night.

"Jay, get our backpack radios and come outside with me."

Though I wasn't a trained communications specialist, I had been learning to maintain our detachment's primary radios. As an intel guy, I ended up using them a lot of the time anyway. We had two set in racks side by side in a hard-shell mount that looked sort of like a ruggedized desktop computer's tower.

I followed Rex to a blast wall directly outside our Quonset hut and about a hundred yards from the perimeter. More flares arched into the blackness around us. The machine guns chewed away the jungles beyond. The 40mm blasted off again as the Colombians ran back and forth, manning positions along the wire or dragging ammo to the guns.

"Here," Rex said, handing me two thermite incendiary grenades.

"What are these for?" I asked.

"Prep them. If we have to leave in a hurry and I tell you, go destroy the radio towers and computer equipment."

The thought of blowing them up drove home the magnitude of the moment. Rex was afraid we were about to be overrun.

Eyes huge, I replied, "All right. I got this."

Rex told me to be ready to slip into the jungle to escape and evade, or E&E, the enemy. This is something we'd trained for a lot. One of the first things we did before reaching this outpost was to develop an E&E plan for this specific area. That way, if the worst did happen, we'd know where to meet up and how to get out. But the reality that we might soon have to be crawling through the dense jungle with the caterpillars and ants and anacondas for miles, evading rebel patrols as we tried to find a way to contact our fellow Americans, left me feeling thunderstruck.

The firing continued for what seemed like an hour. The Colombians raked the jungle, blew trees to splinters, and popped off thousands of dollars of star shells and parachute flares. I stood alone beside the blast wall, rifle ready and scanning for targets, but all I saw was erratic, confused Colombian soldiers running back and forth. I didn't see a single rebel soldier. At length, the spectacle suddenly ended.

The jungle grew quiet. We waited for the enemy's response. Nothing. The Colombians organized a couple of patrols, and I watched as they left the wire and disappeared into the torn and shattered foliage on the edge of our perimeter. They crept through the darkness, searching for any signs of the enemy.

When they returned, we learned the rebels had just probed us with a few men. They'd opened fire to test our defenses, and our Colombians retaliated with all guns blazing 360 death that probably slaughtered a lot of innocent jungle life but killed no rebels. They'd also revealed the positions of the heavy weapons and the firepower we possessed.

Perhaps it was that intelligence, carried back by those rebel scouts, that convinced our enemy not to try a full assault on our outpost. Perhaps they never even intended to hit our base, but the next day we received intel showing the four-hundred-man force had turned away and gone around us.

Nobody wants to be overrun, and standing ready to blow up our radios in case the worst happened was something that left me a little shaken. That said, a big part of me was disappointed we didn't get into a fight that night. Later, as we sat around as a team talking about it, we wondered if we should put in for combat action ribbons. We were in a fight for sure, but none of us fired our weapons or took direct fire. Because of that, we decided not to put in for those coveted ribbons. In the '90s, only a few SEALs had seen combat and wore them, and as new guys we all looked up to them.

More than anything, I wanted to wear one too. After all, it was our job. We trained harder for combat than almost any other organization, and I wanted to put myself and that training to the ultimate test.

Looking back now after experiencing combat, I cannot even fathom that attitude. But I was a hard charger, totally invested in being a SEAL. I had nothing else in my life—no family commitments, no wife or children. The brotherhood of Naval Special Warfare was the entire extent of my life.

That Colombian deployment launched my career and served as the way I judged many of our operations and deployments in the years ahead. I returned to Panama flush with success, feeling more aggressive and capable than at any other time in my life to that point. I felt I had proved myself and stood up to the challenge.

After that first platoon, I went into communications instead of becoming a SEAL medic. I had a knack for radio gear and could get the most out of our sometimes fussy systems where others could not. Maintaining hundreds of thousands of dollars of supremely technical radios and computer gear was a considerable responsibility, especially for somebody only in his midtwenties. I took pride in that ability, and I knew that my skills were some of the most important in our platoon.

Unfortunately, I knew it too well and began to think too highly of myself and my skills. That feeling of being indispensable led me to do some childish and immature things. I was always a great operator. I was a good marksman, and I handled myself well in the field. I was thorough; I studied hard and knew my equipment inside and out. I practiced my field craft, was willing to follow when called upon and to lead when rare opportunities presented themselves.

Yet, as the confidence I took from my Colombia experience grew, in some ways it became my Achilles' heel. At times, when I needed to learn a lesson, I was too arrogant and cocky and overlooked the opportunity to grow.

Two years after Colombia, I took part in one of the most intensely realistic training exercises of my enlisted career. In some ways, the level of intensity surpassed some mundane combat operations I conducted years later.

Naval Special Warfare had developed a relationship with the National Space Agency and we were invited to test the perimeter security of one of America's most strategic and vital space facilities. Our platoon received the honor to carry out the mission. It was tricky and had a lot of moving parts, but we planned thoroughly and studied the base's security rings.

We started the mission by diving into a dense mangrove swamp in the dead of night. We used underwater gear to move stealthily along the bottom of a ten-foot-deep boat channel that was so dark, a tiny emerald glow of my dial compass was the only thing I could see, like a jewel glittering on black velvet. Beyond it, the blackness was total. Swimming underwater long after sunset is like sailing across an alien world.

I enjoyed the silence. It was an opportunity to focus on the task at hand and put the cares of the world behind me. All the normal hubbub of human activity doesn't exist down here. No chain saws or lawn mowers puttering in the distance, no horns honking or jets passing overhead. We coursed through the depths, measuring every movement, accompanied only by the soft *pssssst* of oxygen being released by our Dräger LAR V rebreather gear.

On the surface, no one would ever know we lurked below. Our Drägers don't expel air, so there are no bubbles bobbing to the surface like bread crumbs for bad guys to follow. The water becomes our cloak of invisibility.

I stared intently at the glow of my dial compass, making sure we maintained the exact heading we needed to reach our objective until a noise welled up from the murk. It sounded like a series of loud, echoing gulps. Something answered it. I glanced up just in time to see the darkness flutter.

A chill rolled down my spine. I had no idea what that noise was. I hadn't imagined it, that much I knew. I started to wonder if we weren't the only predators in the water that night.

I focused on the task at hand and kept swimming. More noises echoed around us.

What the hell is that?

We swam on, the darkness little hindrance to our progress even though we didn't have underwater night vision. Years ago, French combat swimmers worked out ways to navigate in these sorts of situations, and we adopted them. The operators work in pairs. One carries the attack board, which includes the compass with its green luminescent dial, a stopwatch, and a depth gauge. He's the driver, and his job is to steer the pair on the proper course and depth over a given amount of time. His buddy swims just above and behind him, also keeping track of time and distance covered while also watching the way ahead so the driver doesn't run into anything. We know exactly how far we go with each kick of our fins. We pace ourselves carefully, count our kicks, and know from that number whenever we've gone a hundred meters. We know exactly how long it takes us to go that distance, and the stopwatch ensures we know precisely when to make preplanned course changes. We call it "flying a bearing." Land navigation works pretty much the same way, except instead of counting kick cycles, we count strides.

Operating submerged in total darkness can be extremely dangerous. Hazards abound and it is easy to get disoriented. Before I joined the teams, one SEAL on a similar training mission lost his sense of direction while under a ship and drowned.

That night in the mangrove swamp, I was our driver. I kept my eyes glued on the attack board as those unknown sounds echoed eerily around us. I tried not to think about what might be causing them and focused instead on getting us to our objective.

Our mission that night was a tricky one. We'd been tasked with "blowing up" key targets inside NASA's very secure perimeter of Cape Canaveral, Florida.

Cape Canaveral sits on an island. The launchpads are surrounded by swamps and inlets. The water serves as the first layer of security for our nation's most important space base. Beyond the white, sun-drenched beaches are fences, cameras, sensors, and guards.

Checking the attack board, I estimated we were coming up on our first waypoint, a bridge beyond which was a restricted area. We slid along the bottom unde-tected, cleared the bridge, and made a course change that took us into shallow water not far from the launch-pad's main fence. As we surfaced and moved through the shallow water, we saw something ominously big slide through the water ahead of us.

It was an alligator. That's what we'd been hear-ing all this time—gators. We were surrounded by them—hundreds of them. At any other point, I prob-ably would have felt real fear swimming among these foul-tempered beasts, but after three hours under-water, I was feeling just as angry as they were. The Drägers we use operate off pure oxygen. Prolonged exposure to pure O_2 that is under pressure has side effects that include irritability, which often escalates into rage. Stay down long enough and you emerge from the water ready to kill anything—including your swim buddy. I firmly believe there is nothing more dangerous on the planet than a combat swim-mer who is suffering from O_2 toxicity when he comes to the surface. He's definitely more dangerous than an alligator.

The reptiles learned this the hard way. One of my teammates surfaced in front of a pissed-off gator, which charged straight at him. Not missing a beat, he slammed his fist into the gator's snout and sent it fleeing into the mangroves, wondering what the hell had just happened.

Several hundred yards away from the gator-punching incident, my swim buddy and I crawled out of the swamp and stashed our Drägers on a mangrove island. We returned to the water and moved silently toward the main fence. We reached our target beach and slid ashore. The fence presented no obstacle. We were through in seconds, darting into the launch facility, staying in the shadows and avoiding the overhead lights. Guards were supposed to patrol the perimeter, but we had yet to see one.

Dashing to a building, we used it as cover to move deeper into our objective. We hugged the wall, then crossed a stretch of open ground to another structure.

A guard station lay between us and the fuel line we were tasked to blow up. My teammate and I both carried a simulated explosive device. Our job was to get the mines on the massive pipes that fueled the Trident missiles. NASA had asked us to try to strike it in order to test their defenses. Aside from NASA's security team, nobody else knew we were coming.

The guard shack presented a tough obstacle, as it stood only fifty yards from our target. We crept closer. Inside, I spotted the security officer, his back to us, watching television. All he needed to do was glance over his shoulder and he would see the two of us creeping through his sector, armed with simulated explosives and M4 rifles. If that happened, game over. NASA would crow that their security was unbreachable, and our team would be embarrassed for its failure.

The guard didn't turn around. Was he watching camera feeds? *Cheers* reruns? I couldn't tell, but it didn't matter. His mistake was our saving grace.

My teammate moved to the fuel line and placed his simulated explosive charge while I provided security and covered the guard. A moment later, he completed his task and tapped my shoulder. That was the signal to switch. He watched the guard as I strapped on the second charge. With our objective complete, we eased back the way we'd come, weaving through the darkness until we reached the beach. We swam with the gators again, retrieved our gear from the mangrove island, and watched the target area for a bit. Cape Canaveral remained quiet. No alerts. No guards running around. The charges lay affixed to the fuel pipes undetected. Had they been real, we would have started a timer, and they would have detonated long after we had made our escape.

Every two-man team we sent into Cape Canaveral that night penetrated the security layers undetected and succeeded in strewing simulated charges all over NASA's most critical facility. One of our operators, a quirky, sometimes unpredictable guy, reached his assigned objective and decided to explore a little farther. He somehow threaded his way through several extra layers of security and got into a restricted area that was out-of-bounds for the exercise. He found a target of opportunity, laid his charge, and escaped. The point he made was a valid one: NASA's most secure area was still vulnerable.

Going off the reservation is never a good idea, and this time it got the entire team in trouble with NASA the next day during the debrief. Our platoon commander pulled us aside afterward and told us although the mission was a success, one man doing his own thing compromised all of us. He talked about how each of us needed to think through our actions and never make selfish decisions. Stay within our briefed profile. Don't go rogue; it could compromise the entire mission. Not surprisingly, NASA never invited us back.

When I look back now, I realize I should have taken our platoon commander's words to heart. His words were valid and wise—to operate with other agencies, we had to be sensitive to crossing boundaries. That's part of what leadership is all about—working well with others, recognizing when and, more important, when not to do things. We didn't do that, and both NASA and Naval Special Warfare suffered for it ultimately.

As I stood there, I didn't really think about what our commander was trying to say. I thought like an arrogant kid: we were awesome; we achieved our objectives; mission complete and successful, and if one of our guys saw a target of opportunity and took it? Well, so much the better for his initiative and daring. That's what we were all about, anyway, right?

I missed a key part of the leadership lesson in that debrief and many more in the years to come.

A few years later, after two more South American deployments and serving time as an advanced training instructor, I was doing well enough to be recommended to apply for an officer commissioning program. Following in the footsteps of my father and grandfather as an officer appealed to me. I wanted a greater role for myself, to have the ability to influence how we did things. But my view of leadership was stunted. While I'd been a successful enlisted operator, the jump to becoming a SEAL officer turned out to be a bigger leap than I even recognized.

In 2001, I was accepted into the Seaman to Admiral Navy Commissioning Program and started college at Old Dominion University in August of that year. I decided from day one that this was my new job, and my goal was to do as well as I possibly could. I put my head down and focused all my energy on graduating with honors and becoming the student battalion commander of the Old Dominion University Navy ROTC program. Three years later, I graduated summa cum laude and made it to battalion commander. I looked at it as my first true leadership test, and I thought I passed it with flying colors and was more than ready to go back and lead in the SEAL Teams.

While I was at school though, another issue emerged. After 9/11, the SEAL Teams went to war. Instead of being one of the few operators who had at least been in the vicinity of a firefight, I became one of the few who did not have combat experience. The fires of Afghanistan and Iraq fundamentally altered our tactics and procedures. I had no idea just how deeply that would affect me when I graduated and returned to the teams in 2004.

My impatience and the sweeping changes in how the post-9/11 SEAL Teams operated came together as my own personal perfect storm. As I returned to the teams, I failed to recognize the leadership I had displayed up to this point in my career was predominantly a simple kind of leadership. I had been in charge of equipment or small groups of people in relatively safe environments. I was about to step into the big leagues of a more dynamic kind of leadership, where the stakes were much higher. But I didn't know that until much later.

Leading large groups of people, motivating and inspiring them to accomplish a common goal regardless of adversity or danger—that's the essence of dynamic leadership.

I excelled in school and displayed some levels of dynamic leadership, but in the military and in the business community, it takes a unique blend of attributes to get large groups of type A personalities to follow you into the fire.

Only those who lead by example and are willing to give everything for the cause and those under their command will succeed in that environment. A dynamic leader must be humble. A dynamic leader must recognize the sacrifices made by those who choose to follow his decisions. Arrogance has no place there. Real leaders need enough confidence to know when to make decisions and when to listen to those around him who may have more experience. A dynamic leader cannot be selfish. He must set the right tone with his commitment every day.

Of course, in 2004 as I graduated college and became a SEAL officer, I did not understand any of this. When I did finally recognize what it was to be a dynamic leader, it was almost too late.

PART I
The Hardening

Loveland Public Library
Loveland, Colo. 80537

Chapter 1

Al Anbar Province, Iraq
September 2007

I am bleeding out. I can feel my life ebbing away as blood seeps from my body into the Iraqi soil. A few brown weeds, splashed crimson now, are crushed around me as I lay sprawled on my back in the middle of this ambush. The weeds offer no concealment; I'm in the open, alone and wounded. Sizzles of pain hit me in waves like pulses of electricity.

A bullet has torn my left arm off.

After I get hit, I reach over to grab my left hand. It isn't there. I hunt around, feeling only the gear on the left side of my body. No arm. I try to move the fingers on my left hand, but my mind sends signals to a station that doesn't exist. Now I can't feel anything but pain.

Bullets kick dirt in my face. Through my night-vision goggles, I see green blooms of light strobing the darkness—muzzle flashes from automatic weapons. Ten meters away, an enemy machine gunner opens fire again. It is a belt-fed, Russian-made, crew-served weapon, probably a PKM. They sound like giant zippers tearing open when the gunners go cyclic, like now. The air around me erupts with sharp cracks, the miniature sonic booms of 7.62mm bullets speeding past me at two thousand five hundred feet per second. The terrorist gunner lowers his aim. A spurt of dust blows across my face again. Several bullets pass so close to my head that I feel shock waves as they go by.

To the left, an AK-47 assault rifle opens up. Then another. I'm pinned in a cross fire without cover or concealment—a crippled sitting duck in a kill zone at least a hundred meters long and seventy-five deep.

With my right hand, I key the radio handset I have mounted on my chest. "Troops in contact! Troops in contact!" I call to my command. "We have three severely wounded, including me."

Static greets my words.

I try again. No response. My teammates and I are on the backside of a gentle sloping field, a patch of dense vegetation between us and the rest of our task unit. We're separated by only about two hundred meters, but the tiny elevation difference and the brush are enough to block my transmissions since our radios are line of sight only. Surely they can hear the gunfire, but without somebody on our end talking to them, they won't send help out of fear of creating a friendly-fire incident. Nobody wants to walk blind into a gun battle and open up on his brothers by accident.

Brad Larkin, our unit's corpsman, is down, hit only a few seconds before I was. Brad's one of our new guys and the platoon's ham who loves to photobomb our Kodak moments with goofy faces. Now he lies as helpless as I am, his five-ten, one-eighty frame torn and bleeding. He begins shouting, but the firefight swallows his words. I've never heard him sound like that. As a new guy, it is his job to take care of the grunt work. Many times new guys partake in silly contests with the older operators. Brad hates these contests but always does them with a smile on his face. We may frustrate him, we may run him into the ground to test his commitment, but we can never get him to lose his cool. Instead, he always fires back at us with his wiseass comments that make us laugh.

He screams again, and I can tell now he has been seriously wounded. It is the sound of a man in severe pain. I can tell he's maybe fifty meters along the slope to my left. If I can pinpoint him, the enemy can too. They're right on top of us.

I inhale deeply before calling back, "Stop yelling! You're only going to draw more fire." My voice is distant, muddy, like I'm trying to yell through a cardboard tube at the end of a long hallway. I try again. Words, half formed, and slurred from blood loss, are lost in the din.

Forget that. I can't lead if I'm dead. Get the bleeding stopped first.

We have been trained for such moments. If we get hit in combat, we are supposed to treat ourselves while the rest of the team gains control of the firefight. In desperate moments, we need every gun pointed downrange and cannot have our brothers working on our wounded. That's the only way to survive and win. After the enemy's been killed or driven off, only then are we supposed to deliver buddy aid until a corpsman can reach our wounded. That's the treatment ladder, and right now I'm on the bottom rung.

Even if the guys ignored our procedures and tried to help, they couldn't reach me. They would have to run across the open kill zone right in front of the PKM—a near suicidal proposition. For now, my survival rests in my own hands. Or hand.

I have a tourniquet as part of my standard mission loadout. I'll need to cinch it around the stump of my left arm to stem the bleeding. I've kept it on my left side, strapped to my Rhodesian chest rack with three thick rubber bands ever since my first mission in Iraq, over five months ago. I've never had to use it, but I know exactly where it is. Special Operations Forces are meticulous about putting gear in the same place on our bodies for every mission. We work in darkness, so we train until we memorize where each piece of gear is and can grab it without looking.

The enemy had not opened fire on us until we were within whispering distance of that machine gun. We had patrolled within ten yards of their position and they had not made a sound. We never saw them in our night vision either, which means they must have dug fighting positions within the concealment of the thicket at the edge of the field. I'm only a few meters from that tangle of bushes and small trees right now. They're hidden and protected. We're as exposed as it gets.

But why did they let us get so close?

The answer dawns on me. They heard our helicopters buzzing overhead, and they wanted to negate our airpower advantage. Lock us into a point-blank firefight and they knew we'd be too close to them to rain bombs or rockets down on their positions. No gunship or jet fighter crew would dare launch a weapon in a tactical situation like that out of fear of killing friendlies. Beyond the horror of a "blue-on-blue" incident are the legal, career, and media ramifications that come along for that ride. We've all seen what happens, so pilots won't release unless they are absolutely certain they are not going to hurt Americans on the ground. At times, it can make some overcautious.

Only an enemy who has studied us and understands how we operate would know enough to try to exploit this. That means we're not facing local guys with AKs who've been paid a few bucks to take potshots at us. We've been ambushed by pros—veterans with skills and knowledge far beyond what we usually encounter.

Reality sinks in. I'm the obstacle to outside help. As long as I'm trapped beneath the muzzle of that PKM, we will not get any air support. Our survival depends on the firepower the aircraft above us can deliver on our enemies.

Stop the bleeding. Then worry about the PKM and finding some cover.

I reach for my tourniquet, but I can't seem to find it. I twist and hunt to no avail. As I struggle, my legs kick me around in a half circle until my boot heel finally digs into the soft dirt and I gain enough leverage to reach across my body again. I pause for a minute to get my breath and will the pain away. It feels like some-body's driven a spike into the back of my head.

Okay, let's do this.

Right hand up and onto my chest. Good. My gloved fingers spider-walk across my gear. I can feel the four extra mags in the pouch on my chest rack. Above them are my chem lights, a pen, and then the all-weather radio handset. The tourniquet is secured just below the handset. I turn my head to the left, but I can't see any-thing. My night-vision goggles are still down over my eyes, focused to ten feet and beyond. Everything closer is just a mess of blurry green blobs. No matter, my fin-gers telegraph everything they touch.

Another spasm of gunfire rocks the night. More shouting. I'm far away, focused only on the task at hand. At last, my fingers discover the tourniquet. It's black and folds up into itself like a small Velcro belt. Some of our medical gear is foreign-designed, such as our Israeli pressure dressings. This little item is American, made by a company called TQS, which is run by a former SEAL. It is a huge improvement over the tourniquets used in prior wars. The days of torn cloth and sticks like you see in movies are long over.

I'm panting from effort, but one tug should break the rubber bands and I'll be in business. I can slip the Velcro belt around my stump, then tighten it with the little black plastic cinch on the side until the bleeding stops.

I have it in my grasp now. I bear down and pull. The rubber bands stretch, but the tourniquet doesn't break free.

What the hell?

The PKM unloads another burst. Bullets flay the ground and claw the air above me. My M4 rifle is attached to my kit with a single point sling. It drapes across my chest, barrel down when we're on patrols. It rests across me like that now, and a 7.62 round strikes the back end of the SureFire flashlight I have mounted on the right rail near the rifle's hand grip. The impact sends bits of plastic and metal spinning into the darkness.

I can't duck. I can't crawl away. There's no place to hide. All I can do is ignore the incoming fire and stay focused. Get the tourniquet. One step at a time.

Task organize. Prioritize what needs to be done, no matter how small or large. Ignore the rest, work through each step. Stay focused. It is the only path to survival.

My fingers play across my gear again until I find the tourniquet and clutch it tight. I yank harder this time, using a sudden jerk with my right-shoulder muscles. Again, the rubber bands stretch, but don't break.

This confuses me. They're just rubber bands, for God's sake. I pull again. Same thing. Now I grow irritated.

Come on, I'm not this weak. When I've done this in training, I've never had this issue.

But I hadn't lost blood in training. Or an arm.

I pull again to no avail. I know I have to stay calm to get through this, but what if I've lost so much blood I don't have the strength to get it off? I'm in trouble. And nobody's close enough to help me. I feel my life draining out of me.

Concentrate. Your life depends on it, Jay.

I reach for the tourniquet one more time. Before I can tug it free, the PKM gunner finds the range. Bullets crack around me. Dirt flies. The terrorist eases up on the trigger. But only for a second. I hear him unleash another burst. Then I hear nothing at all.

Chapter 2

Flares of red-orange light puncture the black night in the distance around me. Snare rolls of machine-gun fire drum across the battlefield. My eyes are open; I see little but the island of darkness that has become my shroud.

My helmet's off; I feel it laying upside down just off from my right hand. My night vision remains clipped to the front of my helmet, which is why I can't see much now. In training, we often pull our helmets off between iterations. They're heavy and awkward, and if you leave them on too long, your head gets sore and you get wicked headaches.

Why did I take it off? I don't even remember doing it.

The question floats away. I try to think, but my brain misfires. Scattershot, half-formed thoughts swirl like smoke, choking my mind. I brush them away as if they were cobwebs in an old barn, but even as they disperse I gain no clarity. When I try to focus, it feels like I'm thinking through concrete.

My helmet lies beside me. The firefight continues. I'm still on my back. Wasn't there something I needed to do?

A powerful thought, driven by some primitive sense of urgency suddenly boils through the concrete.

Something is very wrong.

The thought—or warning?—vanishes.

My arm is gone. I already knew that. What then?

Another thought, ethereal and without form, spirals through my mind.

Where is the pain?

I can't feel my left arm. The spike in the back of my head is gone. The bolts of electric pain have ceased. I'm not numb exactly, more like the nerve impulses can't breach that concrete wedge in my brain.

What's wrong with your face, Jay?

The thought lingers longer than the others. It is a warning signal. It drives me to lift my right hand up. I see it coming toward my eyes, a gloved, dark shadow. My fingers reach my right cheek, and I expect to feel the pressure of their tips on my bare flesh. Instead, I feel nothing.

My face is not my own.

This part of me I've touched countless times while shaving or washing up feels utterly foreign. In its place, there is a hole that extends from where my cheek once was to where my nose should be. My fingers recoil. In the strobe of a muzzle flash, I see my glove is damp with blood.

I've been shot in the face.

A thought crystallizes. *My nose and my arm are gone. I'm going to bleed out.*

Both sides are easing up on their triggers now. The firing becomes more sporadic and directed. The enemy, without night vision, aims for sounds. I can't tell what our men are doing. I can't see anyone.

I let my right arm drop to the ground beside me.

Now what?

Zombies. I think of zombies. I see an image of them storming humanity's last outposts as the few survivors blast away at them with shotguns and assault rifles. A last stand in a giant shopping mall.

Fucking figures.

"If I ever fall on the battlefield, I want those to be my last words."

Who said that . . . me?

My mind races. I'd watched zombie movies with—who?

Al. Al Joliet. He is our platoon's senior team leader. In a rush, I remember now. The neurons fire, and I see Al's house back in Virginia. You can't go anywhere in it without practically tripping over a weapon. He's convinced the zombie apocalypse will break out any day now, and he's equipped himself for the mother of all last stands. He's hidden away knives under the sofa and battle-axes elsewhere in the living room; pump shotguns and handguns lace the kitchen and bedroom. The man is the arsenal of democracy.

My mind finally clicks. Al's nearby. My friend and brother. I need him now.

"Al, I've been hit in the head," I call out.

No response. Al is our assault team leader and air controller tonight. I can't see his six-foot-two frame, or his black eyes that are always slow to anger even in the midst of tension, but I know he's out there somewhere across the bullet-swept darkness.

I hear his voice. "Red?" I hear surprise in his deep voice. He grew up in Kansas and still has a faint Midwestern accent.

I'm going to bleed out.

"Al, how long till the medevac bird gets here?" My words slough out of me in a jumble even I can barely understand.

"Red, it's still too hot. I can't bring it in."

Not long ago, we watched *Dawn of the Dead* together, one of the great zombie movies. As one of the characters got overrun by the undead, he lamented, "Fucking figures." His last words. That's what I told Al I wanted to say if my number was punched. I should be saying it now, but I'm having a hard time concentrating.

The PKM crew hears this conversation. The belt rattles as the gunner shifts fire. A moment later, the ground around me erupts with bullet strikes. The gunner lays on the trigger and walks his barrel back and forth, aiming by sound. Rounds streak overhead. I feel one hit me in the side. No pain. Just a kick, and not even a hard one at that.

More bullets. My helmet, still laying beside me, takes a round directly in the top about an inch above where my forehead should be. If my head had still been in it, I would be dead right now.

Far overhead, a dragon snarls. A tongue of flame ignites the sky over a mile away. A moment later, the *crump . . . crump . . . crump* of cannon shells impacting in the brush behind the PKM team crushes the sounds of the firefight.

Grrrrrrrrrrrrrr. The shells, traveling a thousand meters a second, pass overhead with gusts of wind blowing in their wake—the dragon's breath.

Crump . . . crump . . . crump . . . Dull explosions spout debris in all directions. The concussion waves roll across the open field. I feel them ripple through me. *Crump . . . crump . . . crump.* Flames spark at every impact point, flaring out in a pall of smoke and dirt. I'm lying less than fifty meters from the barrage.

The dragon snarls again. The brush is saturated with bursting cannon shells.

Somehow, Al's called in air support despite the fact that we are danger-close to the enemy's positions. The dragon overhead is our savior—an AC-130 Spectre gunship armed with a battery of powerful cannons, including a weapon we call the Equalizer, a five-barrel Gatling gun powered by an electric motor that spews sixty-six 25mm cannon shells per second onto targets thousands of meters away. The AC-130 loiters over nocturnal battlefields far out of sight. There is no warning that it has arrived overhead. Its turboprop engines cannot be heard on the ground, for it flies too high. The *grrrrrrrr* of the Equalizer is all you hear once it starts pouring death on the enemy.

The Equalizer is the smallest-caliber weapon on board. It also carries 40mm and 105mm rapid-fire cannons. It is a fire support platform in the sky, capable of delivering all its destructive force with pinpoint accuracy.

The explosions come one atop the other now. I lie in the lee of the storm, feeling detached. My brain's disconnected from my senses. Time feels wildly elastic. Some moments feel like an eternity, others fly by rocket-fast. Through it all, the PKM never ceases. Its crew chews through belt after belt. They reload and reengage even as the Equalizer pulverizes the ground around them. I listen to the onslaught until it all becomes a cacophonic blur.

The firefight contracts and expands. Noises. Silence. Darkness. Blinding light. The world has no order or progression anymore. It lurches and jerks and slides around as time grows slippery again. I lie helpless, a prisoner trying to make sense of the chaos with a misfiring brain.

At length, I realize my eyes are open and I'm staring at the leaves of a tree just off to my left.

Where did that come from?

I try to move my right arm, but it weighs a thousand pounds. I try to lift my fingers. Too much effort. I can't turn my head; I stare upward, broken and exhausted.

The warm summer night is still. No breeze flutters the dark leaves overhead. Yet a chill sets in deep within my bones. I'm cold now. So cold.

The enemy has hurt us badly. Three of us are down. We have seen pure evil since our arrival in this wasteland. Barbarity. Cruelty beyond compare. The men we fight tonight are the bodyguards of that evil, whose professions to their faith justify the twisted acts done in their god's name. Torture. Beheadings. Suicide bombings. Marketplaces filled with broken bodies of women and children, slain for sheer terror's sake. We have seen them kill their own family members in their attempts to kill us and then justify it as the will of Allah. They are instigators of chaos and hate. Murder is their means of manipulation. They cow the local populations by making gruesome examples of those who stand against them.

I have always seen us as their reckoning, as agents of justice, swift and true, who will mete out their fate. My task unit came here earlier this night hoping to take down one of the most ruthless and violent al-Qaida leaders in Al Anbar Province. He eluded us, slipping away as our helicopters bore down on this village. He bolted even as his men prepared this ambush and were fighting to the death for their cowardly leader.

Now evil is winning. Me. Rob. Brad. Our life force flows from our bodies while our brothers struggle to save us and survive in this deadly cross fire. The thought of evil triumphant fills me with rage. They cannot win. They cannot beat us. I refuse to accept that. I want justice.

No. I want vengeance.

Grrrrrrrrrrrrrrrrrrrrrrr. The dragon growls. Seconds later, the ground quivers. Dirt and debris cascade around me.

An anguished wail rises over the din. The PKM goes silent. The terrorist who has torn my body with his machine gun now lies bleeding in the barren soil less than fifty feet from where I lie doing the same. Pain-racked and fearful, he calls out for his god.

"Allah! Allahu Akbar!"

You want your god now?

"Allahu Akbar, Allah!! . . ."

Grrrrrrrrrrrrrrrrrrr.

Stand by. Here he comes.

Chapter 3

For a brief moment, in the middle of this maelstrom, silence reigns. The gunner no longer cries to Allah. His PKM is silent. The lull lasts until another PKM begins to chatter farther to the west. AK-47s crack, and I hear some of our own rifles respond. Despite the air support, the enemy has not left the fight. Before this night, we've only encountered one group that was this determined. Most of these terrorists run away at the first sign of danger from the sky. We've seen them beg for their lives and claim they love America and George Bush as they surrender to us. But once before, several months earlier in June, we faced men willing to fight to the last round and die in place. That night, we had to call in helicopter gunships plus an AC-130 Spectre to finally end that battle.

Al is next to me, talking to the AC-130 crew to get more rounds on the enemy.

"Juliet Alpha, cleared hot!"

Grrrrrrrrrrrrrrrr.

Explosions to the west. The sounds seem unnatural and muted, like somebody's turned the volume down on my life.

"Al, when's the medevac bird getting here?" I ask.

A long pause. "Five minutes, Red."

I can't tell if he's serious or humoring me. We play poker together most nights, and he's legendary for his ability to bluff. He'll take big risks and lay down serious money to back up his bluffs and do it so well we never know if he has a full house or three high.

Right now, I'd just like some certainty.

Al goes back to working the radios. He's trying to orchestrate our defense, coordinate with the gunship crew, and guide in the rest of our team while talking in the medevac helicopters to our location. His voice is flat, calm, and professional.

Prior to deployment I had watched a show called *Baghdad ER* and heard that wounded warriors have a ninety-seven percent chance of survival if they arrive at the combat support hospital with a pulse. All I need to do is hold on until the medevac helo gets here.

My fingers feel like stone. Breathing becomes hard. I grow colder. My eyelids drop down. The darkness seems like peace. It calls to me.

"Red! Red! Red!" Al shouts at me. My eyelids fly open. I'm looking straight up into the night's sky. The tree off to my left—*how did it get there?*—obscures part of my view. Beyond it lie the stars. They're so vivid. The Milky Way stripes the blackness like a diamond belt. The majesty of the view leaves me awestruck. What's happening here seems insignificant next to such vastness. Who am I compared to that?

The firefight starts to lose steam. The shooting grows ragged and intermittent. Something's crashing around in the brush not too far away. Another wounded terrorist thrashing in his death agony? Or is somebody trying to escape the holocaust from above?

I have to will myself to breathe now. Each intake of breath becomes ever more difficult. My body feels compressed, like a brick wall has fallen atop it. I exhale heavily. One more breath. One more.

So cold. Cold as a winter grave.

"Al, how long till the medevac gets here?"

"Five minutes, Red. Five minutes."

"You said that ten minutes ago," I reply weakly, knowing now he's been humoring me. The exchange leaves me winded, and I can't catch up. Each breath is shallower than the last, less satisfying. I feel like part of me has already stepped out of this world. My life force is failing. Another breath, and it takes all I've got to get it into my lungs. It draws most of my remaining strength. When I exhale, I realize I've got nothing left.

During BUD/S (Basic Underwater Demolition/ SEAL) training, we spent hours in the water, the surf battering our hypothermic bodies until we could hardly stand to face the next wave. Over and over. Guys gave up and rang the bell. I watched them from the surf, eyes burning from the salt water, body aching from the abuse. I swore I would not follow. I would not quit.

A sure way to destroy a man's will to endure is make him cold and keep him that way. It saps everything from you, like a slow power drain on a battery. Your body can't fight it. The shivering that is your natural response simply accelerates the energy loss. You wear yourself out chattering and shaking. It crushes morale, destroys the spirit. Only a very few can find the reserves needed to stay in the water and persevere.

Hour after hour, I hung on. I stayed in the surf and clung to my dream. I'd get through. I'd wear the Trident. Toward the end, I shivered uncontrollably until I felt a whole new dimension of exhaustion set in. Those nights in Coronado near San Diego were some of the coldest of my life.

Back then, the instructors were careful not to push us too far. There were limits to BUD/S training. They can take you to the brink, but never beyond.

Out here in the Iraqi desert, there are no controls. No limits. Nobody to say we've been pushed far enough and have the instructors pull us from the water.

I feel myself slipping beyond that threshold. There's no escape. No walk up the beach to a waiting heated van, hot coffee, and a one-way ticket back to the fleet. This is different. It is an otherworldly cold, a spiritual one. It is the chill of creeping death, like I'm freezing from the inside out.

So this is it. This is how I'm going out.

Fucking figures.

I accept this. If I have to go, this is the way I want to exit. Here, with my brothers, in battle against a ruthless and evil foe. It beats slowly wasting away in some nursing home, body ravaged by age and kept functional by a beeping machine.

It beats a sudden death in a car wreck. There's no honor in that. My mind stops on that thought. A memory forms and sends me back years to one of the pivotal moments of my life.

The Jeep slides off the road, spinning over black ice in the midst of a blizzard. Blasts of winter air on my face, I fight the wheel until the rig impacts.

Why was I out that night?

Erica.

Bullets lace the night. The firefight gains intensity again. Al's on the radio, calling to the AC-130 crew. The Equalizer growls and belches shells. They inundate the enemy to the west.

A short gasp of breath. The weight on my chest is crushing now.

Erica. Long blond hair. Warm eyes; doe eyes. I was drawn to her the first moment I saw her. I nearly died in that Jeep trying to win her love back. My Hail Mary play to save myself from a life without her.

I hear voices. Al's still on the radio, but others are near too. I can't see who they are. Can't turn my head. No energy. It's all I can do to keep my eyes on the Milky Way.

No air comes with my attempt to draw a breath. The weight is too strong.

The other PKM rattles off a long burst. The 25mm shells explode. Men shout.

"She has squinty eyes," I said as Erica held her.

Mackenzie. My youngest girl.

"That's 'cause she looks like you, Jay."

Blue eyes. Full of fire.

Phoenix. My boy. When he was seven, I took him snowboarding for the first time. I was so proud to see him stand and slide down the mountain on his own.

Angelica. We'd tried forever for her. Erica broke the news to me on April Fools' Day. I didn't believe it, didn't believe the tests either. Erica had to go to a clinic to confirm that those little sticks were indeed accurate. When it finally sank in, it was one of the best moments of my life.

I love being a dad. I've not been around enough for Erica and our children. We all know this. We all accept it as the price of what I do.

The kids at the Great Wolf Lodge—going there became our postdeployment ritual. We'd swim and play.

My girls. Every Daddy Day Out I'd take them to their dance studio, then to have manicures and pedicures next door. I'd sit with them as they delighted in getting pampered and tell them how pretty they were when they were done.

How many men have I known who have come home from war, only to miss anniversaries and births, holidays and family weekends because they're already in the training pipeline for another deployment? How many families has this taken down? The divorce rate within the community is close to ninety percent. This is the hidden price, what Fox and CNN don't often report. Every warrior/parent pays it. The cause is just, but we all suffer for carrying its burden.

Do I hear rotors over the firefight? I strain and listen, but I can't tell for sure. AKs bark. A few of our M4s reply.

A sudden thought grips me about what I'm going to miss. Birthdays. Graduations. Halloween—we love Halloween. Our Christmases, decorating our tree and great food, gifts and laughter. I'll miss all these events and milestones; I'll miss the chance to celebrate the highs and help them through the lows.

Erica. Her smile could ignite a room. People are drawn to her.

She'll be left alone. Someday, she'll find somebody else. I'd want her to. I've told her that.

Some other man will raise my kids.

I try to take another breath, but the weight on my chest is too much for me. I feel a tiny bit of air seep into my lungs. Not enough. Not nearly enough.

I'll use your light to guide the way
'Cause all I think about is you

That 3 Doors Down song is one of my favorites. It has kept me company through dark times.

I'm not ready to go.

"Lord," I say. Are my lips moving? Am I talking aloud or thinking? I'm not sure, and I don't care.

The enemy has his god he cries out to in his moment of judgment. So be it. I have mine. I've wandered from the church I grew up in. I've been a terrible Christian these past years. When I finished BUD/S and earned my Trident, I told myself God has no place in the teams. I used that excuse to live without a conscience at times. Truth is, I never stopped believing. At times, I prayed. But I rarely went to church and let His guidance keep me from nights on the town with the boys.

I was wrong. God walks with us, always. No matter where we are, or what we do, He's with us, ready to forgive. That is my Lord. Not one of vengeance or wrath, in whose name unspeakable acts are committed. Mercy, love, and salvation—those are His foundations.

"Lord, give me the strength to go home."

The Equalizer growls. Al's called in one more fire mission. The shells fall somewhere off to the right.

"I want to see my wife again. See my kids grow up."

My eyes are open. The Milky Way, resplendent overhead. I lie beside this tree, the echoes of battle in my ear. And I take a breath.

The weight is gone. In a rush, I feel my failing strength return. I can move my fingers, turn my head. A prayer answered.

Erica, I'm coming home to you.

Chapter 4

Louisville, Kentucky
2000

Seven years and three South American deployments into my career as a SEAL, I found myself in Fort Knox, Kentucky, working as a basic warfare instructor with a small group of fellow operators. We worked eighteen-hour days, but being twentysomething and single, once the gear was stowed, all we wanted to do was get out on the town and blow off some steam. Work hard. Play hard. That was our pre-9/11 mantra.

One Wednesday evening, we finished up a long field exercise and got ready for the night's festivities. Before we headed into town, we discussed our cover story for the evening. Operational security concerns kept us on the down low, that was true. We had to be very careful what we said as a result of those boundaries. I rarely mentioned that I was born in Ohio, but lived most of my life in North Carolina, Florida, and the Virgin Islands.

Professional concerns aside, we discovered long ago that if we told people we were SEALs, we'd get one of two reactions. Women usually thought it was a line and didn't believe us. The men who did believe us would either pester us to death with questions or they would try to pick a fight. We'd either get blown off or end up in a bar fight, mixing it up with the locals then dodging the authorities so we didn't end up in jail. That got old quick, so before nights on the town, we'd always have a cover story that had nothing to with the military. After a while, it became sort of a contest to see which one of us could invent the biggest whopper that people would believe. Many a team guy has succeeded in convincing some attractive young lady that yes, it is true, my friend is a lion tamer. Or yep, John really does drive the space shuttle crawler!

Sometimes when we rolled out in large groups, we pretended to be a visiting baseball team or a lacrosse club, or a group of business executives on a retreat.

That night, we decided to be a boxing team. It made perfect sense to us since we had a guy in our platoon who looked so much like Oscar De La Hoya that people used to ask him for his autograph. We planned to tell the locals we were in town to spar with the US Army's team at Fort Knox.

We rolled out that evening, crammed into a nondescript, fifteen-passenger Chevy van. We spent considerable time in these vehicles, crisscrossing the country in them as we attended various training events. Of course, putting a bunch of type A guys into such close confines for prolonged periods of time led to some creative ways to combat boredom. One was a straight-up fight that we affectionately called the "Van Brawl." Somebody would throw a punch, and a close-quarters battle would erupt between the backseats. Only one rule was enforced: don't hit the driver. "Radio" was another exciting game we played. New guys always had to sit in the back of the van. One of us would shout "Radio!" and one of the new guys would have to fight his way forward to change the tunes blasting on the van's sound system. Of course it was everyone else's duty to prevent him from doing so.

A significant number of team guys showed up to training with black eyes and bruises from the melee that occurred in our travel vans, and it was utterly astounding the ignorance we pleaded when we turned the vans back in to transportation and they would inquire why there were footprints on the ceiling or why all the backs of the seats were broken. We would shrug our shoulders of course and have no earthly idea. Probably happened during training or maybe it was the last guys who had it.

That night, we were too tired from training for any van shenanigans. We saved our energy for the night ahead. I'm sure the motor T guys appreciated this interlude from the normal damage repair they had to do for us.

Anyway, we reached Louisville and hit Baxter Avenue in search of the nightclub one of the guys had researched the weekend before. A few blocks later, we lurched to a halt in front of a ramshackle, sprawling mess of a building that must have once been an antebellum-era warehouse. After years of subsequent construction, the building had grown into a jigsaw pattern of red and beige brickwork, postmodern retractable glass roofing, and massive wooden beams. It took up the bulk of a city block across the street from a century-old cemetery the locals swore was haunted. Nearby stood an abandoned funeral parlor whose basement crematorium had been taken over by transients.

Between the bar and the cemetery, a crowd milled in the street. Cars came and went. A limo inched through the throng, passing our gray navy van. Looking at the diverse crowd, we knew we had found the perfect place.

As we dismounted and headed for the front entrance, a stylized neon sign blazed with a nineteenth-century chuck wagon loaded with beer kegs. It bathed the people and cars out front in an orange glow and cast long shadows in the street. Music from four different live bands thundered and boomed so loud the sidewalk quivered. We paid the cover and gained entry into Louisville's oldest, and wildest, nightclub.

We stepped into a crowd that spanned the reaches of American demographics. Rednecks and cowboys drank alongside sorority girls and frat boys. We ogled the barely legal hotties in skintight skirts next to the cougars on the prowl. There were gangbangers and wannabes and druggies and hippies who roamed among the hoochie mamas and wide-eyed teenagers taking their fake IDs for a spin. It was fifty-cent beer night at the Phoenix Hill Tavern.

The Phoenix Hill was a maze. Five bars, four stages, three stories, and live bands or DJs in every nook and cranny. The floors were ancient unfinished wood. Potted plants hung from the rafters beside colorful piñatas. The walls were covered with Americana, and the rooms were decorated with junk store antiques.

It was our kind of place.

We paid for our drinks and ventured among the nightlife. I posted myself a ways in from the door and watched the muscle-bound bouncers check IDs as a river of new arrivals poured inside. Pretty faces abounded. It was going to be a great night, of that I had no doubt.

Then a doe-eyed girl stepped up and flashed her ID. Her hair was long and golden blond. She was simply dressed but looked stunning in her blue-and-white-striped halter top, white slacks, and flip-flops. When she smiled at Muscles studying her driver's license, I saw she had a beautiful smile. It complemented her perfectly tanned skin. Hulk Hogan motioned her inside, and I followed her with my eyes as she threaded through the crowd.

I had to meet her. I judged my timing and caught up to her near the bar. She regarded me with those doe eyes, hooded with long dark lashes, and I couldn't help but feel a little taken by her.

"Hi. I'm Jay. How you doing? Can I buy you a drink?"

I cringed at my lack of wit and charm and the weakest pickup line ever.

What the hell? That's the best I've got?

"Hello," she replied. I got the sense she was mildly amused by my pathetic attempt to be witty.

I tried to make small talk over the music. She listened politely for a few minutes, then blew me off.

"I'm here tonight to meet with some friends. They're upstairs waiting for me."

I was crashing and burning here.

"Great, I'll come up later and find you," I said, trying to salvage something.

She nodded and said good-bye. I watched her, transfixed, as she disappeared into the throng of people.

I rejoined my buddies. Soon, we were five bucks into fifty-cent beer night, having a great time. But I couldn't get my mind off that girl. There was something about her—that smile, the way she looked at me like she was vaguely amused—that made me want to know more about her.

Let it go. Enjoy the night.

I had another drink and considered the situation. I wasn't after anything serious. I was just getting out of a relationship with my ex-girlfriend—a woman who was still living in my house back in Virginia despite my best efforts to get her to move on. It was a complex situation since she had kids. They were great kids and I cared about them, so I had allowed her to stay until she found a new place for them. But time was dragging on and I was leaning on her to find a place soon. I knew that was going to come to a nasty confrontation when I got home after my stint in Kentucky.

I finished my drink. The music blasted our ear-drums until they were almost numb. I stood up and headed for the stairs.

I got to the second floor and began searching for the blonde as I worked my away around knots of people drinking or dancing. I spotted her standing on a bench on the far side of the room. Some guy was talking to her.

No. No. This will not do at all.

I walked toward them. The guy looked like he'd been mass-produced from the pages of an L.L.Bean catalog. He was talking away excitedly, but she had that *Please help me* sort of look on her face. Lucky me . . . a damsel in distress.

I threw caution to the wind. When I reached the bench, I stepped up right between the two of them. With my back to Dr. Dork, I pinned my eyes on the blonde's and unleashed a confident, "Hello again. Remember me from downstairs?"

Dr. Dork was taken by surprise. I ignored him and asked the blonde her name.

"Erica," she told me.

"Are you single?" I asked. I honestly couldn't believe somebody like her would be.

"Yes." She smiled this time. Dr. Dork hadn't moved, but he hadn't said anything either.

"I don't believe it. How is that possible? Why are you single?" I asked.

She held my gaze. "I know what I'm looking for and I haven't found it yet."

"Maybe you just have."

Dr. Dork finally got hit by the clue bat and stepped down off our bench, never to be seen again.

While there were tons of beautiful women in the bar that night, Erica had an energy about her that was utterly unique. We hit it off immediately, laughing, drinking, and sharing stories. We headed downstairs and linked up with my teammates, where we spent the rest of the night talking and dancing. She was engaging and intelligent, quick to laugh, and always ready with that flawless smile. When I left her that night, I couldn't stop thinking about her.

The next day, she invited me to a barbecue. I showed up and Erica greeted me warmly—with her seven-month-old son, Phoenix, in her arms. That was a surprise. I was still sort of reeling from this development when the kid whacked me in the face with his bottle.

I rubbed my face and thought any kid with a wicked right hook like that was one I wanted to get to know. I spent a little time with him as Erica and her friends put me to work assembling the grill for the barbecue. He had Erica's same big brown eyes, a thick head of hair, and no off switch. Her boy was always in motion. I was soon convinced the secret to nuclear fusion lay inside that kid.

By the end of the night, the two of us had really taken to each other. At the same time, I got along well with Erica's friends, always a big plus at the start of any relationship. I ended up spending the weekend in Louisville with Phoenix and Erica. Soon after, I commuted into town from Fort Knox whenever I had any time off from my training duties.

A month later, I met her family on Easter Sunday and introduced myself as a boxer. I hadn't told Erica the truth yet. Her grandmother, whom we called G.G., made defusing this lie a little tougher too. G.G. was a feisty lady who loved the fact that I was a boxer. As I said good-bye to her at the end of the night, she said, "Remember, Jay, protect that head and keep your dukes up!"

A few weeks later, I decided this charade had gone on long enough. I sat down and told Erica that I wasn't a boxer, I was a US Navy SEAL. After I finished explaining the lie and why it was necessary, she went quiet for several minutes. In the silence, I worried. We'd grown close, but I was leaving soon for Virginia and she knew it. I figured we'd never see each other again. Price of the job. You meet a person. You see potential there, but the navy pulls you away before it can develop. Often, I liked it that way. But not this time.

This was a big moment. Being a SEAL and understanding the impact of what we do is a game changer for a lot of women. They don't want the military life—it is a hard, lonely life for our wives and girlfriends. Raising children and running a household while husbands and boyfriends are gone for months at a time can be a crushing grind. Most women aren't looking for that. On the flip side, there are some who fall for the image and the coolness factor, who dive headlong into relationships with team members for all the wrong—and superficial—reasons. That almost always leads to drama and divorce.

I knew Erica wasn't one of the latter. But she was a single mom. Her life, her family, her entire support network were all in Louisville. What could a transient military man possibly bring to this situation while always being on the go? As amazing as the last few weeks had been, I knew this was the moment reality set in and sent this beautiful little love affair crashing to the ground.

At length, she finally replied, "This is the craziest thing I've ever said or felt, but I am willing to pick up and move to Virginia Beach."

I was blunt. "You have no idea what you're getting yourself into. You should run."

She didn't run.

I **left** for Virginia a short time after that. Though we hadn't formalized anything, I wrote to her every day after we'd finished our training iterations. Our e-mails gave us time to measure our thoughts, share with each other things that would have been difficult to say face-to-face this early in our relationship.

We just enjoyed being together. We liked the same stuff, had the same taste in music, enjoyed playing games together, found the same things funny, and loved the same films. We talked about hopes and dreams and the future. We shared a love of scuba diving and she had dreams of opening a dive resort some day. We both came from families where our parents had divorced, and we both had stepparents. That gave us perspective on how we wanted our own marriages to be. If we were ever to tie the knot, it would be forever. Period. We never wanted our kids to have to go through a divorce and deal with the drama of dysfunctional families.

Erica and Phoenix came into my life and everything fell into place. We fit, and the comfort we felt was unlike anything we'd ever known. Parts of me long walled off from the world became hers. Her presence completed my life.

I made one more trip to Kentucky for training and we spent every waking moment together when I wasn't training. Every time I was away from her, I only looked forward to being with her. It grew into a cycle, and as we drew closer, the periods we were apart felt increasingly hollow.

When my last training trip to Fort Knox came to an end, I packed up and prepared to head back to Virginia and my house there. Before I left, we made plans for Erica and the two-legged plutonium reactor to come visit me as soon as possible.

When Erica and Phoenix did get out to Virginia a few weeks later, we spent a lot of our time exploring together. We all have adventurous spirits, and we found common ground going to new places, doing different things. We went to the local pool, strolled the boardwalk, and lay on the beach. One day, we went hunting for a Christmas tree ornament. Erica has a tradition of buying one in every new place she visits. In a Virginia Beach tourist shop on Atlantic Avenue, we found a shark figurine with its mouth wide open, ready to devour its prey. Erica loved the idea of our first ornament being a reminder of that trip. She talked about hanging it on her tree for years to come. She bought it, and then put a tiny photo of the three of us on the beach in its mouth.

When they left to go back home, I felt their absence deeply. It was quiet too. Phoenix had only two speeds:

full throttle and unconscious. Seriously, the kid never stopped moving. He'd race around my house for hours, crashing into walls, breaking stuff. We chased after him, cleaning up the minicatastrophes in his wake only to see him suddenly drop to the floor, sound asleep.

After they left, I drove out to Louisville whenever I could. Erica reciprocated and came to Virginia Beach as her schedule allowed. The distance grew wearisome, and the circumstances of our enforced separation ever more heavy. But moving to Virginia Beach would be a huge step for both of us. For Erica, she would be giving up her friends, her family, and her support network for Phoenix. On my end, I'd be giving up the freedom I'd enjoyed ever since leaving my mom's house for the navy seven years before.

Yet, when we were together, it just worked.

Which of course meant I had to screw it up. I had a knack for doing that back then.

At Thanksgiving, I invited Erica to come meet my family in North Carolina. We had a terrific weekend. Erica got along great with my sister and mom, and everyone's reaction to her was universally positive. As I watched her fit in so well, two things happened. First, I realized I may have found my perfect match. I wanted to spend every minute with her, wanted to always know what she was thinking, what her opinion was on things, how she felt about whatever we encountered on our adventures together. I wanted to make her laugh and be rewarded with that Caribbean sunrise of a smile.

With Erica, it was effortless. We just agreed on everything.

I believe everyone has a soul mate perfectly matched by God. The hard part is finding that one among the many who are almost, but not quite, right. Settling for that is probably why the divorce rate is so high. That Thanksgiving, I knew I had found my mate.

Then of course, testosterone, probably a little alcohol, and the looming threat of "forever" all came together to start choking me out. I could almost see the cold, dark hand of commitment reaching for my throat. Truth was, I hadn't been free for ten months—I mean, in reality my single-guy freedom had been cast aside at the Phoenix Hill Tavern. These past months had been some of the best of my life. Of course, that never occurred to me. It was as if I had the proverbial devil and angel sitting on my shoulders. The angel weighed in with how perfect Erica was and that I would probably never find another like her. The devil jabbed me in the neck with his pitchfork and yelled "Freedom!" like William Wallace.

The devil won.

At the end of the weekend, we drove home to Virginia Beach in silence. I sat behind the wheel exuding tension. Erica asked me what was wrong. I deflected. We'd had a great weekend. Although neither Erica nor I saw the invitation to meet my family as some sort of test she had to pass, I think we both realized the truth. We'd just reached a milestone in our relationship, one that would set the stage for moving forward to something more.

And here I was, being a sullen jerk. Talk about a slap in the face for her. She tried to roll with it for a few more miles, then asked me what was wrong again. This time, instead of deflecting, I grew impulsive— something that I did frequently in my younger days. I opened my mouth and just unloaded on her. I laid out every reason why we shouldn't be together. My job, Erica losing her support network in Louisville. I mentioned the pain of long-distance relationships—which my job would force on us even if we were married. I did everything I could to leverage my job as a get-out-of commitment-free card.

It didn't work. Erica was unflappable. I couldn't believe it. I'd thrown the kitchen sink at her and she was solid. I went for plan B.

Although Erica and I complemented each other very well, we did have one fundamental difference. After years in the military, I had grown accustomed to structure. I liked a plan and I liked order. In my house, everything had a place. Erica was a free spirit. She didn't always have to have a plan and didn't mind chaos. Stuff didn't always have to be put away, and a little mess never bothered her. Many nights, I would look around the house and suggest we clean up. Erica would flash me that killer smile and say, "After we go do something fun!"

Some of our best times were when I threw caution to the wind and stopped worrying about these little things. She drew me out of my rigid sense of order— and secretly I loved that.

That night, I used this beautiful difference as the final wedge that broke us apart. I railed at her until she burst into tears and asked, "What does all this mean?"

"It means we're through," I said coldly.

When we reached my house, Erica scooped up Phoenix, put him in her car, and packed their things. After midnight, they sped off, Louisville bound. Erica kept one song playing on her stereo.

Got a lead foot down on my accelerator and the rearview mirror torn off
'Cause I ain't never lookin' back, and that's a fact.

As the miles spread between us, she sang her way through the anguish with Jo Dee Messina. None of this boded well for reconciliation.

I stood on the porch and watched her taillights fade from view. I felt like there was a cable tied to her bumper firmly wrapped around my heart, and suddenly it got torn right out of my chest. I kicked myself and wondered what the hell I had just done.

I couldn't sleep that night. I just lay there, paralyzed by the utter senselessness of what I'd done. What's that line from *Say Anything*? "The world is full of guys. Be a man. Don't be a guy."

I'd been the quintessential guy.

I stewed in my misery for a couple of weeks, too proud to call her.

Meanwhile, Erica punished me with silence. She could not have picked a better weapon. Had she called me up to tell me what an idiot I was, I would have jumped at the chance to talk to her. At least we'd be engaged voice to voice, spending time together—even if she was hammering on me. I'd spent ten months in constant communication with her. She was the first thought I had every morning, the last before I went to bed at night. I loved to write to her, and I still had every e-mail she had sent to me.

Now the line went dead. Connection broken. I felt severed. The silence deafened me. I moped; I wallowed. I tried to lose myself in work, but that had no effect. I stumbled through each day, missing her more and more. You know how they say you have to hit rock bottom before you can start working your way up? In this case, there was no bottom. I kept spinning downward; a free fall with no impact, just the awful realization that there was no escape from this descent.

Believe me, I tried to put it behind me. I went out with the boys and tried to drink her memory away. That just made it worse. So I tried to call Erica. By then, I was way past the point of pride holding me back. She answered the phone, heard my voice and shouted "Drop dead!" and then hung up. Or maybe she just hung up on me and I heard her scream "Drop dead!" all the way from Kentucky. I'm not sure; things were pretty sketchy by that point.

I kept calling. Usually, I got the answering machine, but at least I heard her voice telling me to leave a message. After many attempts, she finally picked the phone up long enough to tell me she didn't want to have anything to do with me anymore. And, oh, if I happened to get hit by a truck, that'd be a good thing too.

A few days passed. I got a call from her. Erica loves hats, and she has a very creative, eclectic sense of style with them. In the rush to leave Virginia Beach after Thanksgiving, she'd forgotten her latest one at my place. She asked me to mail it to her, then hung up before I could tell her what a mistake I had made. It dawned on me that Erica really considered us over.

Message received. I stopped calling and switched tactics. I tried to rationalize what had happened. It wasn't meant to be. She and I were too different—like oil and water. She was messy. The navy taught me order and cleanliness are the keys to a successful life. Erica called that being anal. Opposites may attract, but they don't last. I waged unrestricted psychological warfare on myself.

Well, none of the lies I told myself worked.

One night, I was sitting with two buddies, vainly trying to find solace in the bottom of a bottle. By this point, Glenn and Jason were probably sick of hearing about my breakup with Erica, but I talked about little else. I tried marginalizing the affair once again, as if my heart would be fooled into believing if my brothers bought the lie. They called me on it.

Glenn listened until his patience wore out. "Hey, dumbass, stop crying. Go get her."

Later that night, I went home and thought about that bit of advice. Before our Thanksgiving disaster, I'd planned to be in Louisville in December for Christmas. Phoenix had been born with a genetic heart condition called ventricular septal defect, or VSD. Earlier in the year, his doctors had recommended surgery to correct it. Erica had scheduled it for December eighteenth. When she had, I'd promised her I'd be there for the both of them.

Then I went and wrecked everything.

I thought about her in Louisville, steeling herself for Phoenix's surgery, and it just drilled me into the ground. How could I have done this to her weeks before such a terrifying event for a single mom?

I made a promise to be there for Phoenix and for the woman I loved. I've got many flaws, and I've made many mistakes, but I have always taken pride in how I honor my word. I'll follow through regardless of any external events.

Go get her.

I knew the night before Phoenix's surgery Erica was having a Christmas party for her friends. I figured if I could make it to her house before her friends got there I might have a shot at reconciliation. If I showed up too late, though, her friends would close ranks around her and I wouldn't stand a chance. The clock was ticking, and I had a long drive in front of me. It was Hail Mary time.

I threw some clothes into a bag and got my Jeep ready for the winter road trip. Winters were mild in Virginia Beach so I rarely put the top on my Jeep. But after checking the weather report, I suspected it would probably get pretty chilly, so I went to find the Jeep's canvas top. Months before, I'd stashed it under my bed and forgotten about it. Now, when I went to retrieve it, I discovered my German shepherd, Shadow, had chewed out the plastic back window.

The weather guys were forecasting a severe storm. Without a back window, this was going to suck. I decided if I was going to suffer, Shadow could too. I put the top on the rig, stuffed the dog in the back with my bag, and rolled for the Bluegrass State.

I drove west toward the mountains, shivering behind the wheel despite several thick coats and a black watch cap pulled over my head. I kept an eye on the clock, knowing that my window of opportunity to reach Erica before her party started was rapidly shrinking. If I drove nonstop, I'd get there thirty minutes before her friends showed up.

Periodically, I'd look up and see Shadow, all happy and warm with his lush brown fur. His nose had a splash of black on it, and he'd stare back at me, just happy to be along for the adventure. I rolled my eyes at him and shivered a little harder. I hoped the plastic gave him indigestion.

I wondered how I was going to approach this. I started envisioning scenarios. Erica flinging open the door in response to my urgent knocks—and? What? Would she throw something at me?

Most likely.

Maybe I should be ready to dodge bullets. Hopefully not, as I discovered years later I wasn't very good at that.

Would she give me a chance to speak? What would I say to her? I began crafting a speech. I tried it out on the dog, who seemed impressed. But he was a friendly audience, and what I really needed was a tougher crowd to help hone the message.

We hit the West Virginia mountains and the universe aligned itself with Erica. Over the radio, I heard news reports of the approaching snowstorm. Snowstorm—ha! Shadow and I plunged straight into a massive blizzard that sent sheets of flakes spinning almost horizontally in our path. Our progress slowed to a crawl. With every minute lost, I knew my chances were dimming.

I could just see what would happen if I rolled up after the party started. I'd bang on the door and her friends would run interference. They'd answer and tell me to beat feet. Even if I made it past that first line of defense, Erica would be somewhere inside the house, well guarded by a phalanx of pissed-off women who'd keep reminding her of what an ass I'd been.

As I reached the heart of the mountains on I-64, the snow fell even harder. Clearly, the universe was telling me not to do this. Turn back, go home. Too risky.

I dropped the hammer and sped through the blizzard.

Despite the heater blowing, the temperature inside my Jeep dropped below freezing. Thank God for being in a job where I got issued some of the best cold weather equipment available on the market. Unfortunately, all of it was still sitting in my cage back at the team. I was soon bordering on hypothermia as the wind whipped through the Jeep's cockpit.

I was doing sixty when the Jeep skidded over a stretch of black ice and I lost control. The rig slid sideways and drifted into the oncoming lane, directly into the path of an eighteen-wheel tractor-trailer. I was about to be T-boned like JFK's PT boat.

I braced for the impact, but at the last second the tires gripped wet pavement and sent me rocketing off the road. The truck blew past me as the Jeep struck a mile marker and lurched to a stop in the weeds at the base of a West Virginia rocky cliff.

Erica had told me to go get hit by a truck, and I almost did. How about that?

The sudden margin between life and death left me exhilarated. High on adrenaline, I pumped my fist and shouted. I think I even high-fived the dog.

I got back on the road and never slowed down. The wind raged. The snow blew in white clouds, and by the time we made it to the Kentucky state line, even Shadow was shivering uncontrollably. I got some measure of satisfaction out of seeing that.

We'd done it without a minute to spare; the party was set to begin in less than an hour. I parked the Jeep in front of Erica's house and jumped out—half frozen, two coats on, and a black beanie on my head. I'm positive I did not look like anyone's future in that attire. Hobo home invader, maybe. Husband material, not so much.

I knocked on the door. I'd rehearsed and practiced for hours. This was my *Jerry Maguire* you-had-me-at-hello moment.

Keep it pithy. Smart. Romantic. If that fails, grovel. Grovel for all you're worth.

The door opened. She looked radiant, all dressed up to receive her friends. Stunning, really. She regarded me first with shock, then with utter scorn. Beyond the doorway, I could see her Christmas tree covered with ornaments, each representing a different place and adventure.

No shark.

I stared wide-eyed at her, thinking back on the night I sent her home crying and the reality of what a fool I'd been. And I choked. The lines that worked so well on

Shadow only a few hours before eluded me. This was my one moment when I had to be great—and I had nothing.

I looked past Erica at the tree and thought of the ornament with the photo of the three of us. I never cared much about such things until that moment. I wanted our shark on that tree. I wanted to call it our own, share it with this gorgeous woman and her tornado-like man cub. I could see in the years ahead, our tree filling with ornaments found on countless great adventures, until someday, when we were gray and our faces lined, it would stand as our testament of a beautiful life spent together.

I stood in the doorway without a clue as to how I could possibly articulate that.

"Hi," I managed.

She glowered. "Hi."

"I told you I'd be here for Phoenix's surgery tomorrow and I am a man of my word."

This did not impress her.

So I groveled. I told her how sorry I was. I told her I loved her. I told her that I wanted her and Phoenix to move in with me back in Virginia Beach.

When she heard that, she said, "The only way I'm moving to Virginia Beach is with a ring on my finger."

I measured her eyes with mine. "Done."

She took me into her arms, and we held each other in the doorway. As we kissed, I realized that I'd just offered the lamest marriage proposal in history.

I'm really going to need a redo on that.

As we went inside, I realized that I still had something in my hands. I held it up and said, "By the way, I brought your hat back."

Chapter 5

Al Anbar Province, Iraq
September 2007

The sound of rotor blades swells in the distance. Normally, it is easy to tell the type of helicopter just by listening to it. Chinooks sound like they are beating hell out of the air with their massive double rotors. The five blades spinning above an MH-53 sound choppy and rough, while an MH-60 Black Hawk is much smoother.

Somewhere in the night, blades spin my way, and that's all I care about. The *chop-chop-chop* of the rotors grows louder by the second. It is the sound of hope.

Al appears beside me again, giving orders, and providing status updates over the radio. Someone else—I can't see who—lies prone not far away. He's taking measured shots with his rifle. No fire is returned.

"Al, do we have a full head count?" I ask weakly.

"Relax, Red. I've got this. You just hang on. The bird's one minute out."

That minute seems like forever.

I lie still, helpless, drifting and staring at the stars. The ground begins to tremble. The throb of the incoming rotors fills my ears.

My tourniquet!

The thought slams into my head with sudden clarity. I don't want to die seconds before rescue. "Al, I need a tourniquet on my arm. I'm going to bleed out."

"Already done, Red."

Once he tells me, I have a fleeting image of him bent over me, putting it on. When did that happen? Everything's so disjointed.

Al gets on the radio and begins talking to the rest of our team. They're moving up the road. I see shadows of men like ghosts in the night, but I recognize their silhouettes as ours. They have linked up with three of my teammates and are spreading out to set security for the incoming medevac. They'll protect the medevac bird and us until we're safely on board and heading for a combat support hospital.

The sound of gunfire ceases. My ears ring like a test of the Emergency Broadcast System. I'm dazed and feeling disconnected, unsure of what's going on around me. But I am not in pain, and the strength my prayer infused in me is holding firm. I just need to hold on for a few more seconds.

A Black Hawk glides like a protective shadow overhead. The pilot deftly sets the helicopter down perhaps seventy-five yards from our position. The timbre of its rotors changes as the pilot lets off the collective and reduces power.

My mind hunts for a crucial piece of information. It feels like I'm standing on a stepladder back home in the garage, reaching up to the top shelf and not being able to see what I'm searching for. My fingers brush it, sense it, but I don't have enough extension to get a good grip.

I will myself to focus. A Black Hawk's waiting for me. And then, the thought clicks into place.

At the briefing before the night's mission, we were told we'd be backstopped by a Special Operations aviation regiment helicopter. Their medevac birds carry flight surgeons, not just medics or corpsmen. I get to that bird, and I'll be under a doctor's care from the moment I climb through the door. For a moment I feel my strength surge. My ride is crewed by the best of the best.

What was I thinking about? Stars. So many stars.

They awe me again, even as part of me realizes something fell out of place inside my brain. My mind is jumping from subject to subject like a stock market ticker tape.

Suddenly I see Al standing over me. His face is smeared with grime and dust. Al's nationality has always been a mystery to all but his closest friends. He could pass for American Indian, or perhaps African American, or even Asian American. It was always entertaining to us that he'd go with whatever worked best for him in the moment, especially when talking to women.

He reaches for me, and I think of all the times we've played poker together.

Do I owe him money? Is this why he's trying so hard to save my ass?

Al grabs me by the drag handle on the back of my body armor and pulls me toward the medevac bird. The sudden movement sends bolts of agony through my body and I can't help but cry out. He doesn't slow down, even as the pain intensifies. I can hardly breathe.

"Stop! Stop!"

He pauses.

"You're killing me. Help me up."

I rest for a second until the pain recedes. Then he helps me struggle to my feet. All the renewed strength

God granted me goes into this effort now. I get my knees under me first. Then, holding on to Al, I stand.

"Al, grab my arm and my helmet."

I don't want my arm left behind in this godforsaken place. Besides, if there's any way to save it and reattach it, I want that option open.

He looks confused.

"Al, grab my arm and my helmet for me. Please."

We're accountable for all our sensitive items. Aside from our weapons, nothing is more sensitive than our night-vision goggles and armor. No matter what, I was not going to leave anything on the battlefield for the enemy.

Al nods then vanishes from sight for a moment, leaving me alone. I suppose he's hunting for my arm and helmet. I wait for him, stooped over as blood pours from my face to splash the ground at my feet. I stare at it, mind spinning, until he returns to put an arm around my shoulder. Together, we start walking for the helo. I try to get my head up, but blood fills my throat, so I stoop forward again to keep from choking. With each step, I leave dark stains in the soil behind us. The world tilts, then begins to spin around me.

We keep moving. Al's with me, stride for stride, making sure I don't lose my balance or trip.

The Black Hawk's whirling main rotor traces arcs of blue-white static-electrical light over the blades while it waits for us. These helicopters are big, vulnerable targets when sitting in a landing zone. We're trained to minimize that window of exposure by getting aboard as fast as possible. But there is nothing fast in my movements at this point.

We reach the Black Hawk to find the flight medic standing by the side door. There's a handle on the door we use to pull ourselves up into the bird. I grab it with my right hand, and it steadies me even as I grow dizzier. Then I struggle inside and lie down on the cold steel deck, exhausted from all the exertion. I drift again, losing touch with the moment.

Does Erica have dinner ready?

This doesn't feel like home. Dark and cold, metal beneath me. This isn't my bed. Where am I?

A scream shocks me back into myself. I'm staring up at the quilted soundproofing that lines the inside roof of the Black Hawk.

I'm in Iraq. I've been hit.

I sense movement and I catch a glimpse of Rob, our third wounded man, as the medics push him into the helicopter. Rob's been hit multiple times in the legs and arm, and moving him is no easy task due to his size. He's got to be at least six two, two thirty.

Normally, he's a quiet man who wears a scowl on his face most of the time. He probably got that visage from his days as a bar bouncer in college. In training, we discovered he is a brutal hand-to-hand fighter. All that toughness hides a well-read, profound intellect. It was months before I found out he had a degree in English literature.

Now, he's in agony. As they load him aboard, his scowl breaks and he cries out in pain. And then he's aboard and ready for the flight ahead.

"Hang in there, Red," I hear someone say hoarsely.

I turn my head and notice Brad already lying next to me. He says something else, but I can't make out his words.

With the three of us secure, the medic climbs back in. The crew chief relays word to the pilots over their intercom system, and the Black Hawk lifts off, pitching and swaying as it claws its way aloft. Its motions are soothing, calming; it feels like I'm being rocked to sleep.

Sleep. I feel so heavy. I want to let myself go. There is tranquility somewhere in the darkness, like a feather bed waiting to give comfort and peace after a long and busy day. I don't want to resist it any longer. I can't remember why I'm fighting it in the first place.

My eyes close.

I'm jolted back to reality as Brad tries to say something over the din of the Black Hawk's jet engines. I can't hear him or read his lips. But back in the moment again, I realize that I have got to keep my eyes open. The cold metal deck feels like a block of ice under my back.

All I have left is my will. If I give up, I'll die. But I can't do this alone. I think of the kids and Erica.

Stay awake for them.

God, carry me home to my children and Erica.

The sun sets on the Appalachian Mountains. We are getting married and we stand close as we hold our unity candles together into the flame. A breeze blows up the hill and blows them all out. We laugh and smile at each other and pretend nothing happened as we put the candles back in their holders.

In my broken mind, I can't help but think of the irony of the candles being blown out as my own flame slowly flickers and fades.

I hear yelling, and it jars me back into the moment. Brad is trying to talk to me, but the engines crush his words again. Rob is silent. The bird flies on, knifing through the Iraqi night at a hundred knots. The pitch and sway of our initial ascent has been replaced by a steady, subtle vibration. It is soothing and sleep inducing. I want to release myself to it.

The flight surgeon is busy working on us. He moves from Rob to me, then Brad. Head down, quietly focused, his hands a blur—I watch him, a consummate professional, and wonder how many broken men he's seen since coming to this desert battlefield.

Seconds tick by like hours. I can't even move my right arm anymore. How did I ever manage the walk to the helo? It would be so much easier to just relax and let go. There is a dark angel with me, waiting for that moment of release and acceptance so he can pull me from this world. I close my eyes, and it takes effort to open them again.

My kids.

My man cub.

My princess.

My angel.

I need to get back to them. I wasn't the best dad. I was selfish. I need this second chance.

You can do this, Jay. Stay awake.

I have to stay awake. As long as my eyes are open and I'm breathing, I have a fighting chance to keep the dark angel at bay. Get to the combat support hospital with a pulse, and I'll be okay.

My eyelids draw inexorably downward. The sound of the Black Hawk drifts away. I give into the darkness.

The darkness is warmth. The darkness is peace.

"Red, stay with us."

The words shock my system. My eyes fly open as I think I hear Brad call my name. Green light glows from the cockpit instrument panel. The Black Hawk's cabin is shades of gray and black. The shadow of the medic moves around me. The Black Hawk's engines whine.

I drift. And fight. I can't give in. I won't be drawn down into the darkness again.

Dear Lord, grant me this second chance.

The helo pitches upward and settles into a hover. A moment later, its wheels slap the ground. The pilots stand on their brakes. The door at my feet slides open. I'm still in the game.

I let my eyes close. For an eternity, they seem welded shut. Noises fade in and out. Unfamiliar voices bark orders I can't understand. Movement in the darkness. Shadows take shape then fade. The glare of halogen lights makes me realize my eyes are open again.

The moment resolves. The sound of the Black Hawk is distant now; its engines' roar diminishes like a fading memory. I'm on a stretcher, loaded on the back of some sort of golf cart next to Brad. I don't see Rob.

Where's Rob?

Brad talks to me. I can't make out what he says, but the intent is clear. He's encouraging me, trying to keep me from giving into the peace waiting in the darkness.

The golf cart rocks forward toward a nondescript building with double doors. Figures wait for us there. I want to talk to Brad, tell him we'll be okay, but I don't have the strength.

My eyelids force their way down again. The scene disappears. Sound telescopes until even the loudest noises seem like a lifetime away.

Splashes of light stripe my vision. Eyes are open again. Now I'm next to the building. There's an overhead platform above me. A man stands on it smoking a cigarette, staring down at me, face unreadable. Then the doors open, and the golf cart speeds inside.

"Hang on, Red. Hang on," Brad says over and over, like a mantra.

We're flooded by light so brilliant it whites out my view. I blink and squint, but I can see little beyond the glare.

Voices of authority fill the air around us. A nurse in brown scrubs and a surgical mask appears over me. I'm lifted off the cart onto something else. I'm not sure where I am or what I'm on, but I'm surrounded by men and women. Something tugs at me. I hear cloth ripping. The edges of the whiteness come into focus. I see equipment. Machinery. Tubes.

They cut away most of my gear and even some of my clothing. Voices, urgent ones, call down a hallway. I think they're taking me directly into an operating room. I close my eyes and feel the ride. Doors open. More voices.

We got here not a moment too soon. I feel the power drawing me down into the darkness again, and I'm too weak to resist. I've given all I've got to this fight, but there are limits even to the fiercest spirit. That barrier's been breached. All I've got now is a sense that I'm in good hands. These docs and nurses know what they're doing, and they'll see me through.

The medical staff lifts me up and places me on a table in the center of the OR. The scene is milky white, pulsing and malleable. Forms move, resolve, disappear. Colors come to life, burst through the glare just long enough to give me a hint of where I am. Then the whiteness smothers them again. I am bathed in light.

I feel something on my left side. Hands? Somebody's touching me, picking their fingers across the remnants of my gear. Something rustles. A tug. Then a frantic female voice: "He's still got a bomb on him!"

In an instant, the white haze vanishes. Adrenaline hits me. Eyes wide now, I watch the entire OR clear out. Nurses bolt for the nearest exits. Doctors scramble away. In an instant, I'm alone. The OR is silent as a tomb.

Not now. Not when I'm so close.

My thoughts jump back to the tug on my left side. Before wounded soldiers are wheeled into an OR, medical staff removes anything they consider to be a hazard. Bullets, grenades, explosives—anything that can blow up or jab them while they work on their patients gets stripped off and stashed somewhere. That tug on my left side must have meant someone had opened a pouch and found the grenade I keep there.

Just a grenade. Just a grenade. Pin is still in it. Taped and stowed. Safe.

"Don't leave me." *I can't tell if I'm talking out loud or not.*

I watch the doors, but they remain firmly closed. I have nothing left, my strength is gone.

The whiteness fades away. I close my eyes. The dark angel is there, waiting.

Chapter 6

Iraq
September 2007

A soft pulse chimes rhythmically in my ear. Others keep cadence, each with a slightly different pitch, like tinny electronic bells.

Beep . . . beep . . . beep.

Interspersed among the chimes, I register a steady, soft blowing sound. Conversations carry on around me in quiet, professional tones. A tray rattles. A cart clatters by. The bells toll in steady intervals. It is the symphony of survival.

A wave of pure euphoria overtakes me. Get to the Baghdad CSH with a pulse, and I'd be okay. That faith was not misplaced. The docs and nurses have pulled me through.

Erica and the kids—they are the anchor that has kept me moored in the storm. I think of them with pangs of guilt. My focus has not been on them over the years. I've been selfish and so involved in other aspects of my life that my time with them has atrophied.

I have to use this second chance to change that. I must make sure my path always leads to them. That must be the center of my new life.

I lie still, eyes closed, listening and drifting in a sort of drug-induced twilight. I've never taken drugs before, so I don't know what a high feels like. I am pretty sure I know now. It feels like I'm flying. What have they given me? Morphine? Probably. God knows what else.

I open my eyes, only to be assaulted by brilliant fluorescent lights. It takes a long moment for the room to come into definition. When it does, I see I'm surrounded by people I don't recognize.

Wait a minute.

Faces and forms start to come into focus. Gray hair, big burly guy, full face. That's my commanding officer, Commander Gil Bradford, standing next to the bed. At first glance, he still looks like the Big Ten offensive lineman he was once in college. He towers over me at six four, maybe two fifty. He's no lunkheaded football player cliché, though. Instead, one conversation with him will tell you he's wicked smart. We always joke that he's got the brain of a four-star admiral trapped in a commander's body.

Next to him is the balding, slightly shorter and stockier form of our master chief, Ernie Johnson. Ernie has almost thirty years in the SEAL Teams and carries himself with a quiet demeanor at all times. Like all SEAL master chiefs he is respected throughout all of Naval Special Warfare.

Seeing them sends my mood soaring even higher. My brothers are here. I want to shout out a big hello, but when I try to speak, no words come out. The bellows sound hitches and an alarm bell dings urgently.

What just happened?

"Don't try to speak," a voice I don't recognize says. A doctor? A nurse? Whoever it is stands beside my teammates.

"You've been shot in the face," the voice continues. "We had to trach you."

Trach? There's a tube running from my neck across my bed to a machine that's feeding me oxygen. That must be what the blowing sound is.

The voice tells me, "You're going to be okay, but you won't be able to talk because of the trach."

I nod slowly and think of the Colombian we trached so many years ago, and then that thought fades away. Nothing can take away the high I'm on. I'm one of the lucky ones: I got a second chance denied to so many others.

The doctor—nurse?—adds, "Because of the extensive damage to your face, we had to wire your jaw shut as well. You were in surgery for ten hours. You lost a lot of blood, but you pulled through."

Okay. No worries. Still on the right side of the earth.

"You were also shot in the left arm."

Out of the corner of my eye, I can see my left arm bandaged like a mummy's. It wasn't torn off during the firefight like I had thought. The realization doesn't really sink in at first. Through the drugs, I stare at it.

Huh. How about that.

I feel like I'm floating above the sheets. Light, detached, head swimming with disconnected thoughts, I lie engulfed in waves of euphoria.

Babe, Man Cub, Angel, Princess, I'm coming home to you.

"How's your pain level?"

I give a thumbs-up. No sweat there. I'm higher than the space shuttle. I don't even feel my body.

I lift my right arm and make a writing motion with it. A quick scramble ensues, and a moment later somebody hands me a pen and a pad of paper. Carefully, I write out three questions.

Are my guys okay?

Has my wife been notified?

Do I still look pretty?

I tear off the sheet of paper and hand it to Gil. He reads it for a long moment, then looks over at me. "Yeah, Jay, Rob and Brad are okay. They're both out of surgery now."

The news that everyone made it out is like an answered prayer. Relief and exultation mingle, sending me into an even higher state of euphoria. We're all going home to those we love.

Not so for the men who ambushed us. No victories for the enemy this battle.

Gil says, "Your wife's been notified. I spoke to her myself."

I try to nod. I want to thank him, but the trach and my wired jaw preclude that.

Gil looks slyly over at Ernie Johnson, then adds, "And the guys wanted me to tell you: you never looked pretty."

I want to write more questions, but the meds are making me float away. Somebody pulls out a camera, and I have enough presence to offer a smile and another thumbs-up before he snaps a pic. A moment later, a doctor (nurse?) fusses over my IV drip. I lose traction with the moment. A sudden and deep fatigue settles over me and I let go. My eyes close and I feel abiding peace.

When I wake up again, I hear all the familiar sounds of a military intensive care unit, but the scene is different. Gil and our master chief are long gone. So are the docs and nurses I saw when I came out of surgery. The place is unfamiliar.

A passing nurse sees my eyes are open and tells me I'm in Balad now, stable and waiting for a flight to Germany. At some point, I was put on a helicopter and flown out of Baghdad—and I don't have any recollection of it. In the space next to me, separated only by a curtain, a US Army soldier lies in a coma. He was hit in the head when a roadside bomb exploded beside his vehicle. If anything, he has even more tubes and wires sprouting out of his body than I do. A chorus of chimes and beeps keeps track of his vitals. They mingle with the ones coming from my heart monitor, IV, oxygen supply—God knows what else—until they form the soundtrack of the ICU.

I drift in and out. Shapes come and go. Nurses. Docs. I have no idea. It reminds me of a time-lapse camera filmed over days and then put into fast-forward. Blurs of motion and light strobe around me with no sense of rhythm or continuity.

Each time I awake, the realization that I am still alive floods me with that beautiful high. It comes on in a rush, then gradually mellows into a warm glow deep within me. The meds stoke the sensation, while at the same time making everything seem surreal and other-worldly. Reality blends with dreams—good and bad—until the line between the two is so blurred there are times I cannot distinguish one from the other.

At some point, I pick up on what the medical staff is giving me. It isn't morphine, but another opiate deriva-tive called Dilaudid. It is the most powerful pain-control medicine currently in use and is said to be eight times more potent than morphine yet substantially less addictive.

The ICU nurses have the Dilaudid hooked up into my IV. When I'm awake, I can self-medicate with the push of a button. Every ten or fifteen minutes, I push it, ensuring I remain in this twilight state of near-pain-free bliss.

I have no idea how many hours or days have passed, but as I come back into the world, I see figures crowded around my corner of the ICU. The scene is hazy, and at first I don't recognize anyone. Then it dawns on me as shapes take form: my teammates are here. John Prince, or J.P., our platoon's officer in charge and my boss, stands at the edge of my bed. With short, graying hair and weathered features borne from two decades with the SEAL Teams, he regards me with a look of mild amusement coupled with burning intensity. It is the same expression I've seen on his face countless times regardless of the situation.

Since my coming aboard the previous year, J.P.'s been a rare mentor and a friend. Seeing him here in the ICU does wonders for my morale. More than almost anyone else, he has shown me how to lead by setting an example with everything he does.

Over the years, I've had the honor to serve under many types of leaders and have developed a concept of leadership that can best be explained by what I call the "fence analogy." Imagine a chain-link fence with a small board that runs the length of its top. On one side of the fence, you've got those who fall underneath your leadership. On the other side are the people you report to in your own chain of command. Most men stand on one side of the fence or the other. Some men have an intense need to be loved by their men, to party and hang out with them. They identify too closely, and in the process, they have moved too far from the leadership fence. They lose the connection to those above them in the chain of command. That creates its own dynamic with a host of issues that can degrade the effectiveness of a unit.

The other extreme are the leaders who are scared to make decisions without the consent of those above them in the chain of command—the other side of the fence. They are often career-focused and ambitious and fail to connect with the men they need to lead, who consider them little more than political beasts. They have strayed too far the other way from the fence. They will tell their chain of command above them anything they want to hear and step on the backs of every man underneath them to make the next rank.

These are the extreme cases. Most leaders fall somewhere in between. The top ten percent stand right against the leadership fence and are respected by both sides. These people are connected, effective leaders.

Then there are the one percenters, men who define leadership and who people follow from both sides of the fence. These men are the tiny few who have climbed the leadership fence and stand on the small platform looking down at both sides; they are keenly aware of what is going on with both those they lead and those they follow. They have the unique ability to jump to whichever side is necessary at the time, connecting with those they need to connect with, before climbing back up to watch and survey the next moment of crisis.

J.P. is one of these men: a one percenter. He has been the epitome of leadership at all times.

Above all, J.P. always takes care of his boys. I've seen it countless times under countless situations, both in combat or with the chain of command. He cuts through red tape effortlessly, and his sense of what is right is absolutely solid. We always count on him to be that rock for us.

I know I can count on him now. As I look around, I don't see Al. He saved all of us that night in Al Anbar, and he has to be recognized for that. After greeting J.P., all I want to do is tell him what Al did for us.

I grab the pad the ICU staff had left for me and scribble,

Where's Al?

When I hand the note to J.P., he answers, "He had to stay behind to keep things running."

Damn jaw and trach. Trying to have a conversation takes forever, like talking to local Iraqis through an interpreter. You never really appreciate the art of verbal communication until it is denied to you. Now I'm reduced to filling blank pages on this notepad.

J.P., Al did an amazing job. We wouldn't have made it out without him. Our team and I owe him our lives. He deserves a Navy Cross.

J.P. reads this and nods. "I heard what he did. I was monitoring the radio through the entire fight. We'll write it up and get it taken care of. Don't worry about that."

Altogether, there are nine men from our platoon in the ICU. That's a full load off a Black Hawk, which was the first bird going from our base to Balad. They jumped aboard to come see the three of us and help keep our spirits up.

The conversation is light and full of wisecracks. They cajole me to stop being lazy and get back to the war. They hit on the nurses and crack stupid jokes. But the underlying current in the room runs far deeper. It isn't spoken about; it isn't even acknowledged. It is just there, a bond forged in combat that has long since made us as close as family.

A doctor wanders in. He senses what's going on, and he says to J.P., "See the private over there?" He motions to the young soldier in a coma, barely visible through the thin curtain that separates our rooms in this combat ICU.

J.P. nods.

"He's been here for days. Nobody's come to see him."

He lets that linger for a minute, then adds, "Your guy was here only a few hours and several Green Berets showed up to be with him for a while. They said they didn't know him, but he was a fellow Special Operations brother. It is amazing the camaraderie your community has."

The connection that fuels that camaraderie is based on respect. The doctor doesn't know it, but it must be earned. Just because you completed SEAL training doesn't give you instant access into the brotherhood. Far from it. You earn that bond and respect every day with everything you do. It is derived from your actions both on and off the battlefield. Screw up, let your teammates down even once, and that connection fails. The bond breaks. The camaraderie on display here recedes until you become a pariah.

As we chat, the AC-130 crew makes an entrance. My teammates greet them warmly, and they tell us that the fire missions Al called in that night were the closest to friendly troops ever carried out during the Iraq War. They bring me a flag and spent 105, 40mm and 25mm shell casings from the fight.

After they leave, J.P. tells me that Tony, another member of our platoon, has packed up some of my personal gear for me. They brought it with them aboard the Black Hawk and it is now set to go with me to Germany. J.P. mentions that Tony will accompany me all the way back to the States. The news is a relief. I won't be alone.

"You need anything? Can we do anything for you?"
J.P. asks.

I think about that. My iPod and speaker dock
are probably in my personal gear. I listen to music
constantly—everything from speed metal to country—
and for whatever reason in my drug-induced high, I
suddenly want to have my tunes with me.

Can you bring my iPod and dock to me?

J.P. nods and heads out of the ICU to search for my
gear. It has already been palletized and is ready to be
loaded aboard a C-17, along with a bunch of other gear
from a marine unit. Undeterred, J.P. starts barking
orders at the young marines as if he is a US Marine
Corps drill sergeant. They quickly break the pallet
down and find my bag, much to the chagrin of the aircraft's crew who had already inspected it.

When he returns to the ICU with the iPod and dock,
I thank him gratefully. I don't know why it was so
important at the time, but I really was looking forward
to some good tunes. If music soothes the savage beast,
it makes the doped-up wounded warrior relaxed and
ecstatic at the same time.

My iPod is dinged, scuffed, and beaten to hell from the
abuse of two deployments and multiple trips around the

world. I've stuffed it with songs for every mood and activity. Tony asks what I want to listen to. I think through the haze and lock in on a group that always gets me pumped and energized. That's the one. I write down one word.

TOOL

Immediately Tool kicks it off. I ask Tony to turn it up, and soon the ICU is filled with the slow power of this metal band.

Problem is, I'm still partially deafened as a result of the firefight. It is hard enough to hear the guys, but now the music seems muffled and distant, like I have cotton in my ears. On top of the muffles, I can barely hear over the constant ringing. I ask the guys to turn it up a bit more. It immediately gets louder.

A nurse pokes her head in and tells us to turn the music down. My teammates laugh at her and turn it up even louder. The ICU turns into a concert venue. The only thing we are missing is a mosh pit, which I'm sure is only seconds away.

A few minutes pass, and a doctor appears and tells us to turn the music down. They laugh even harder and chase him away just as fast.

Turn it up! Can't hear.

The volume edges higher. I watch as my teammates laugh and joke. The heart monitors beep on. Tool blasts through the ICU. My teammates make fun of one another and me. They tell me that I should have moved faster and that getting shot in the face will be an improvement. To an innocent bystander who just glanced in, I'm sure we appear like degenerate teenagers dressed up as soldiers. What they don't know is that this is how men who have walked with death act. The horrors of battle are far too serious. Keeping it light is what we do best. But below the surface, it is a different story.

I click my pain pump button and feel the warmth of the drugs wash through my veins. Euphoria once again. Despite what's happened to me, the show of unity here in the ICU is something, at one point in my past, I thought I would never see again.

I had severed the bond once. Few men get a shot at redemption after losing their brothers' trust. Not so long ago, through my own mistakes, I'd become a pariah. But I'd earned my way back, and this moment in the ICU was the expression of that triumph.

I steal a glance through the curtain at the young soldier lying motionless one bay over. His breathing is steady, thanks to the ventilator. His heart monitor sings a rhythmic tune. Alone, somewhere lost in his head, his body lies here without a single familiar face to stand watch over him.

If I had been wounded at the end of my previous combat deployment in Afghanistan, I wonder if I would have been alone. Through many poor decisions and one pivotal moment on the battlefield, I had destroyed the trust of my brothers. I became a leader without men willing to follow him. It turned me bitter. I lost my way, and it almost cost me everything.

Just as there is nothing like being part of the brotherhood of warriors, there is no greater pain than being exiled from it. It makes me realize the importance of the moment.

I glance at the young soldier again.

That could have been me.

PART II

The Breaking

Chapter 7

Bagram Air Force Base
Afghanistan
July 2005
Two Years Earlier

Before the entire Special Operations Task Force, including my deployed SEAL unit, a Humvee rolled across the vast aircraft parking area at Bagram Air Force Base and drew near the waiting Boeing C-17 Globemaster. The huge transport's cargo ramp was down, exposing its cavernous interior that could hold hundreds of combat-ready troops and their gear. Today, instead of carrying soldiers into a combat theater, it was taking a hero home.

Other operators joined my teammates to form a double line ten yards apart that stretched a hundred yards out from the end of the C-17's ramp. The sun shone high above us, blazing with all its desert intensity. We stood at attention, shoulder to shoulder, waiting while the blast-furnace heat baked us in our tan camouflage uniforms, taking part in a ritual done all too many times since the first American fell in this arid and desolate place four years before. No Special Operations warrior has returned to the States without this ceremony.

The Humvee drove in between this corridor of honor we had created with our bodies and parked a short distance from the end of the C-17 ramp. Six men stepped forward. They were the warrior brothers, the closest men to the hero going home. Together, they carried the flag-draped coffin from the Humvee to the waiting air force transport.

As one, we raised our hands in a final salute to Sonar Technician Second Class Matt Axelson. Matt was a native of Cupertino, California, home of Apple and countless other high-tech companies. He was a Monta Vista High School Matador, a '93 graduate who went on to college at Cal State Chico. It was the path that for decades had become a rite of passage for the children of Silicon Valley. In most cases, that path led back to the Valley where bountiful careers, McMansions, and stock options awaited.

That was not Matt's path. He chose service over salary and joined the navy to become a SEAL. On June 28, 2005, during Operation Red Wings, he was part of a four-man reconnaissance team inserted into a remote area of the Hindu Kush. Lieutenant Michael Murphy was to take his team to an overwatch point above a village where an enemy leader was supposedly hiding. Ordered to observe and confirm the leader's presence so a capture/kill mission could be launched, they were detected the next morning. A Taliban force assaulted them, and a fierce running battle ensued. Axelson and his team were overwhelmed during an intense firefight. One by one, they all were killed while fighting, except for Axelson's teammate Marcus Luttrell. Marcus and Axelson were the only two left when an RPG ripped in and exploded, sending them in opposite directions. Marcus notes that he never saw Axelson again and assumed he died from the blast. Though gravely wounded, shot in the chest and head, just before the RPG impacted between Marcus and Matt, Matt told Marcus to stay alive and "tell Cindy I love her." These were the last words spoken between the two. Marcus continued on as the last man standing and was later found and protected by a tribal Afghan village before eventually being rescued by American forces. When Matt's body was recovered, he was found with only one magazine left for his M4 rifle. He'd fought to his last breath, an act of bravery for which he would receive a posthumous Navy Cross.

As I stood at rigid attention, I initially felt awed to be here, honoring one of our fallen. Then his six brothers passed me, and my eyes fell upon the coffin. Matt was three days past his twenty-ninth birthday when he was killed. Somewhere on the other side of the world, his widow and his parents waited for him. The finality of it all, the lost potential of a brilliant life cut so short, struck me in that instant and crushed that sense of awe. What was left was like a cold vise around my heart, an aching sorrow that I could see mirrored on the faces across from me in our formation.

Though I did not know Matt personally, our lives had similar trajectories. I was class of '93, just like he was. My wife and family waited for my return, just like Matt's. Truth is, all of us in our community shared ties as Americans. As SEALs, we shared the risks inherent in our calling.

While we looked on, I realized it could be any one of us going home at the next ramp ceremony. With the war heating up in Afghanistan, we were under no illusions. There would be more of these. Red Wings underscored that. Nineteen Americans, including eleven SEALs, were killed in what up to that time was the worst disaster in the history of Naval Special Warfare.

The coffin was lowered to the metal deck inside the C-17 with a dull thump. Not far from the slate-gray Boeing, Bagram's runway stretched almost two miles through a board-flat valley. Beyond the stripe of asphalt towered a backdrop of mountains that rose thousands of feet from the valley floor so steeply that they could have come straight off the set of a fantasy movie. The terrain of Afghanistan, like the cultures that have survived there for eons, is one of extremes.

When the ceremony ended, we broke ranks and headed to the Combined Joint Special Operations Task Force (CJSOTF) camp, the main compound for US Special Operations Forces and their headquarters elements. The Naval Special Warfare compound, Camp Ouellette, was down the street from CJSOTF and was named in honor of Petty Officer First Class Brian Ouellette, a fellow SEAL I had worked with when I was younger. Brian was killed here in Afghanistan in 2004 when his vehicle was destroyed by a roadside bomb.

Having been here less than a week, Bagram was still unfamiliar to us, and finding our way around was a challenge. The place was a rabbit warren of new construction, B-huts, and leftover Soviet-era buildings that still showed the scars of the civil war that raged here in the 1990s.

At times, the Northern Alliance held one end of the airfield, the Taliban the other. The no-man's-land that filled the space between them became a crater-scape of skeletal buildings, wrecked aircraft, and burned-out vehicles.

It'd been almost four years since we'd taken over the place but there was still a lot of work to do. Much of the wreckage had been cleared out, but National Guard engineers and civilian contractors worked daily to clear the tens of thousands of mines left behind after twenty years of constant warfare. That was a hard way to earn a living. We lost people in those minefields, and locals who wandered into them were still coming into our aid stations with limbs blown off.

We reached Route Disney, the main avenue that ran north–south through Bagram. Humvees, armored vehicles, and colorful local contractor rigs we called "jinga trucks" made up the traffic flow that seemed never to slacken regardless of time or day. We made our way across it and merged into a crowded flow of people on the sidewalk.

I'd been all over the world since joining the navy, but I'd never seen so many nationalities represented in one place before I came here. South Korean medics walked

side by side with Polish infantry. Egyptian army doctors hurried along past Canadian officers and French
aviators. German, Czech, Japanese, and Jordanian uniforms salted the flow of American desert camis on both
sides of the avenue. The place was like a military melt-
ing pot drawn from across the free world.

We reached the CJSOTF camp, where we held a
memorial service to our fallen from Operation Red
Wings. In addition to the three men killed from
Lieutenant Murphy's recon element, eight more of my
brother SEALs died when the Taliban shot down the
Chinook helicopter trying to insert the quick reaction
force to help our beleaguered men. This was a severe
blow to my unit, because five of those men belonged
to Echo Platoon, our sister platoon. We also lost our
task unit commander, LCDR Erik Kristensen, in the
crash.

I had been part of Echo Platoon for a brief time and
knew all five of those men. Some of them were friends
I'd trained with for much of my navy career. One I had
known most of my career. We had shared barbecues
and compared notes watching our young daughters
grow up. Our youngest were only months apart. Now I
was sitting in a memorial service for them before we'd
even gone on our first combat mission. It bordered on
the surreal.

We grieved as warriors do. We took turns getting up and talking about the good times we shared. Some told raucous stories. Some told poignant ones. But that's how we get through these things. The irreverent tales later attracted attention and created controversy within the community. Truth was, those who were upset by those stories failed to grasp the dynamics working below the surface.

When the memorial service ended later that afternoon, we stowed our grief and prepared to get to work. We could not let our sense of loss destroy our ability to do our jobs. We had to suppress it, taking solace in the thought that our fallen brothers would stand watch over all of us as we took the fight to the enemy.

In fact, we all continued to mourn on some level. I know that even now, not a day goes by that I don't think about them. These days, when the American national anthem plays, I hold a roll call in my mind for every SEAL I know who has fallen. I am saddened to say, that after eighty-six losses, I can no longer complete the roll call before the last words of the "Star-Spangled Banner" are sung.

All that suppressed grief quickly morphed into a sense of outrage and a thirst for revenge. Our first mission was supposed to be conducted with Echo Platoon as a way in which the experienced outfit could show the new one the ropes. The mission picked for this battle handoff seemed perfect for us. A local Taliban leader had been identified by our intelligence network as the head of a cell responsible for launching rocket attacks against Bagram. We dubbed him the "Rocket Man," and capturing him became our first task in theater. In the days following the ramp ceremony, our team worked up a plan, sent it up the chain of command, and waited for the green light to execute it.

In the meantime, we helped the remaining members of Echo Platoon pack up their gear and get ready to rotate back to Germany. We'd been in Europe when Red Wings took place, working up to our Afghan deployment, which was scheduled to occur only a few weeks later. As soon as the magnitude of the loss became clear, our chain of command accelerated our rotation and sent us straight to Afghanistan. Now we'd take over for Echo as they assumed the watch rotation in Europe we'd been assigned to before arriving in Bagram. Basically, we were flip-flopping spots early because of the Red Wings disaster.

As Echo prepared to rip out, they shared as much information and knowledge as they could with us. We listened carefully and tried to absorb everything, but it was no substitute for experience. We needed to get our boots in Afghan sand somewhere beyond the safety of Bagram's HESCO bag walls. There is just no substitute for combat experience.

Every afternoon at 1600, we'd gather in our planning room for our daily update brief, which was delivered by Pete Kerry, our senior chief. He'd start off with a rundown of all the significant events in our area that had taken place the previous twenty-four hours. Then there would be a description of the weather expected for the next twenty-four, as well as what other units would be doing over that period. If we had a mission of our own, Senior Chief Kerry would tell us at that point and detail how we were to execute it.

Those early meetings after Red Wings became morale busters. Each afternoon, we arrived amped and ready to go get the Rocket Man, only to be told we had not received the go order yet. The letdown got worse and worse as the weeks passed. Our brothers had been killed in a last stand against a vicious enemy, and here we were stuck in our fortress within a fortress. Few of us had seen combat yet, though we'd trained for it all our adult lives. Now, finally in a combat zone, we had yet to clash with the enemy. It was incredibly tough to take.

The delay cost us our chance to work with Echo Platoon, whose members finished packing up and began to depart in mid-July. When and if the word came down from on high to launch the mission, we'd have to do it without our sister platoon backstopping us.

Three weeks after the ramp ceremony, we walked into the afternoon brief to find Chief Kerry waiting for us with news.

"The mission is on," he announced.

The mood in the room instantly shifted. Gone were the long faces and sense of frustration. This was really going to happen now. We sat down, alert and keen and ready to go.

The chief walked us through the mission, though we all knew our roles since we'd had little else to do but prepare for it since the ramp ceremony. As he talked, a sense of nervous anticipation mingled with our excitement and made the atmosphere in the room almost electric.

At length, he wrapped up the brief. "We go at 0100. Try and get some sleep."

The meeting broke up and I went back to my hooch to get my gear prepped and ready. I sat down on my bunk and inventoried everything. I kept my helmet, body armor, chest rig, and M4 on a wooden H-rack next to my bed. All my gear was already attached to it so that all I needed to do was put it on and go.

My rifle was cleaned and ready. Six magazines sat snug in my chest rig, each one within easy reach so I could reload with maximum speed. That gave me almost a hundred and eighty rounds of 5.56mm ammunition for the M4. I also carried a Sig Sauer P226 pistol with three fifteen-round clips. Frag grenades and flash bangs rounded out my offensive firepower.

I checked over my night vision, radios, and medical supplies and made sure my CamelBak held a full bladder of fresh water. When I finished, I pulled my boots off and climbed into bed. Time to sleep.

I lay there trying to let myself drift off, but my mind kept jumping from one thought to the next. I'd been close to firefights in South America during my early years with the teams back in the 1990s, but I'd never been under direct enemy fire before. After the 9/11 attacks, I thought I would miss the war on terror altogether. A month before the towers fell, I had started college at Old Dominion University. The year before, I had applied to the Seaman to Admiral program, something the navy started to encourage top-performing enlisted to become officers. Only fifty candidates a year were accepted back then, so the competition was fierce. I gained a slot, and the navy sent me to college just in time to miss the outbreak of the war.

As I watched the towers fall, I recognized the magnitude of the moment and left school in a daze fully aware that our country was heading to war. With three years of college ahead of me, I feared I'd miss my chance to be a part of it. A few days later, I drove back to my old SEAL team to see my former CO and mentor, Commander Vince Peterson. He had stuck his neck out for me more than once and had been instrumental in getting me a slot in the Seaman to Admiral program.

I told him I wanted to drop out of school so I could get back to a platoon and help with the war effort. Commander Peterson sat listening quietly as I explained my desire to come back. He was a legend in the SEAL Teams. He had been a former marine before joining the navy and headed to SEAL training at the age of thirty-six. He was highly respected both up and down the chain of command. In my leadership fence analogy, most men fell on one side of the fence or the other, while there were those small few who had the unique ability to stand on top and move back and forth. For Vince Peterson, there was no fence.

As I sat down with him and asked him to put me back in a platoon, he looked me dead in the eye, and said, "Red, this will not be a short war. It is going to go on for years, and we're going to need strong warriors and leaders for the upcoming battles. You need to stay in school. Then come back and lead."

His wisdom resonated with me and I headed back to school, still agonizing over being left on the bench as my brothers went into battle in Afghanistan and later Iraq. At times, after hearing of amazing battlefield successes or the loss of friends, I'd think I'd made the wrong call and I'd reflect on Commander Peterson's words. Unfortunately, it would be years of hardship and trial before I would bring his wisdom full circle and understand what it meant to be a good leader and what level of character it took to lead men into combat.

Since I had committed to staying in school, I decided to make the most of it. I threw myself into my studies and campus life. I excelled at school, graduating with honors, and ultimately worked my way up to become the student battalion commander of the largest US Navy ROTC program on the East Coast. At the end of my senior year, as I prepared to graduate and return to the teams, I organized a charity event that gained national media attention. We called it the Run for Freedom. On April 3, 2004, navy and army ROTC candidates, midshipmen, and cadets, along with other ODU students, faculty, and staff, joined community and military members in running the American flag nonstop on a one-mile course around the campus.

Each mile, completed by a solo runner, was in honor of a single serviceman or -woman killed in the war on terror. At the completion of each lap, a small flag bearing the service member's name was placed in a pegboard as a visual memorial to the more than seven hundred troops who had been killed since September 2001. Some of those flags represented men I'd served with in the '90s, a painful reminder that I was not out there alongside my brothers where I belonged.

As we completed the run, I recognized, in only a few weeks, I would finally have a chance to prove myself and contribute to our nation's defense. I'd be out in the field, doing what the other teams had already been doing for the past three years. The thought of returning to lead these men was somewhat intimidating, but I quickly put the thought behind me.

When I graduated in May 2004, I couldn't wait to get back to operational status. But I also knew that, as I left school, my family would go through a painful transition. Erica and Phoenix had grown used to me being at home every night. Those three years were the most stable and concentrated time we shared together. No sudden trips. No deployments, no temporary duty on the far side of the country. We established our household and domestic life during those years. Angelica was born in my second year of school and I felt blessed to be home and spend the time with my new daughter. Shortly before graduation we found out Erica was pregnant again. I was convinced it was a boy and when the sonogram technician told me it was a girl, I was adamant she had made a mistake. I inquired how long she had been doing this job and she gave me a dirty look and replied, "Over thirty years, Mr. Redman." Looked like we were having another girl.

Shortly after that, the navy commissioned me an ensign and everything changed. Our lives together became more episodic than consistent. I was gone for increasingly longer periods of time, which put the onus of running the household and caring for our children on Erica. It was a difficult phase for us, but that foundation built while I was at school became our saving grace.

That summer of 2004, I joined my new SEAL team as my new platoon's assistant officer in charge (AOIC). I was excited to be back within the brotherhood again, and thought that I'd have a leg up as a leader with all my prior experience as an enlisted operator.

I could not have been more wrong. The three years away from the SEAL Teams turned out to be the biggest time of change for Naval Special Warfare since Vietnam. Combat had taught us that many of our tactics and procedures simply were not effective in this terrain and against this ambiguous enemy. As battle-hardened operators returned home, their experience percolated throughout the community, prompting a full-scale rewrite of how we did business.

Instead of having an advantage, I found myself left behind. Everything had changed, and as our platoon went through its training cycle, I always felt like I was playing catch-up. I made mistakes in exercises that I'd never made in the '90s. It made me edgy and tense feeling the pressure of trying to be a leader and drinking from that training fire hose at the same time. I got tight and held on even harder, which only made things worse. In our time off, I drowned my frustrations in booze and routinely made an ass of myself. None of this was helping my credibility with the men I was supposed to be leading. But I didn't see that in the moment.

It also didn't help that Senior Chief Pete Kerry and I despised each other almost from our first introduction. He was a good, skilled SEAL, and I respected his tactical abilities. But I felt his people skills were lacking. Rough and abrasive at times, his leadership style clashed with mine, which set us on many a collision course. While I privately railed against Kerry, I was too blinded by arrogance to see my own flaws. I wasn't making a good transition to being an officer. I'd been enlisted for so long. I identified with my enlisted teammates more as one of them rather than as one of their leaders. It put me too far away from the fence.

The senior chief and the AOIC are supposed to work closely together to make sure the team functions effectively. The AOIC is also supposed to learn from the chief's tactical experience. That never happened in our platoon. Instead, I refused to humble myself and listen to the senior chief. As the predeployment workup wore on, we couldn't conceal our dislike for each other. The feud spilled out into the open and culminated with a public screaming match in Europe after a tactical exercise with some NATO allies.

In the weeks that followed my arrival with the team, our relationship became the cancer in our locker room. By the time we got to Afghanistan, we refused to even be civil to each other. I had lost touch entirely with what it meant to be a leader. During the daily briefs, we took open shots at each other. I'd talked about this dynamic many times with my superior, the platoon's officer in charge. One day, the OIC finally said, "Look, you two have to work this out. I'm tired of it."

We never could or did work things out.

As I lay in my bunk a year after graduation and coming aboard, I wrestled with this. I realized that the time had passed for Kerry and I to resolve our differences. As a result, we'd be going into combat within a matter of hours with a dysfunctional dynamic within our platoon.

However much we hated each other, I knew we would have to find a way to function in the field together. Later that night, he would lead one assault team to the Rocket Man's compound. I would be part of that element and would have to follow his orders. It grated on me.

Different platoons structure things in different ways. In our platoon, senior enlisted members acted as fire team leaders with chiefs and some more experienced officers acting as the assault force commanders. I had been assigned as neither. If I had taken a step back, I might have realized I hadn't given my bosses much confidence in my leadership. But I didn't see that. I only felt slighted and embittered.

Given the opportunity, I'd have to prove myself tonight.

Sleep forgotten, I checked my watch. Two hours until showtime. I sat up and went through my gear once again with meticulous attention to detail. All those years of training drilled into me that the little things could serve as the margin between life or death in the field. A misplaced magazine, a radio on the wrong frequency, or a grenade not properly taped and ready to go and you could end up having a serious problem at the worst possible time. There was no way I was going to let that happen.

Tonight's mission was as complex as anything we'd ever done in training. We'd be using both helicopters and Humvees, explosives and simultaneous entries into darkened compounds within which we would face a host of unknowns. Would the Rocket Man make a stand inside his house? In training, with enough firepower, we'd found we could almost always overwhelm any resistance inside a building, but at times it came at a heavy price.

I finished my second pass and sat at the edge of the bed, lost in thought. As AOIC, I should have been in a leadership position. Senior Chief Kerry probably made sure I would have to report to him until we secured the target. In retrospect, such thoughts were just compounding my mistakes. I wasn't focused on my task. I was focused on what I *wasn't* doing, which only added to my resentment.

The minutes dragged by. At last it was time to go. I strapped my gear on, grabbed my rifle, and headed out the door.

A half hour later, I stood on the tarmac with my teammates, making last-minute preparations for the mission. Four MH-60 Spec Ops Black Hawks were standing by and waiting for us, their crew chiefs making last checks on their birds. We'd be wedged in tight tonight. The plan called for twelve to fourteen men in every Black Hawk.

We were minutes away now. A short flight and we'd be on the ground. I looked around. My teammates were mostly quiet and focused. The usual banter was absent tonight. Since almost none of us had combat experience, we didn't know exactly what to expect. That unknown factor made us draw into ourselves.

Say a prayer, Jay.

The thought crept up and stopped me in my tracks. I hadn't thought about God in ages. The days of going to church every week ended during my senior year in high school when I left North Carolina. I stowed my spirituality the day I joined the navy. I lied to myself for years, saying there was no place for God in the SEAL Teams. Impending combat has a way of changing the most resolute mind.

I stepped toward my teammates. "Hey," I said, "if you all don't mind, I'd like to say a prayer for us."

The team gathered together beside one of the Black Hawks. The night was windless, still and humid. A waning moon hung low on the horizon and cast a silver glow across the tarmac. Heads bowed, I prayed for my brothers and for a safe, successful mission. When I looked up, the moment was gone. The Black Hawks' auxiliary power unit began to whine. Rotors were soon spinning. It was go time.

We climbed aboard our assigned birds. Special Operations Forces are some of the few in the military who are waived from the requirement to have seats in their helicopters. Due to the nature of our missions and the need for speed and space, we fly with no seats. We secure ourselves to a lanyard from our belt clip to the helicopter's deck so we don't tumble out in the event of an emergency or radical maneuvers.

The best spots were in the doorway, feet hanging out, ready to run toward the target the second the bird landed. Those not hanging out the doors were stuffed inside the helo, where it soon got so cramped we felt like sardines in a can with spinning blades overhead. I was smashed deep inside the stack, as far from the doors as one could get. Fortunately, this flight would not last long. The Rocket Man only lived a few miles from the runway.

A moment later, the Black Hawks lifted off into the night. I left my thoughts of God back on the tarmac.

Chapter 8

Outside of Bagram Air Force Base
July 2005

The Black hawks sped low over the flat Afghan countryside en route to our target area. Below us was a crazy quilt of *qalats*—walled compounds—farmers' fields, and clustered mud-walled villages. As we reached our infil point, the pilots nosed up and bled speed off until we settled into a hover about thirty feet off the ground. Suspended in the air over a bad guy's house made us sitting ducks for anyone with an RPG. It made every second that passed in that vulnerable state feel like forever.

"Movement on the roof," one of our snipers reported as he studied the Rocket Man's house.

The report added urgency to our movements. My teammates tossed thick braided green lines overboard, then began fast roping into a field beside our target's outside wall. My turn came and I found myself in the door, looking out over the Rocket Man's compound. I clutched the rope and went over the side. I was the last one out. It took perhaps ten seconds to empty the Black Hawk.

I slid down the rope and landed almost atop one of my teammates. Our assault element had come down in a mulberry field. The plants had been arranged in rows between deep irrigation ditches, making the place look like a thigh-high version of the Normandy hedgerows. It caused a bottleneck at the bottom of our rope as the guys got channeled into one of the irrigation ditches. For a minute there, I'm sure we looked like Keystone Cops.

We untangled ourselves and moved to the target area. As we reached the edge of the mulberry field, one of my teammates suddenly disappeared. He popped up a second later and gave a thumbs-up. He'd fallen into a dry sewer ditch.

As our assault element reached the Rocket Man's thick metal gate, I could see our second team already placing their explosive charge on the brother's door a few dozen meters away from us. The walls of the two compounds adjoined and made an L. Our team was on the north–south leg of the L, the second team on the base.

We stuck our explosive strip to the door, prepped it, and backed up along the wall to wait for its detonation. A moment later, it exploded and blew the gate to pieces. That was our cue to get inside as fast as possible. We set off, weapons at the ready, just as the second assault team blew the brother's gate. The blast wave struck us and nearly knocked us off our feet. We'd been almost directly across from the explosion, and it rocked our world far worse than any flash bang I'd been hit with in training. I was seeing stars.

This was a critical moment in the mission. Going through a door is dangerous enough—they are channel points that we call the "fatal funnel." If somebody's on the other side with a weapon, there's no missing the men coming through the doorway. Training and combat experience has shown the only way to deal with such a vulnerable moment is to get through the doorway as fast as we can, always ready to engage anything on the other side. Speed, surprise, and violence of action are the key elements to taking down a building and crushing any attempt at resistance. Now, at the crucial moment, we'd had our bells rung.

Fortunately, we did not stop. Stars spinning in our heads, we plunged through the doorway into the Rocket Man's courtyard. A small building stood to the right, while the main house was on the left. Overhead, a figure appeared on the roof. Our interpreter yelled for him to come down as part of the assault team covered him. The rest of us drove headlong into the buildings.

I went right and cleared what turned out to be a small storage shed. I came out and got into the main house long enough to clear a couple of rooms on the first floor. Thirty seconds later, Senior Chief Kerry called "Target secure!" over the radio.

That was my cue to take over the objective. I'd been assigned as the sensitive site exploitation (SSE) commander for this mission, which meant, once the target was secure, it was my job to organize the detainees, get them processed, and make sure the compound was thoroughly searched. If the search teams found anything compromising, we would bag and tag the evidence, and I would report it up to the ground force commander (GFC), J.D. Richardson.

J.D. was our SEAL Team's executive officer but took over the task unit after our original task unit commander, Erik Kristensen, was killed during Red Wings. J.D. was about five ten, one hundred ninety pounds, with close-cut brown hair. He was a fast runner. I was pretty quick back then too, and I frequently found myself racing with him back in the States before we deployed. He was an Academy grad and had a polish about him that many Academy grads maintained. Not that it made him good or bad; it's just the way he carried himself, like a career businessman or politician. I know it made some of the guys dislike him. They felt he came across as disingenuous at times.

J.D. asked for a status report as I moved through the compound. These compounds housed a lot of people. Though we'd shown up in the middle of the night, we encountered well over three dozen men, women, and children. With the assault force now in search mode, I took several of our guys and separated the military-age males, the men who appeared over sixteen, from the women and children. Our second wave, the ground mobility force, rolled up in Humvees after the target was secure. They brought with them several female military police officers, or MPs, to help search the women we'd encountered. With the cultural sensitivities regarding women in Afghanistan, it was rare if we went on a target without women MPs. As they arrived, I directed them to take the women and children to a room inside the main house where they would be safe.

We began identifying the men and questioning them. The Rocket Man had been the figure we'd seen on the roof. We positively identified him and were set to transport him to his own personal cell at Bagram. The other men we weren't so sure about at first. As we talked to them though, it became clear that some were coconspirators of the Rocket Man. We'd have to take them with us too.

While we were busy with that, Senior Chief Kerry led some of our team to a few nearby outbuildings beyond the compound wall. After trying one of their doors and finding it locked, he called on the radio to me, "Hey, ask one of those guys if they have a key to this place."

"Roger," I replied.

Our interpreter spread the word we needed a key. The men all played dumb. Shrugs and blank looks abounded. Like we're stupid enough to think they don't have keys to their own properties.

At length, I reported back to the senior chief, "That went nowhere. Go ahead and breach it."

We tried to avoid doing this as much as possible, as the US taxpayer was on the hook for all damage we inflicted during these raids. If a door got broken, we replaced it. If a goat got killed somehow, we'd buy a replacement goat. It was part of our hearts and minds campaign to not put any undue hardship on the local population.

Senior Chief Kerry and the men with him kicked the door in and searched the structure. It turned out to be clean.

That just cost us about two hundred bucks.

The search continued as our other assault team from the brother's compound brought over their military-age males as well. Soon, we had about twenty of them in the compound's courtyard. They seemed in remarkably good cheer given the circumstances. They stood together, smiling and joking as they waited for their turn to be identified and processed.

By now, dawn was fast approaching. A kid poked his head out of the main house. He watched the scene, then darted into the yard. Several others followed. Soon, we had kids racing back and forth all over the courtyard, playing games and laughing. One of them noticed that our youngest team member, Seth, was the only SEAL on the team without a beard. To better blend in and interact with the locals, Special Operations units are allowed to wear beards, and growing them often becomes a competition. Many of us had already grown bushy, Rasputin-like beards even though we'd only been in-country for a short time.

Seth's smooth skin and lack of whiskers drew considerable interest, and soon several boys crept closer to Seth, giggling and smiling.

"Baby! Baby!" they began to chant in Pashtun.

Seth smiled back at them, a good sport.

They ran up to him and stroked their bare chins, as if they had beards, before scooting back a short distance to laugh again. Finally, one of the military-age males shouted at the children. That killed the moment, and the kids went back in the house to be with the women.

The sun was climbing higher in the sky, leaving us more vulnerable. We needed to finish things up and get out of there as soon as possible. To protect us while we searched the compounds, our snipers had established overwatch positions on rooftops of nearby buildings. Together with some of our other teammates, they formed an outer cordon to make sure we would not be surprised by an enemy force entering the area.

Now one of the snipers reported, "We have unarmed people coming our way here. Lots of movement."

About then, our men searching the Rocket Man's house struck pay dirt. They uncovered a secret cache of explosives, IED-making equipment, and a homemade device for launching rockets. Our intel had been spot-on: these were the guys responsible for attacking our base. As the search team bagged and tagged the evidence, we finished identifying the military-age males. After questioning them, it looked to us as if about half had some sort of involvement with the rocket cell. We separated and zip-cuffed them. When we did, they grew sullen. The detention facility at Bagram was well-known among the Taliban, and it was no picnic.

The snipers reported more movement as a crowd gathered on our perimeter. A small group broke away to walk straight for the Rocket Man's compound. The snipers warned us that they were coming. A few minutes later, an aged, bearded Afghan walked imperiously up to the door of the compound, followed by several others who looked to be his aides.

"What are you doing here?" he demanded through our interpreter.

J.D. was the senior man on target and was waiting to meet him. He tried to explain, but the man angrily cut him off. I watched as the local elder stomped his foot like a petulant child. He was supposed to be notified anytime American forces came to his village. "Why wasn't I notified?" he asked.

J.D. tried to calm him down. He ignored the effort and began cataloging his complaints. "You come to our village in the middle of the night! With helicopters! You blow things up and scare my people! We had an agreement. I am to be notified!"

We tried to mollify him without any luck. Instead, he ordered us to release our detainees into his custody. "If they are bad, we will deal with them ourselves," he assured us.

Yeah, right.

Commander Richardson excused himself and took me aside. "Red, take your SSE team and the Rocket Man along with the other detainees and get them off target. Okay?"

"Roger, sir."

The commander rejoined the elder and listened to him carp on as I got our team together with the eight detainees. They looked very nervous now and barely said a word.

A helicopter would come to extract my group, while Humvees would pull the rest of the team out of the objective area. We needed a good landing zone for the Black Hawks, so we patrolled north of the compound in search of a good stretch of open ground. We found an excellent spot about a hundred and fifty meters from the Rocket Man's back wall.

As I busily got everything ready for the helicopter's arrival, Chief Mike Peters came out of the compound to see what we were doing. I'd known Mike for a couple of years, and he was one of the most senior, and respected, NCOs in our task unit. At the same time, part of the crowd saw us and began to drift our way. Another wall, this one about six feet high, flanked one side of the field, and the civilians gathered there to climb on it and watch. They looked pretty agitated with us.

Mike walked to our landing zone, looking pissed off. Considered the air expert for East Coast Naval Special Warfare Teams, he knew everything there was to know about helicopters and operating with them. He was also a joint tactical air controller (JTAC) and could call in air strikes using everything from marine AH-1 Cobra gunships to air force B-1 bombers.

"Listen up," he announced gruffly. "Here's what we're going to do."

I stood, shocked as he changed the entire configuration of my team. What the hell? I stormed over to him and began to argue.

Mike cut me off. "Shut the hell up. Get you and your people and your prisoners lined up how I tell you. The helo's inbound now."

As I simmered with rage over the smackdown, more people appeared on the wall at the edge of our landing zone. This was starting to get hairy; any one of them could have a weapon. An RPG gunner could be hiding behind the wall, just waiting for the moment to inflict maximum damage. We needed to get off target before this got out of control.

Mike repositioned everyone just in time. A Chinook appeared in the morning light, made a circuit overhead, and set down in our landing zone. Nobody had told me we were getting a Chinook instead of a Black Hawk, and that makes a huge difference on how you configure the LZ. One Chinook can carry four times the number of men that a Black Hawk can. Plus you enter and exit the Chinook from the rear, as opposed to the sides with a Black Hawk. I felt like a fool and burned over the incident as we streamed aboard.

Right after we started to lift off, somebody in the crowd opened fire. Our teammates still on the ground shouldered their weapons and returned it. A scattered, brief fight ensued until our ground force commander decided it was time to get everyone out. As we landed back at Bagram, the rest of the team climbed into Humvees and drove back through the gate as my team and I took the Rocket Man and his confederates to the detention facility.

We linked back up at Camp Ouellette. Our first time beyond the wire and we'd found our targeted bad guy. We had fast roped out of helicopters, blown two doors to gain simultaneous entry into a pair of compounds, and taken both down without a single shot fired. We'd ended up with eight captured Taliban and enough evidence to keep the Rocket Man in Parwan Detention Facility for the foreseeable future. Never mind the hiccups and the argument in the LZ, we'd done what we'd set out to do.

We'd trained for this all our adult lives. The victory was a culmination of all the work and preparation we'd done for years. Seeing how it all paid off filled me with a sense of deep pride. And this was just our first mission—there was much more work to be done in the weeks and months ahead.

We went to bed that morning pleased with our success, but we stopped short of the celebrating seen in so many war movies. The ethos of the quiet, professional warrior reminds us how to be in such moments. Besides, we knew that in the upcoming missions, we would surely have as many missed opportunities as successes. At least, that was the experience of our friends who had preceded us into battle. Still, our first time out and we scored a solid victory. It did wonders for our morale.

While we slept, though, everything went to hell.

Chapter 9

That morning, the crowd that had congregated at the Rocket Man's house followed our Humvees back to Bagram. More and more people gathered at the front gates, until one estimate put the total at over two thousand. They screamed and chanted, burned tires, and gave interviews to journalists who ventured among them. When a convoy showed up to gain entrance into Bagram, the mob rushed the vehicles. The Americans, unsure of what was going on, fired pistols into the air to drive the crowd back. The mob replied by pelting the rigs with rocks. When the Afghan guards opened the gate, the Humvees pulled inside even as knots of protesters charged after them. Energized, the mob tried to force the gates open and gain entry into the main base itself. The Afghan soldiers on duty waded into them, swinging clubs and firing their AKs into the air. The onslaught drove the protesters back into the street, but they refused to leave. They chanted "Death to America!" and kept calling for the Rocket Man's release. Some of the protest was filmed live by CNN, and we watched part of it in our operations center later that day.

It was not hard to see the village elder's hand in all this. When he came to speak to us, he had complained that nobody had discussed the raid with him. Later, when journalists interviewed members of the crowd, they all said the Americans should have consulted with local authorities before launching the mission.

The protest earned coverage across the globe. Reporters chasing the story approached the US military and wanted to know why the local elder hadn't been consulted. Well, the truth was obvious—we didn't trust him. Instead, the public affairs officer, LTC Jerry O'Hara, told the press that both the US and Afghan forces tried to inform the local authorities that we were coming, but that they could not reach them.

The media reported that we'd taken eight villagers into custody, including a local cleric and a former senior leader of the Northern Alliance. We didn't know if that was true or not. But there was no mistaking the outrage that flowed our way from Kabul. The Rocket

Man turned out to be friends with Afghan president Hamid Karzai, whose office sent our chain of command blistering demands for his immediate release.

Despite the evidence we'd found, our command gave in to Karzai. After less than two days in lockup, the detention facility released the Rocket Man and his confederates. The news came like a sweep to the legs. Here we'd risked our lives to execute the mission. We'd come off target with eight bad guys, only to discover they were friends of our ally's senior governmental leadership. This first blow we'd struck for the brothers we'd lost in Red Wings turned into a political firestorm, and all the evildoers returned to their homes. Where was the justice?

That night, the team received a second blow. The general in charge of all operations in Afghanistan had issued an order prior to our arrival that all planned night raids using fast rope infils and explosives had to be personally approved by him. He didn't know anything about our raid until the effects of it hit the international media. Outraged that we'd gone off his reservation, he stood the entire team down and initiated an investigation.

Until it was finished, we would not operate. It felt like house arrest. We stayed at Camp Ouellette and feared for our futures. The next day, Commander Richardson was ordered to appear before the general. I saw him nervously gather up his things and head out the door. Around the base, we wore civilian clothes, which, combined with our beards, gave us an unmilitary bearing that rubbed many traditional military officers the wrong way. J.D. went to meet the general dressed that way, which only made things worse for us. When he returned from the face-to-face, he mused, "I should have put my uniform on for that meeting. It may have gone a little better." Apparently, the general had chewed him out for his attire and grooming on top of everything else.

The forces of political correctness aligned against us, and we could feel the storm surge heading our way. All this over a successful operation where we did what we were trained to do left our morale in the tank.

Senior Chief Kerry took a philosophical view. As long as we had downtime, he wanted to keep us focused on what we could do in the future and start planning future missions so that we would be prepared to go once we received clearance. Our intel shop had already prepped a small mountain of portfolios on Taliban operatives who needed to be taken out; we just needed to plan the best ways to go get them. Then go do it, of course. But as long as we were sitting on our hands, he argued that we might as well lay the foundation for future operations.

My boss, Fred Derry, the team's officer in charge (OIC), had some ideas for me too.

"We need to get you your own mission to plan, Red," he said after one of our daily meetings.

I relished the chance to have such a hands-on role and opportunity to lead and couldn't wait to get started. I was given a civil affairs mission. Nothing too risky, but a great one to learn the planning process. Our team would provide security for an army civil affairs unit that wanted to go into a remote village, meet the elder, and begin talks on public works projects that they needed. We were tasked to plan the most secure route and provide security for the civil affairs team while they were in the village. I threw myself into this mission and spent hours working with the other members of the team to develop our plan.

Meanwhile, the investigation wrapped up and it was concluded we had done everything right. The mission plan had been sent by our team up the Special Operations chain of command, where it had been approved and routed to the general's staff. As it turned out, the general had been away from his headquarters when the request came in, which is part of the reason why he never saw it. His staff approved it, sent word back to our chain of command, then somebody at his HQ forgot to tell the general about it. The error was on his side of the house, not ours.

We breathed a collective sigh of relief when we were returned to operational status. After this mess, we couldn't wait to get back out there and go to work. We had almost forty intel packages in our to-do box, with plenty of missions already prepped and ready for approval. Within a day, we began sending them up the chain of command, awaiting the green light to go out and conduct operations.

Our first one was denied. We fired another one up the chain. The general denied it as well. At first, we were puzzled. These were good missions based on solid intel against serious bad guys. What was the hang-up?

A week passed, and every mission we'd requested had been shot down. Morale wavered again. Two weeks into this dynamic, and it felt like the general was still punishing us. What good were we doing sitting on the safest FOB in Afghanistan? Doing nothing hurt. It would have under any circumstances, but in the aftermath of Red Wings, this box we'd been stuffed into seemed doubly cruel. We grew bitter and edgy. We planned more missions, thoroughly debriefed the one we'd executed, and spent the rest of the time exercising, sleeping, or watching movies.

Toward the end of August, firefights raged all over Afghanistan while we sat on our hands. Even my civil affairs mission got denied. This made no sense to us. It was drawn up in line with the general's own guidelines: a daylight op without a fast rope infil, no explosive breaching, and no entering of homes. Either we were still being punished, or the general simply did not trust our platoon to operate outside the wire.

One morning, I walked to the chow hall with one of my teammates, Mark Jenkins. Mark was a fantastic SEAL, very capable and skilled. It never ceased to amaze me how after a full night on the town he would consistently smoke us all in training the next day. After we finished eating his dust, he'd light up a cigarette and laugh at us. Nothing fazed him. He also was a legendary smart-ass, which chafed our leadership because he didn't have much of a filter.

We walked inside, grabbed trays, and got in line, Mark cracking jokes all the way. He'd say whatever came to mind, no matter who was around to hear it. We got our food and made our way to a table, where we were joined by two other operators who'd been attached as "augments" to our team. As we sat down, Mark noticed the general sitting a few tables away. A couple of his aides—both lieutenant colonels—sat with him.

We all made a couple of comments about the general sitting there and our frustration with our inability to get outside the wire. Mark then glanced at me, then back to the general. "Hey, Red," he began, "you don't have a hair on your ass if you don't go say something to that guy."

I was an O1 ensign, the most junior officer around. Jenkins wanted me to go confront one of the top generals in theater?

I thought it over. Maybe this was just what I needed. We'd been suffering for weeks, but here was an opportunity to go talk to the man behind it all.

My teammates watched silently as I worked it out in my head.

What would my fellow team members say if they heard I had a chance to go talk to him and didn't? Maybe this was an opportunity for me to prove myself as a leader. I could show them I wasn't afraid to stand up for them. I'd been searching for ways to prove myself ever since I'd come aboard. Now the opportunity to do so had just fallen in my lap. I had to take it.

In time, I learned there is nothing more dangerous on the battlefield than an immature and arrogant officer who feels he needs to prove himself. It can lead men to their death. Thankfully in this situation, lives weren't at stake, just my reputation.

Instead of recognizing any of that, I decided this was my way to prove my leadership abilities to my teammates and to the leadership above.

"You're right, Mark. I'm going to go talk to him," I said as I stood up. Mark and the other two operators looked surprised. Good. I figured they'd tell the rest of the guys that I didn't hesitate when we got back to Ouellette.

I walked over and stood beside the general's table. "Excuse me, General. Ensign Redman, Naval Special Warfare. Do you have a couple of minutes?"

His aides glowered up at me. Stamped on their faces was a *Who the hell are you?* look that made me waver momentarily.

The general invited me to sit down. His aides looked frosted and grew more so after I began to talk.

"Sir, I just wanted to talk to you about this operational pause we seem to still be in," I began. The general's face registered nothing but interest. I continued, "I know there was a miscommunication with our first mission. But we know the enemy is out there, and we'd really like the opportunity to go after them."

The general heard me out, then replied diplomatically, "Well, Ensign, I've got to look at all the strategic factors here. We must always weigh the strategic impact with impact on the civilian populous and there are implications to going out and operating at night."

"I understand that, sir."

"Right now, we're at a crazy time in the war, and we have to balance what we are doing."

"Well, General," I said, "we really feel like we can contribute in a positive way by going after men who pose a clear and present threat to coalition forces."

The general was noncommittal, but remained polite. I don't think his aides took their eyes off me through the entire conversation. I could feel them boring holes through me. I thanked them for their time, got up, and headed back to my table.

Mark and the other two operators were gone. Why hadn't they stuck around? Their disappearance surprised me. I walked back to our compound thinking over the incident. The more I thought about it, the more I began to wonder if I'd just done something really stupid. Throughout my career, I had always excelled. As an enlisted man, I had been regarded as one of the top communicators within our team and had even been selected to become the primary training instructor for communications. I always took pride in that. Until I had to learn all the new tactics and procedures after graduating from Old Dominion the year before, I'd also always been a solid tactical operator.

But I had one major flaw. Every now and then, I'd do something rash that got me in trouble. I was spot-on where I needed to be ninety-five percent of the time. But those five percent moments where I wasn't usually hit like a freight train. I'd do something impulsive or impetuous and go off the reservation. My motives were usually good, but the consequences had been pretty harsh sometimes.

I thought of how those lieutenant colonels sitting with the general reacted to me. Then I saw in my mind the empty table where my brothers had been when I went over to speak to the general. How quickly had they taken off? That was not a good sign.

Maybe this had been one of those five percent moments of mine . . . again.

I reached Camp Ouellette and headed for our operations center, figuring I'd better fess up to my leadership before something came down from above. I found Captain George Walsh, our SEAL Team's commanding officer, and asked if we could talk.

In his office, I explained what had transpired at the chow hall. When I finished, George nodded slowly and said, "Okay. Well, thanks for letting me know, Red."

He seemed to contemplate what to say next. At length, he asked, "Tell me something. Why did you feel the need to do that?"

I thought about all the reasons I had in the moment after Mark Jenkins had baited me. I boiled it down to, "Sir, I felt like I would not have been a good leader if I hadn't gone and said something. I did it for the boys."

George stared at me with an odd expression on his face. I couldn't read it, and that unsettled me. Had I said something wrong?

"Okay, Red. Thanks. That'll be all."

Sticking my neck out like that ended up doing no good. The days dragged by, and we languished at the FOB while everyone else, including Reserve and National Guard units, patrolled beyond the wire. For warriors who have devoted their lives to the craft and art of warfare, there is nothing worse than being inactive in a combat theater. Our own command kept us on a leash.

It was a rude wake-up call for all of us. Our first mission had demonstrated the nature of this war, and we despised the implications of it. Our forces operated in a gray world between actively targeting the enemy and letting them live for the sake of political calm. I have always been a black-and-white kind of person, and this reality was frustrating. We'd been shown that having the right friends was more important than taking down enemies of our country who had killed or wounded our fellow Americans and our allies. It was tough to stomach.

Morale within our platoon all but collapsed. Every day, we continued to go through the motions. It became Groundhog Day. We worked out. We slept. We planned, and we would send yet another new mission up the CJSOTF chain of command. We ground our teeth with every rejection.

I hoped that a bright spot in this dark time would be my willingness to confront the general who'd shut us down. After all we'd been through that summer, I thought I'd look like a hero to the rest of the team. Instead, there was a lot of grumbling throughout the platoon about what an idiot I'd been. Nobody approached me directly about it, but I heard enough whispering to know that my teammates thought very little of what I'd done. I thought I'd be proving myself as a leader, but ultimately it had the opposite effect. It left me confused and more determined than ever to prove myself to the men. I just needed a chance.

Chapter 10

Southern Afghanistan
September 2005

The Chinooks ducked below the ridgelines on either side of the valley, their pilots flying through the darkness with the aid of night-vision goggles. This was a vulnerable moment. A few weeks before, the Taliban had caught Mustang 22, a National Guard CH-47, as it flew below a ridgeline and into a valley in Zabul Province. Firing an RPG down on the bird from higher ground, they'd scored a direct hit, killing all five aboard. Combined with our own loss a few months before during Red Wings, the flight crews were hyperalert and edgy.

The big helos clattered and rattled as we sat in back waiting in tense anticipation for the moment we got wheels on the landing zone. We fully expected contact on this mission. A week before, we'd infilled into this area and ran into a group of Taliban fighters moving on a hillside about seven hundred meters from us. We engaged them with small-arms fire, but they were just beyond the effective range of our M4s. Mark Jenkins took matters into his own hands, unslinging a Carl Gustav rocket launcher he was carrying and let one fly. He vaporized two of the enemy fighters with a direct hit. One of our snipers picked off a third. We spent the rest of the day blowing up the caves the enemy was using as their base of operations.

Now we'd been ordered back into the area after several coalition patrols had been ambushed. We would get on the ground and sweep through the area, engaging any enemy who attempted to resist, and destroying any cave complexes we came across.

Our Chinooks hugged the slope of one side of the valley as the pilots pushed their Vietnam-era birds beyond a hundred knots. Above and behind us, a pair of Apache gunships flew escort, ready to pounce on anyone willing to open up on us. Having the Apaches with us usually meant we wouldn't take ground fire during our infil or exfil. The AH-64 carried guided and unguided rockets, plus a massive 30mm auto-cannon that poured out ten shells a second. Such airborne fire-power inspired terror in the hearts of even the stoutest terrorists. When overhead, the Taliban usually ditched their weapons and tried their best to look like unarmed locals.

Except here. The cell operating in this valley was full of fanatical fighters—al-Qaida foreign volunteers and die-hard Taliban. In recent days, they'd lit up several passing Apaches. It took a special brand of crazy courage to do that, especially after they watched their comrades get blown to pieces with Hellfire guided missiles and cannon strafing runs only minutes after pulling their triggers.

We closed in on our landing zone. The pitch of the rotors changed as we made our final approach. I looked left and right at my brothers beside me, and for a second my mind flashed on Operation Red Wings and the Chinook the enemy had shot down. We'd been told to expect contact and that we could be going into a hot landing zone. The walls of the Chinook were thin aluminum without any armor plating to protect us. One well-placed burst of machine-gun fire could riddle our team with bullets.

"Remember," I yelled over the engine and rotor noise, "if you get hit as we're landing, stay in the helo. Do not get off."

Nods all around. This way, the bird could get the wounded to an aid station quickly. If somebody got hit, kept going, and left the Chinook, we'd have to call in a medevac helo and risk another aircraft.

We all rose, ready to run off the ramp the second the helo touched down. We were packed into the bird with several ATVs for carrying extra ammo. The Chinook swung into a hard flare, and we touched down in the landing zone. The rear ramp lowered, and we streamed off the aircraft to establish a perimeter. In seconds, the Chinook lifted off in a cloud of brown dust kicked up by its rotor wash.

All across the valley, Chinooks hopscotched around and inserted our teammates in critical locations until we'd sealed off all the ways in and out from the southern bowl of the valley to a T intersection that defined its northern side. Now, it was a matter of sweeping through to find the bad guys.

Our leadership landed at the south end of the valley. J.D. Richardson was our ground force commander again that day.

On the west and east sides, we deployed snipers and overwatch teams. To the north, the valley intersected with another valley that ran east and west, making a natural T. The element that set down at the top of the northern T immediately detected large groups of enemy fighters moving around below them. The walls of the valley were steep and rose from the floor at least a thousand feet in places. Our northern group stayed on the high ground and counted over fifty Taliban in their area.

A UH-60 Black Hawk working with the northern element passed the T intersection. The Taliban below didn't hesitate. An RPG streaked through the predawn darkness and narrowly missed the bird. Seconds later, the air around it filled with zipping tracers.

The northern team immediately called in air support. A pair of A-10 Warthog attack jets raced to the rescue and shot up the enemy below. The Apaches followed with a second gun run and reported seeing Taliban bodies lying in the dirt, killed by the A-10 drivers.

As the battle raged a few kilometers away from my position, I took my four-man team along the valley's eastern slope and moved north. I had two snipers and a machine gunner with me, and our job was to secure the high ground on the eastern side of the valley as our main assault force, the maneuver element composed of two other squads of SEALs reinforced by some Afghan National Army troops, swept along the valley floor. My boss, Fred Derry, was in charge of that group and was the acting assault force commander (AFC).

We were in a remote area, without a single Afghan village for miles. The valley's isolation made it a superb base of operations for the local enemy fighters, and it did not take us long to discover their fighting positions. Dugouts, trenches, and makeshift bunkers with overhead cover to conceal them from passing aircraft studded the area. But as we advanced south to north along our ridgeline, we detected no enemy movement. In the distance, our aircraft pulled off target and climbed out above us, ready to intervene again when needed. A stillness fell across the valley, but that made us even more wary. The surviving enemy had gone to ground. Any one of our elements could trip into a well-concealed ambush now. The sun broke the horizon as the maneuver element made their way down into the valley to begin their sweep.

Hours slowly ticked by as the late-summer Afghan sun beat down on us in our overwatch positions. The only thing that moved was the maneuver element, thousands of feet below us. At one point, the maneuver element came across a Taliban camp site. A quick search revealed that whoever had been there had only recently departed. They'd seen us coming and bugged out. The ground force relayed all this information to us and we stayed extra alert as they continued north. The sun climbed higher in the sky and shone down on us with merciless intensity. We maintained our overwatch position as the assault element picked their way along the slope's broken terrain. My team did all we could to remain vigilant as we baked under all our gear. The team below never slowed in their progress, though. We had six hours to clear this place and make it to the extract point where the helos would pick us up. The aviation guys had told us that if we weren't there at 1600, they wouldn't have any birds available to get us out for several days due to the stacks of missions lined up across southern Afghanistan. The fighting in this part of the country had grown so intense that our assets were being stretched to the limit.

The entire morning, I chomped at the bit, wanting to find the enemy we had seen earlier. Though there'd been firefights in several of the missions since the general relented and deployed us to Kandahar, I had yet to come under direct fire. After years of training for it, I felt robbed.

Combat theaters are a series of concentric circles. The largest circles are the bases like Bagram and, aside from random rocket attacks, living there is almost like a peacetime post. The FOBs out in southern Afghanistan bring you a ring closer. Going on missions outside the wire tightens the circle, but it still doesn't put you at the center of the war until you finally find yourself in the middle of a firefight. So far, I'd been a ring away from that pinnacle moment of my career, and it was driving me crazy.

I wanted that moment not only because I would finally be able to do what I'd been training for, but also to prove to myself that I had what it took to perform well under fire. No warrior can truly know what he is made of until he is put into that moment. In the words of one of my old commanding officers, "No man truly knows what he is made of until he goes up and slaps the dragon."

In the hottest moments, you see the best and worst in men. I ached for that moment. Unfortunately, the desire to prove myself was in danger of blinding me to my duty to lead. Good combat leaders not only know when to fight, they know when not to fight. In that moment, all I wanted to do was slap the dragon.

Noon came and went without any enemy contact in our area. The terrain grew even more rugged as the ground team continued to make its way to the northern end of the valley. As they reached the T intersection of the two valleys, they saw evidence of enemy movement and began to move west in the east–west running valley. The radio communication between the ground elements and our ground force commander began to break down. When J.D.'s HQ team to the south lost contact with our two squads in the valley, I started to relay messages between them, as I still had comms with everyone. Having the high ground became even more tactically vital, as my team became the communication link that kept everyone in contact with our GFC.

Another hour passed without incident. We were getting close to our extraction time, so with no contact with the enemy, Commander Richardson decided to call it a day. He radioed to my element and the other overwatch team on the west side of the valley and told us to fall back to his HQ group to the south where we would prepare for extract. Meanwhile, the two squads on the valley floor would push up the northern ridgeline to the T intersection and climb up the slope to link up with our northern element.

I went ahead and sent our two snipers back to the HQ team but decided to stay where I was a little longer with our machine gunner. I figured the guys below could still use some eyes watching over them. Besides, I could continue to relay radio messages to them since they were still out of radio contact with our leadership.

A spasm of gunfire suddenly erupted from the valley floor. AKs echoed. Machine guns rattled into a swell of violence. Furious return fire followed from our own rifles and automatic weapons. We scanned the valley floor, but couldn't see the fight.

Fred Derry, who was in charge of the two squads in the valley, came over the radio. He and I were among the smaller men in the platoon—he was about five six or seven. We called him Joker because he always had a smile on his face and was quick to laugh.

Between bursts of gunfire, I heard him report, "Troops in contact! Troops in contact! We're facing at least twenty enemy fighters."

A wash of static followed. Then I heard Joker add, "One of our Afghan soldiers is wounded. We need reinforcements."

I relayed this back to J.D. Richardson, then thought about the situation. Our guys were in trouble and needed help. But the other elements were scattered all over the valley. Some to the south, some to the north. It would take vital time for them to converge on the battle, and by then it could be too late to help out.

My teammate and I were the two friendlies nearest to the fight. And we had a machine gun.

Jay, here's your chance. Your teammates are in trouble.

I looked down into the valley a thousand feet below. The slope was steep—perhaps sixty degrees in places. Getting down there would be a serious climb. Once at the bottom, we'd have to maneuver to the sound of the guns through broken terrain and vegetation. That would complicate approaching our guys without getting shot by accident.

I called to Fred and asked if the western overwatch team was still in place.

Gunfire erupted over the radio as he keyed his mike and answered, "I think so."

Okay, good. That gave us eyes above, and control of the high ground over there.

This is the moment, Jay. Go prove yourself.

The situation was not a good one. If we went down, it would complicate the situation. We're trained to maneuver only one element at a time so we can make absolutely sure we don't end up in a blue-on-blue engagement. Also, I'd be giving up the high ground. If there was a Taliban group anywhere nearby, they could cause some real trouble if they got onto our ridge. Combat is an intricate ballet, a balance of firepower, movement, and strategy. Leading in these moments is more art than science.

I toggled my mike and told Fred, "We're coming down to you. We'll be coming to your position from the east on the valley floor."

Through static and rifle reports, I heard him acknowledge. Fred was our team's OIC, and I worked directly for him. I had his approval. That was good enough for me. Without reporting what I was doing to the HQ element and Commander Richardson, I turned to my machine gunner and said, "Let's go."

He looked at me like I was crazy but didn't say anything. I led the way down off the face of the slope and clambered hand over hand in places when the going got nearly vertical. It took probably fifteen minutes for us to finally get our boots on the valley floor. As we dropped off the lip, Senior Chief Kerry called to me over the radio and wanted to know what I was doing. "We're going down," I told him.

He went ballistic. "Absolutely not! We need to link back up. Fall back!"

The boys needed help and we were closest. If it had been anybody else, I may have thought twice about his call, but my own personal quest to prove myself coupled with my intense hatred for him clouded my judgment. I ignored him and we pressed on.

As we dropped farther into the valley, we lost all communication with the headquarters team. I began to realize what a hairy situation I had just placed the two of us in. We had given up the high ground to move down a thousand feet of vertical terrain to try to link up with an element under fire with an enemy force almost one kilometer away. I pushed this thought to the back of my mind. The boys need help. Focus on that. But where was the fight? The sounds of the battle echoed all across the valley, making it difficult to calculate distance and direction.

A broken transmission filled my earpiece. I couldn't tell what was said, but I recognized J.D.'s voice.

We moved farther down and finally reached the valley floor. One enemy fighter in a good position could have decimated us. We paused and I tried to reestablish contact. A moment later, through washes of static, J.D.'s voice came back.

"Where the hell are you?" J.D. demanded.

I told him we were right at the T intersection on the valley floor.

"Get your ass out of the valley, NOW!" he said with so much anger that I could almost feel a blast of fire shoot out of the earpiece.

I was about to explain my intent when he added, "Those guys are in a major fight and we can't call in close air support because we don't know where you are!"

That shook me. There were aircraft overhead waiting to join the battle with rockets and bombs. Yet they could not make their runs because of my decision to go into the valley.

I should have thought about our air assets, but I was too blinded by my own ambition. With my combat inexperience on full display, it started to dawn on me at last: Had I made a mistake? What if somebody got hit during the delay I'd caused? I keyed my radio and reported that we would be pulling out of the valley and climbing the north face of the T intersection to link up with our element there.

If anything, the north face was even steeper than the east one. We scrambled up it as fast as we could. All the while, the sounds of the firefight echoed through the valley. At the top of the eight-hundred-foot climb we had to make, I radioed in our new position. Within minutes, the squads in the valley pulled back as a pair of attack jets moved in to pummel the Taliban defensive positions with five-hundred-pound bombs. A moment later, they swung low out of the clear blue sky, looking like long-nosed birds of prey as they lined up on their targets below us. Seconds later, they loosed their 30mm Gatling guns. Hundreds of explosive rounds riddled the valley floor with eruptions of dirt and debris. Trees were blown apart, branches sent spinning in all directions. Smoke rose in small, spiraling columns in their wake.

A Black Hawk arrived on the scene. It buzzed back and forth, picking up our scattered elements and delivering them to the northern slope so we could all link up and form a perimeter for the night. J.D. called to my position and told me the Black Hawk would pick up me and my machine gunner and link us back up with the main element. The firefight had lasted well over an hour, which blew our timetable. We had missed our extract time with the Chinooks, and now we learned that one of the Chinooks that had inserted us that morning had been shot down and all five crew members had been killed. The five crew members were Chief Warrant Officer John M. Flynn, Sergeant Patrick D. Stewart, Warrant Officer Adrian B. Stump, and Sergeant Tane T. Baum of Pendleton, all of the Army National Guard's 113th Aviation Regiment; and Sergeant Kenneth G. Ross, of the 7th Battalion, 159th Aviation Regiment from Giebelstadt, Germany.

With this sad news, I thought of these brave men who would never make it home, and knew we might have to wait several days to be taken out. And I wondered what else I was about to face.

Once we were consolidated on the north ridge and our security was set for what surely would be a long night ahead, J.D. came looking for me.

As he approached, I could see he was livid. "What the hell were you doing?"

Indignantly, I told him I was trying to go to the aid of my brothers.

He looked at me like I'd just spit on his wife. "That was a stupid thing you did, Red. You could have gotten people killed."

His words made me even more righteously indignant.

I fired back at him, "The boys were in trouble and I went to their aid. I did what needed to be done in the moment."

J.D. refused to accept that. I tossed out a similar situation that occurred in Afghanistan a few years before as if establishing precedence would help my case. J.D. knew of the mission too, and he cut me off with, "Not the same at all, Red. They didn't have air support available."

"I didn't know we did!" I shouted back.

"You delayed it with what you did!" J.D. roared.

At last, when it was clear to J.D. that his words were not sinking in, he ended the argument. Curtly, he said, "We'll deal with this after we get back to Kandahar."

He turned and stalked off.

I watched him leave and struggled with my thoughts. Had I really made that big of a mistake? *No. No way. I went to go help. When is that ever wrong?*

That evening, as the sun started to fall, I sat next to one of the snipers from my team, a guy I had served with for years back when I was still enlisted. I talked to him about the situation. I walked through everything that happened, justifying everything I'd done. When I finished, he just stared at me. No comments, no thoughts, no "You did the right thing, Red."

His reaction prompted another moment of self-doubt.

But how was I supposed to know there was air on the way?

You messed up, Jay.

No way. You did the right thing. Action is better than doing nothing.

You could have gotten your teammates killed.

I soon found myself alone. With darkness came a chill wind that blew across those desolate, ancient mountains. We had not expected to be out for more than six hours, so I had lightened my normal load-out and left behind much of my cold weather gear. I hunkered down in the dirt, wearing a watch cap and a windbreaker—and froze. Through the night, our jets executed intermittent bombing runs in the valley below. The gunfire and explosions woke me from a light and fitful sleep, and I stared skyward as I thought about the events of the day. As I shivered and tried to fall back asleep, I tortured myself with a step-by-step replay of every decision I had made.

As the sun rose in the morning sky, we sent a team down onto the valley floor to investigate the enemy's bunker complex and carry out what we call battle damage assessment (BDA)—a fancy term for seeing how much punishment had been inflicted on the enemy. I was ordered to take my team to the top of the cliff face and cover our brothers in the valley below as they examined the damage. We found a place about two hundred feet above the battlefield and settled down to search for any signs of enemy movement. As we scanned the valley floor, I noticed none of my teammates were speaking to me.

Whatever. I did the right thing in the moment.

The BDA team found over a dozen bodies, or remains of bodies, scattered through the enemy base. As they swept through the area, they came across a single al-Qaida survivor. He had been shot but somehow escaped the bombs and rockets from the aircraft. He had begun to crawl away, but karma kicked him in the teeth. The bomb that had his name on it was a dud. It hit the ground and skipped through the bunker complex before it slammed into a tree, knocking it over onto the lone terrorist survivor. The trunk was so heavy, it pinned him in place. Our BDA team found him stuck under it, badly wounded and unable to offer any resistance.

What to do with him? If the tables had been reversed and it was somehow one of our guys that the Taliban had found, they would have promptly decapitated him and defiled his body in the name of jihad. Fortunately for him, the US military, along with some of our closest allies, still adhere to the Law of Armed Conflict and the Geneva Convention. Both state that an enemy combatant is entitled to medical care after the immediate conflict is over.

Fully knowing our enemy would not have provided us the same treatment, our BDA team freed him from the tree trunk, and our medic set about stabilizing him while we called in a medevac helicopter. Once again, a Black Hawk thundered into the valley and dipped below the ridgelines. I watched the scene, remembering how this guy's al-Qaida brethren had opened up on our helicopter yesterday morning after we first landed. Maybe he was one of the trigger pullers. Now this brave helo crew was risking their lives for him.

The Black Hawk pulled into a hover over the ruins of the Taliban bunker complex with a thousand feet of cliff wall looming above it. One fighter with an RPG, still alive and willing to fight, could take the bird down, but the crew did not hesitate. The winch lowered a stretcher to the ground. The seconds ticked by. The terrorist was carried to it and loaded aboard. A hand signal from the ground and the helo's crew chief winched the stretcher upward. A moment later, he was safely aboard, and the Black Hawk pulled up and out of the valley.

I don't know what happened to that wounded, tree-smacked terrorist after he reached the helicopter. I don't know if he even survived long enough to be treated at a coalition aid station. Or perhaps he made a full recovery at American taxpayer expense.

I do know this: in that moment, despite the internal war raging in my mind, as I watched the Black Hawk disappear over a distant ridgeline, I felt honored to be a part of this scene and proud to be an American. We are a benevolent and merciful people who have rushed to the aid of people in peril all over this globe. That strength will always be our path to victory against those who know only brutality and murder.

Chapter 11

B ack at Kandahar, I heard the first whispers about me floating around the team. The men had nick-named me "Rambo Red." Though some may think being compared to Stallone's lone wolf silver screen icon was a compliment, within our community it was a supreme insult. In the SEAL Teams, there is no room for individualism; the foundations of our success rest on mutual cooperation and communication. A lone wolf like Rambo could destroy a team, with catastrophic effects on the battlefield.

I was beginning to see the tidal wave coming toward me, and I knew I needed an ally. I went to speak with

Fred Derry. Outside the chow hall, as I recounted what happened that afternoon several days ago, I mentioned that he approved my decision to come down into the valley.

"I don't really remember that; there was a lot going on," he said, his eyes leveled on mine.

So there it was. I couldn't believe it. It was the first hint to me that something more than a chewing out was going to happen here.

The Rambo Red snickers turned out to be just one symptom of the derision the rest of the team felt for me. After we debriefed this mission, J.D. Richardson took me into his makeshift office and said, "Red, your operational abilities have been called into question. We're sending you back to Bagram to meet with the CO and we'll discuss this further when the rest of the team gets back."

I was stunned. At worst, I was starting to expect something more than a wrist slap, but nothing like that. I was being sent back to the rear, out of combat. Nothing can ever be more humiliating for a warrior. I'd trained my entire adult life for this, and now I had been told I didn't measure up. It felt like a mule kick to the gut.

I heard rumblings that Senior Chief Kerry wanted to see my Trident taken away. Behind the scenes, he was pushing for a Trident review board to determine my fate. The months of infighting between us had been bad enough. Now he was trying to destroy my career.

The next day, I packed my gear up and left our compound. Accompanying me onto the plane were three other members of our task unit. One of them was Mike Peters, the highly respected chief petty officer who had ripped into me during the extract after the Rocket Man mission. He'd won navy-wide awards and had a stellar reputation as a combat leader. Next to him was Chief Garth Johnson, a silver-haired veteran who'd been with the teams for over twenty years.

As the transport swung onto the runway and the pilots pushed the throttles forward, I stole a last look at Kandahar, lost in thought. I was the freshly minted ensign exiled for his conduct in battle. And my senior chief wanted to take away my Trident.

Outside of my family, nothing meant more to me than wearing it. It was the symbol that guided me through a rocky childhood. It was the beacon that led me to the teams. As a kid, I stared at it and marveled. To wear the Trident was all I had ever wanted.

Two hours later, we landed back at Bagram. The bird taxied to the tarmac, and I walked down the ramp to find my gear. When I got to Camp Ouellette, the place was a ghost town. Almost the entire task unit had forward deployed to Kandahar, including the support staff. A skeleton crew kept the lights on here, but that was it.

I stepped into my hooch and dumped my stuff on the floor.

Now what?

I had no idea. I'd achieved everything I'd ever set out to do since high school. Now my fire was gone. I was safe now, out of harm's way. The men I'd trained with and wanted to lead in battle were still out there in the fight. That thought cut through me like a blade. No operator ever wants to be out of the fight when his teammates are in combat. We were only weeks from going home, but I fully recognized the gravity of this moment.

My days in the field are over, maybe even forever.

I needed to report in with George Walsh, the commanding officer of our SEAL Team. I had no doubt he was well aware of what happened and was waiting for me to come see him. I was not looking forward to that meeting. I decided I'd better lose the beard before I did that.

In Afghanistan, you are judged as a man by your beard. The locals won't take you seriously if you don't have one. Because of this cultural demographic and our mission requirement to directly interface with the locals, Special Operations Forces are granted modified grooming standards, which is a fancy military term for being allowed to grow facial hair. I grabbed a pair of scissors, a couple of razors, and rummaged around my hooch until I found my electric clippers. Gathering it all up, I went over to the head and began to go to work.

Clippers first. Chunks of beard fell away into the sink. I couldn't look myself in the eye. With each pass, I stripped away more hair—and more of myself as an operator. It became almost an act of self-flagellation. Scissors next. As I cut and trimmed, I couldn't help but think I was saying good-bye to the life I'd loved so much. Baby-faced once again, I cleaned up and went to see the CO.

I reported to Captain Walsh and the team's command master chief. After perfunctory greetings, I told them my side of the story. I pleaded my case as best I could. When I finished, they collected their thoughts. I waited, outwardly stoic but dying inside as I silently prayed they'd validate what I'd done. They were the senior leaders in the entire two-hundred-man SEAL Team. Both listened attentively, then they spoke, one at a time, first Captain Walsh then the master chief.

They told me I'd made a bad decision. "We will reassemble and discuss this further when the rest of the task unit returns from Kandahar." My anger flared, but I stowed it. It quickly gave way to despair.

After I was dismissed, I made my way back to my hooch. I sat down and wrote to Erica. This was our marriage's first deployment, and she'd been my rock. Every chance I had, I would either write to her or cut video together for her and the kids so they could see what my life was like over here. A few weeks before, I'd taken photos they'd sent me and edited them into a video I called *A Day with Daddy* that showed what I was doing at the same time their pics were taken. The kids loved it and Erica told me they watched it all the time. If a song came on the radio that I used in the video, they would tell Erica, "This is Daddy's song."

Where to even start? My fingers hovered over my laptop's keyboard, mind racing. Much of what happened fell under operational security, so I couldn't talk about it. But I needed to tell her something. More than anything, I needed someone on my side and I knew Erica would support me.

I tapped out a note and hit Send.

Sitting at my desk, I tried to force my mind away from what was happening to me. I decided to send a short e-mail addressed to all my closest friends, giving a general and vague view of what happened. I suppose

I was trying to win my friends—and myself—over to the idea that I was the victim here. One of those friends was the owner of the bed-and-breakfast we had used for our training operations in the Virginia backcountry. The owner, Bill Holliday, was a retired US Army veteran who always welcomed us with warmth and friendship. Bill and his lovely wife were tremendous Americans and they had become like a second set of parents for us. Erica and I held our wedding up there. In happier times.

I started to laugh, thinking of the night before the ceremony. Erica had planned for the wedding party to have a scavenger hunt around the grounds of the bed-and-breakfast. My side of the party—not so much into that. My groomsmen, who were close SEAL buddies of mine, had other ideas. So after we started the scavenger hunt, we let the women head off into the woods while we went back inside the bed-and-breakfast to do what many SEALs do the night before one of us gets hitched.

We drank. And brawled.

I remembered walking through the door and getting blindsided with a stunning, vicious tackle from one of my groomsmen who weighed around two hundred sixty-five pounds. The blow sent me flying over the couch and onto the floor. The rest of my groomsmen piled on before I had a chance to get up. I kicked and punched and fought furiously to regain my feet, but there were just too many of them.

I had become friends with the local sheriff during our training exercises, and he had joined our soiree for the evening. Just as I thought I might escape, he waded into the fray, fists swinging. The guy stood six feet six and had to weigh three hundred pounds. Getting hit by him was like a puppy being hit by a two-by-four. Still, I fought like a banshee and ended up breaking one of his ribs. The battle raged in epic fashion: fingers were broken, and deep bruises and contusions multiplied as the brawl played out across the furniture in the room. At last, they pinned me to the floor long enough to tie my hands and feet. When they finally got me tied up, they began pouring liquor down my throat.

A few hours later, the girls burst in, furious that they'd been out doing their scavenger hunt alone. Needless to say, they were shocked to find me bruised, battered, and tied up, drunker than ten monkeys with an almost empty bottle of booze sitting next to my head. I was so drunk the world was spinning.

While all this rough-and-tumble stuff is par for the course within our community, it is not something that civilians really understand. Seeing her future husband trussed up, covered in welts and bruises, and being force-fed whiskey by his groomsmen left Erica momentarily speechless. As she recovered from the shock, she demanded they untie me and then dragged me down to the house where she was staying. She chewed me out with a vengeance. I'd never seen her so angry. I tried to tell her I did my best to fight them off, but I had no way to keep from drinking after they stuffed the bottle in me.

That didn't help the situation.

We talked all night. She cried and considered walking away from the whole thing. The wedding party hovered in nearby rooms, getting updates from family members who came in to check on us. Was the marriage on or off? It hung in the balance that night, believe me.

We loved each other with fierce devotion. As the anger of the moment drained away, that became increasingly clear. In the end, that all-night talk wasn't about whether we were going to go through with the ceremony or not—bruises and all—it was an affirmation of what we meant to each other. I just had to convince her of that.

Now in my darkest hour on the far side of the world, I needed her more than ever. I'd been through tough times before with this team, and she was always a refuge for me. Where others might judge, she always stood in my corner. At times when I had said or done something stupid, she never jumped on me for it. I'd seen other wives do that. They'd nitpick at their husbands' shortcomings or mistakes. To me that seemed like poking a stick in a wound. Erica never did that. Her loyalty never wavered.

I stared at the computer screen, trying to figure out what time it was in Virginia. Would she be awake? Could I just go call her on one of the satphones? Man, I needed to hear her voice.

Until Erica came into my life, I'd been fairly self-reliant. Any problems I had, I dealt with them myself. With Erica, we shared each other's burdens. Our relationship made it easy. Other wives within our community had told her more than once, "Not everybody has what you and Jay have."

All I wanted to do was see her now. But then I thought of the disgrace I'd suffered. I'd be going home under a cloud. I'd humiliate her and our children by the very fact that I was coming home a complete failure.

Slowly, e-mails from friends began to trickle in offering words of encouragement. Some I received no reply from, and our relationships were never the same afterward. In that moment on top of everything else I was fighting, I began to realize who my true friends were.

When I checked my e-mail later, I saw Bill Holliday had written back. I opened his message and stared at it in disbelief.

Jay, I'm sorry this happened, but I am not surprised. I've worried your arrogance would be your downfall.

Bill

I considered Bill a close friend. Apparently, he had issues with me he'd never hinted at before. It felt like a kick to the groin—like the whole relationship had been a farce. The realization sent my mood spiraling even further downward.

When the sun came up in Virginia, I called Erica on a satphone and told her everything I could without violating OPSEC. When I finished, the line was silent for just a moment. Then I heard the reassurance in her voice.

"Jay, we'll get through this together. You know I'll always stand behind you."

Her words eased my pain and made me feel slightly better. But it did not dull my misery. At least I knew, no matter what happened here or what my fate would be within the community, I would always have a family to go home to—a family that would offer nothing but warmth.

I hung up, and the waiting game began. Nothing fuels apprehension like waiting. (Remember those days when you were a kid and your mom said, "Go to your room until your father gets home"? It was kind of like that.) It would be several days before the rest of the task unit came back from Kandahar. In the meantime, I was in limbo, and it did not take long for my mind to start up again. I stayed in my room and tormented myself. I walked through that day in the valley second by second until it seemed like I was trapped in those vital moments, my life unable to move on from them.

Gradually, a narrative took shape in my head. Yes, I'd made a mistake, but my actions were well intended. It was a minor mistake, blown far out of proportion in an effort to prosecute a personal vendetta against me. Boil it down, and what was this? A witch hunt by Senior Chief Kerry.

That was how I would defend myself, and I set about putting together a PowerPoint presentation to lay out my case. I took painstaking care with this preparation. My career—my way of life—was on the line, and I would not give it up without a fight.

The team returned from Kandahar several days later. By this point I was deep into wallowing in my own misery and had no desire to see any of my combat brothers. It soon became obvious the feeling was mutual. Even some of my teammates whom I considered friends never came by to talk to me. I felt so disgraced that I stayed in my room twenty-two hours a day, venturing out only at odd hours to get food when the chow hall was virtually empty. When I ran into my brothers on the way to the showers or the head, they barely acknowledged me. Men I would have gladly given my life for now shunned me like cancer. I withdrew deeper and deeper into myself, flooded with self-pity and a bitter growing conviction that I was being thrown under the bus.

About a week after the task unit returned, I was called into a meeting with Captain Walsh, the command master chief, J.D. Richardson, Fred Derry, and Senior Chief Kerry. This would be my chance to present my case and defend my actions. I knew the cards were stacked against me, especially with Senior Chief Kerry out to destroy me.

The meeting began, and the sides quickly aligned. Senior Chief Kerry laid out his case by describing the mission in question. Then he surprised me by stating my supposed error was the culmination of a series of bad decisions and poor leadership I had displayed since coming into the platoon. He talked about my heavy drinking during the predeployment workup, especially with the enlisted men. He went into detail about other incidents where we clashed, and he finished by saying, "Ensign Redman has demonstrated a consistent pattern of bad decision making. His Trident should be taken."

Lieutenant Derry, my OIC, weighed in, saying that he had talked to me repeatedly about my drinking and conduct unbecoming a leader.

I sat and listened to the both of them, bitter over all the personal dirty laundry getting aired. Senior Chief Kerry jumped back in, adding more detail from the last eighteen months. As he continued, it dawned on me: *Man, I've given him a lot of rope to hang me with during the workup. My drinking had gotten out of control. At times I had acted like an ass. I'd behaved at times more like a buddy to my teammates and not a leader.*

A memory came to me of my thirtieth birthday while we were still in Germany. Several of the guys took me out to a nice Asian restaurant in a small German town, where I proceeded to drink myself senseless. I was so inebriated that, midway through the meal, I started trying to catch the koi fish out of the pond in the middle of the restaurant with my bare hands.

And what happened next, Jay?

The guys dumped me off by myself at a local bar outside of base because I was being an ass.

Why had I not understood the implications of that before now?

In the SEAL Teams, you always have a swim buddy with you. It is a lesson that is instilled from day one of Basic SEAL Training and we enforce it for a SEAL's entire career, both on the battlefield and even out at the bars. If I had been smarter, I would have thought about that after they left me alone on my birthday. What a telling indicator.

I gave a spirited defense, but finally admitted I'd made a mistake in the valley, compounded by poor communication and the fact that I was unaware that we had air assets overhead. I argued that it was being blown out of proportion as part of Senior Chief Kerry's vendetta against me.

As the meeting concluded, Captain Walsh brought up the day I went to talk to the general. "Jay, remember what I asked you?"

"Yes, sir," I replied, thinking of that morning I confronted the general in the chow hall. Walsh's words returned to me: *Why did you feel the need to do that?*

"Jay, your answer really puzzled me."

He let that hang in the air. A moment later, he said they would discuss the situation and get back to me with a verdict. I turned and walked out of his office, feeling like I'd just seen the end of my career.

I stepped outside. The late afternoon was still warm. In a few weeks, winter's biting chill would settle in over Bagram and make these late afternoons increasingly miserable. But for now, the stillness and heat of the day made for shirtsleeve weather.

Across from the entrance to our tactical operations center, I saw our platoon's leading petty officer, Charlie Wingate. He was sitting at a picnic table beside a concrete wall, just outside our tactical operations center.

Charlie was a straight shooter. He was our lead sniper and had been the glue that often held our dysfunctional platoon together. Some leaders are politicians. They choose their words carefully, always with an eye on the implications to their career. Not Charlie. His only concern was the well-being of the men in the platoon, and he didn't care what others thought as long as he knew that his boys had the support they needed. He commanded respect from everyone on both sides of the leadership fence because of his priorities and his blunt honesty. If he told you his opinion on something or someone, you could take it to the bank that his thoughts were well considered and were the plain truth devoid of spin intended to advance his own agenda.

I went over and sat down with him. I decided not to hold anything back. Charlie had been a sounding board for me ever since I joined the platoon at Virginia Beach the year before, and I had known him my entire career.

I began to talk. I walked him through everything that had happened and gave my side of events. I told him how I felt like I'd been thrown under the bus. When I finished the story, I said, "I just don't know how I can recover from this."

In our community, a man's reputation is everything. Among operators, there is a network constantly at play, telegraphing information about how individuals perform under stress and in combat. A man with a stellar reputation will always be welcomed into new platoons or task units. A man who comes aboard a new unit with a cloudy reputation will be closely scrutinized. Those with bad reputations will be shunned. At extreme times, the operators take matters into their own hands and will flat-out refuse to work with somebody if the person's reputation warrants it. There's no room for weakness or slackers or cancerous personalities in our line of work. It is policed so closely because our lives depend on one another. Nobody wants to go into combat with somebody he can't completely trust.

Now I was one of those individuals under a black cloud. No matter what resulted in the days to come, whether I was allowed to keep my Trident or not, this would be the scarlet letter that would doom me within the community. One way or another, the senior chief was going to destroy me.

All of that was running through my head and out my mouth as Charlie listened quietly. I finally said, "I just don't know how to go forward."

Charlie regarded me with a steady gaze. I waited for his advice. He would tell it straight, whether it made me feel better or not. I opened this door, and I waited for his reply.

"Red, I have to tell you, I've always kind of wondered about you," he said. "I guess the biggest question I've had about you is why you joined the teams."

My motivation for becoming a SEAL? This came out of the blue. For a moment, I couldn't react. I just sat there, looking back at Charlie, memories of everything I did and sacrificed to get here spinning around in my mind.

I finished boot camp with pneumonia and a collapsed lung. I lost thirty pounds but I graduated.

Charlie continued. "There's two types of people who join. There are those who want to be the best and be part of something larger than themselves."

That has always been me. Ever since my freshman year of high school. All I have wanted was to wear the Trident.

"Then there are those who join for the 'cool guy' factor."

Charlie said, "I gotta tell ya, Red, the more I've been around you, the more I think you're one of the latter."

I'd sat down hoping to find a way, a future within the teams. Instead, Charlie questioned the philosophical underpinnings for my entire career. I was caught by surprise and shocked. I didn't even know how to reply. I had dedicated my life in the pursuit of this profession. Months spent in adverse conditions away from friends and family. This was not a job; it was a lifestyle that one had to dedicate oneself to and I had spent years trying to do just that. Now I was Rambo Red who joined the SEAL Teams because he thought it was cool. Was this how I was viewed? I thanked Charlie for his honesty and returned to my hooch.

Long into the night, I considered Charlie's words. And when my indignation drained away, I was left with my memories—and the hard truths they contained.

Chapter 12

North Carolina
1990

When I was younger, if you told me I couldn't do something, I'd use your words as fuel to prove you wrong. Call it a blessing, or a curse. It has been both throughout my life.

Believe me, I've heard it all before. Jay, you're too small, too skinny, too unfocused, too reckless, too cocky, too wild. Not good enough, not smart enough, a loose cannon, a "social hand grenade."

Yeah, keep talking. You're just feeding the inferno.

When I was three, my parents gave me a fireman's helmet that came equipped with a flashing light and a siren. I ran amok through the house with that thing, siren wailing as I rescued invisible people and the family pets from make-believe blazes. My parents must have been ready to stab their eardrums out. That was my first vision of a heroic future. Later, I grabbed on to the military. I came from a family with a rich tradition of service, so in retrospect this made sense. My dad was a US Army airborne rigger at Fort Campbell during the Vietnam War. My paternal grandfather earned a Distinguished Flying Cross while piloting a B-24 Liberator bomber over the flak-filled skies of Hitler's Europe. I also had a great-uncle who flew fighter aircraft in the Southwest Pacific during World War II. He made the ultimate sacrifice in battle against the Japanese.

I dreamed of adding to that legacy—a life of combat, medals, and service. I was young and naive and had a long road to travel before I could truly understand what my grandfather and great-uncle gave for our country, but that idealism became a very big part of me. I wanted to carry a rifle for a living.

My dad watched this desire grow in me and decided to focus it. My freshman year in high school, he sat me down in our tiny living room and said, "You know, Jay, we had these guys come through airborne school. They were US Navy. Called SEALs. They jumped out of airplanes, swam, they blew stuff up . . . given how you love the water, maybe you ought to look into them."

That was the spark that ignited the defining fire of my life. I went in search of everything I could find about the SEAL Teams—which in the early 1990s was virtually nothing since I lived in a small North Carolina town and the SEALs were far more secretive then than they are now. I pestered my dad to tell me everything he knew, which wasn't much more than he'd already shared. He said again, "They swam, they blew stuff up, they jumped out of planes, and they were crazy."

I was hooked, but further information eluded me. This was 1990; we had no Internet, no Wiki entries, no access to archives across the globe. The world was smaller, and the SEALs were a secretive, quiet lot. That made their mystique ever more fascinating. In the absence of fact, I dreamed.

I set off to find new sources on the SEAL Teams. I figured I'd give the local navy recruiting office a try. It was close to my dad's place of work, so I figured I'd go down there after school some afternoon.

With a Cheshire smile and earnest eyes, recruiters are famous for glad-handing walk-ins and telling them anything so they will sign on the dotted line. I wandered into the office and told the recruiters there that I wanted to be a SEAL. They looked me up and down, which didn't take long since I was only five one. After exchanging glances, the room erupted in laughter. This kid—a SEAL? Yeah, right.

They handed me a pamphlet on getting to BUD/S and showed me a video called *Someone Special*. You'd think with a title like that, this flick would be a love story to be shared with your girlfriend on date night. Instead, it was all about America's maritime commandos. Frogmen. US Navy SEALs. I don't think I breathed through the entire thing. It was my first glimpse at my future.

It was late-'70s Defense Department media spectacle at its finest, full of overacting, bad cinematography, and vaguely Cuban-looking communist bad guys. The film showed a SEAL sniper team inserting over a beach, picking off AK-47 armed enemies as they tried to shoot at another SEAL element coming in aboard Vietnam-era Huey Iroquois helicopters.

Okay, so it was campy and poorly produced. I barely noticed. I was a small-town kid, an Ohio transplant living in Lumberton, North Carolina, in my stepgrandmother's house that used to be on an old tobacco farm. We were a working-class family with barely enough money to cover the basics and little else. *Someone Special* opened a window to a world beyond Elm Street, beyond the tobacco fields. I saw Lumberton as a dead end for me, one of those places where if you don't escape early, you end up stuck.

On the screen, a battle took shape. Those helos roared over the target area in tight formation, their door gunners blazing away with their M60 machine guns. Suddenly, the birds pulled into a low-altitude hover just long enough for the SEALs to fast rope to the ground. I couldn't believe how swiftly it all happened. One minute the Hueys were scooting along the treetops. The next, they were paused in midair while black-clad, Uzi-armed operators pitched overboard. In seconds, the whole team was assaulting a building. Bad guys died left and right; the SEALs breached the structure and cleared it room by room. Once secured, they set an explosive charge atop what looked to be a big radio set, then bolted for the extraction point. As purple smoke filled the air around the SEALs, the Hueys returned and picked them up. They were gone like ghosts before the reeling enemy could even react.

Until this moment, I had only a vague image of what SEALs did in battle. Seeing them in action blew my hair back. I left the recruiting office in a haze, counting the days to when I could enlist and start my journey to BUD/S.

A few weeks later I returned. The chiefs rolled their eyes when I asked if they had any more information on BUD/S. They didn't. So I asked if I could watch the video again. I think just to get me to stop hounding them, they parked me in front of the TV and pressed the play button.

I watched the training sequences and saw what BUD/S would be like. Rows of prospective SEALs enduring flutter kicks, push-ups, and sit-ups filled the screen as the narrator said, "Calisthenics harden flabby muscles grown used to soft living." In a stylized, slow-motion scene a few seconds later, the camera followed the men as they jogged along a beach. The narrator explained, "They begin to learn that there is nothing quite like running to make a man reach deep down inside himself."

For six months, I came back to the office every chance I had. It became my ritual. My dad worked only a few blocks away so I would leave school and walk over to the recruiting office on my way to Dad's office. In a town of seventy thousand there were only a few recruiters, but I could tell from their comments behind my back, they thought I was a joke.

Why are we letting him waste our time? That kid'll never make it as a SEAL.

Yeah, no kidding. He barely weighs a buck.

I ignored them. And dreamed.

Later that year, I turned sixteen. One more year and I could enlist. I kept going down to the office to watch the same video, week after week. Then one day, I showed up and a crusty old petty officer first class barred my way inside the office. The recruiting staff had rotated out, and a new regime now ruled the roost.

"Whaddyou want?" the old salt demanded.

"I want to become a SEAL."

He bellowed with laughter. I stood there, feeling foolish until he pointed to the door and said, "I heard about you. Stop wasting our time; you're never gonna be a SEAL. If you want to do something else in the navy, then come talk to us and let's be serious. If you want to keep chasing rainbows, go elsewhere. We got better things to do than babysit you."

I stared at him, unable to move.

"Get the hell out of here," he barked as he jabbed a weather-beaten finger at the door again.

I turned and stormed out, enraged and humiliated.

I'll show him.

I stewed over this for weeks, trying to figure out how I could prove that petty officer wrong. If the video was any indication, SEALs needed to be in excellent physical shape. They needed to be rugged and tough. I decided that I would develop myself physically until I was old enough to join the navy.

Football seemed like the best way to accomplish that. For years, I had wanted to play, but my father wouldn't allow it. "Forget it. You're too small. You'll get hurt."

My sophomore year, a friend told me the team needed more players. I was barely a hundred and ten pounds at this point, but I ignored my dad's objections and went out for the team anyway. I showed up on the practice field looking like a two-eyed version of the kid in the movie *Lucas*. The other players towered over me. Among the biggest was a barrel-shaped two-hundred-fifty-pound Lumbee Indian named Kevin Lowery. When I showed up, he called out, "Hey, Red. If you're gonna play football, you're gonna have to learn to take a hit."

That seemed self-evident.

He moved closer, a wicked smile on his face.

"Why don't you let me hit you?"

He was the team's nose tackle, the big guy on the D line whose job was to plug the middle with his sheer size and wingspan. But one thing I had learned as a smaller guy: act crazy and people will believe you are. That makes them cautious around you.

"All right," I replied. "Let's go."

He slammed into me so hard he knocked the snot out of me. No joke. Ropes of mucus spun out of both nostrils and striped my face. He went through me like a locomotive through a cow lingering on the tracks. I lay on my back, gasping for breath as my brain did a warm reboot. Then I realized I needed to make a statement. With the back of one hand, I wiped the snot off my face and got to my feet. There he was, looming over me, grinning wider than ever.

"All right," I said, "now it's my turn." We lined up again and I ran into him with all I had.

That first day set the tone for my football career. I made the team, but never started. I ended up as one of the tackling dummies the first string pounded on week after week between games. I played wide receiver and cornerback and flung myself headlong into every catch and tackle. Practice left my body covered in bruises, but I refused to give up. It earned me respect. Plus the bruises served as my red badges of courage. I knew I had a lot to prove.

I learned a lot about myself playing football. I learned how to take a beating, how to work hard, how to be part of a team. Most of all, I learned that heart and insanity could make up for size and speed . . . or at least earn you respect before it got you killed.

The August before my junior year, we were working out one summer afternoon. We sweltered in the hundred-plus heat, the humidity so bad it seemed at times we were breathing under water. I'd been assigned to the defense while the first string offense learned a new play. Our defensive coordinator called our squad together to tell us to give it all we had, make the O's earn the new play. Message understood.

We blitzed with reckless abandon. Each time, I slipped through the offensive line and broke up the play. By the fourth or fifth snap, I could see I was really starting to piss off the center. Not such a good thing. The dude was two hundred twenty pounds of muscled fury who had wrecked other kids with his devastating blocks. They ran the play a few more times—same result. Each time, I got around the line to break up the play.

At that point, our coach got annoyed with me as I kept interfering with his new play. He moved me from cornerback to defensive tackle, which was sort of like throwing blood into shark-infested waters. The center called his offensive line together and told them, "Kill Redman on three."

The quarterback took position under the center. We dropped to our stances. The O line peered out from their helmets and snorted with rage. At the snap, they gang tackled me and planted me in the turf. They got up laughing—which only pissed me off.

I peeled myself off the turf and did my best to break up the play on the next snap. The center fumed. The O line erupted. They wanted my head. Suddenly, instead of learning a new play, each snap became a game of Smear the Skinny White Kid. I got crushed, hammered, thrown like a rag doll. Dumped, dropped, and destroyed. They beat the living hell out of me on that sun-baked football field.

But they couldn't get me to quit. Tell me I can't do something, and I'll use your words as fuel to prove you wrong. This was one of those moments. Those linemen laughed and jawed every time they buried my face in the grass. That only made me more determined not to let them win. Crush my body, maybe. Crush my heart—they never had a chance.

Walt Locklear, one of our assistant coaches, joined me as I walked. "Jay, that was one of the bravest things I've seen on the football field. You refused to back down. You showed me you have more heart than most of the guys on this team combined. Heart and tenacity ultimately will outplay talent and strength every time. Never lose that fire."

I have never forgotten his words. You don't have to be big. You have to be relentless. You have to refuse to quit. Little did I know at the time, this is the secret to becoming a US Navy SEAL.

I continued to search for anything in print that could give me more insight into the SEAL Teams. One day later that year, I found a paperback with a quote running along the top that read, "Makes Rambo Seem Like a Harlequin Romance." Below it was a group of SEALs in a boat somewhere in Vietnam.

I read the title. *SEALs: UDT/SEAL Operations in Vietnam.* The author, Tim Bosiljevac, had been an officer in the teams. I brought it home and pored over it for weeks. It was not an easy read for a high school kid, but it gave me a complete picture of what SEALs did in wartime. It also provided insight into the cost of those missions. Bosiljevac wrote about every one of the forty-nine operators killed during Vietnam. At the time, I had no concept of loss, or of grief. I was young and nobody close to me had died. If anything, the danger their deaths represented made the SEALs seem even more romantic.

Today, after all I've experienced, I recognize the dangerous immaturity inherent in these thoughts. It is common in most young warriors until experience and combat alters their perspectives. For some who don't grow out of it, they become dangerous to themselves and their brother warriors. I fell victim to this view as a kid and clung to it for far too long while serving my country. Life has a way of reshaping how you look at things. Today, I can't even fathom thinking there is romance in losing friends and brothers.

When football season ended that year, I kept up my physical conditioning by joining the wrestling team. At our first practice, I weighed in at a hundred and fifteen pounds, which was bad for me as I was paired with a hundred-and-nineteen-pounder who happened to be the state champion in our weight class. Once again, I got crushed and humbled nearly every day. I didn't give up; I made him fight for every win. When the defeats took their toll on my morale, I stayed motivated by thinking about SEAL training. Each practice got me one step closer to BUD/S.

At the same time, I fell in with the wrong crowd. I got a job my junior year, and my work friends were drinkers. I started sneaking out of the house by sliding down the antenna pole outside my window. I'd meet friends and we'd go drink. I'd stagger home drunk at odd hours of the night, scaling the side of the house with the help of that pole. My family tried to nudge me into a course correction, but I had a chip on my shoulder and refused to listen, especially to my dad. Things got worse. My relationships with my father and stepmom spiraled into the ground. Months of this wore us all down as the slide continued.

When I turned seventeen, things were almost unbearable at home. I asked my dad if he would sign for me to join the navy in the delayed entry program. He gladly agreed, hoping it would stabilize things and keep me out of any more trouble. I went back to the recruiting office and found that the old salt had been replaced by Chief Petty Officer Henry Horne, who welcomed me with honest warmth. To the dismay of his colleagues, he happily showed me *Someone Special* every time I came in, and he never failed to encourage me and my dream.

Thanks to Henry, the navy inducted me on September 11, 1992. I went to boot camp after graduation in the summer of 1993. From there, I'd have a chance to screen for BUD/S. Henry walked me through every step I'd need to take to have that opportunity, and his guidance proved crucial. I never got a chance to thank him though. By the time I came home, he'd moved on and I've never been able to track him down.

Truth is, if I hadn't enlisted at the start of my senior year, my life would have been very different. As things spun out of control at home, I delved deeper into the party scene. Yet even when I was out raising hell, I knew I had to be careful lest I lose my shot at BUD/S. A criminal record would have doomed my chances, so I avoided the drugs that some of my friends were using. Yet I pushed the envelope and lived right on the edge of that line.

Soon another series of fights erupted, and my dad and stepmom kicked me out. I moved in with my older sister for a while, but that couldn't last either. I worked nights and weekends to pay the bills and went to school during the day. On my few nights off, I partied hard and began to drink more. I developed a bad temper and a penchant for impulsiveness. Both were character flaws that would later haunt me through much of my career. It tested my sister's patience to the limit.

One night, while my sister was at work, I had some friends over to our apartment. We were hanging out and watching a movie when my girlfriend and I got in a fight. It escalated until I was so enraged that I turned away from her and punched a hole through a nearby door. My sister had paid for the deposit on the place, which put her on the hook for the damages. She threw me out after seeing it. I was good at burning bridges back then.

Halfway through my senior year, I went to live with my mom in Florida. I think everyone was hoping the change of locations would be good for me.

My mom saw me struggling and did her best to support me. Shortly after I unpacked, she took me over to Fort Pierce to see the UDT/SEAL museum. UDT stands for Underwater Demolition Team. Members of the WWII-era UDTs were called frogmen, and they became the forerunners of our modern-day SEALs.

I wandered through the place, fascinated by the displays that traced the development of the SEAL Teams, starting with the early days in World War II when their primary task was to sneak onto enemy beaches and blow up the landing obstacles. The marines used to say, "First ashore and first to fight!" The frogmen of World War II would quip, "Right behind the UDT."

By Vietnam, the SEAL Teams had grown into a far more flexible force. They undertook raids in the Mekong Delta, a swampy region used by the Vietcong as a base of operations. The teams ambushed the enemy, blew up vital installations, and caused mayhem wherever they went. By sea, by air or land, the SEALs infiltrated enemy territory and struck fear into the hearts of the Vietcong, who called them the "Men with Green Faces" because of the camouflage paint the operators wore.

In the gift shop, I found a license plate embossed with the SEAL emblem. I bought it and hung it on my wall opposite my bed. I'd heard about the emblem's creation. In the post-Vietnam years, the SEALs submitted a variety of emblems for official navy approval. Officialdom canned each one. The frogmen grew frustrated. They tried again. Same thing. Big navy always found something to gripe about.

One night, a group of operators were hanging out, discussing this dilemma as they killed a case of Budweiser. SEAL lore has it that the Bud logo inspired them, and they put to paper a fierce eagle wrapped around an anchor as he clutched a flintlock pistol and

Neptune's trident. The guys submitted it, fully expecting big navy to balk again. To everyone's astonishment, it was approved and adapted.

I was spellbound by it. The symbolism was obvious: the eagle represented America, the anchor represented the navy. The weapons the eagle held in its talons hinted at the versatility and reach of the teams.

Since Vietnam, only about ten thousand men have worn the Trident on their chests. Wanting to be part of that elite community drove me relentlessly that year. I stopped getting in trouble; I took advanced placement courses at school. I focused and applied myself in everything that would help me get to BUD/S. To be a SEAL requires a level of physical conditioning that few Americans possess. With less than eight months before I would depart for boot camp I was determined to get in top physical shape.

I gave my mom free license to tell me to drop and do push-ups at her whim. She'd call to me, and I'd hit the deck, whether alone or with friends, no matter where we were. I found a pull-up and dip workout station at the mall, which my mom helped me purchase. I'd stare at that Trident as inspiration to push myself to do just one more.

I saw the Trident's eagle as the quintessential symbol of American strength. It represents everything right with America. With that fierce gleam in his eyes, he looks at once resolved, ferocious, utterly confident. I'd lived enough to know that the nine-to-five route was not for me. The Trident was my road map, the emblem of my future. It was all I focused on; it kept me going when the consequences of my immature behavior threatened to beat me into the ground. In truth, I became infatuated with what I thought it represented.

I had always loved military history. Now I devoured everything I could find on the subject, reading about the great units of the past. I grew convinced that the SEALs represented the last of a long and storied heritage of superbly trained elite warriors. Aggressive, capable, they formed our nation's Praetorian Guard. When all else failed, the SEALs were the one go-to unit. Their courage and dedication helped shape history, securing victory even in desperate hours.

In retrospect, I bought into the glamour of battle so many books emphasize. In my youthful ignorance, I never thought to check if any of those authors had seen combat themselves. I had no clue of the hardships and horrors of combat. I had no idea that even if you survive battle, your body and mind carry its scars in ways that redefine your life. No human survives contact with the enemy and emerges unchanged. It is a question of degrees. But such nuances were totally lost on me at age seventeen. Later my senior year, Dick Marcinko's book *Rogue Warrior* hit the shelves. If Fort Pierce gave me insight into what SEALs do in combat, *Rogue Warrior* taught me how a SEAL should live his life.

Marcinko's book portrays SEALs as epic partiers who make rock bands look like Mormon choirs. When not on the job, they live without rules. They drink harder, play harder, womanize harder than any other men alive. They blaze through every day with throttles firewalled and no off switch. The normal or laid-back need never apply. To be a SEAL meant you joined a brotherhood of warriors who had no peer on the planet. The lessons I took from the book turned out to be contrary to the quiet professional values the teams actually espouse. I was too immature and too ignorant to know that then. Instead, I bought the picture Marcinko painted and sought to emulate it.

In the end, I made it. I graduated from high school in 1993, went to basic training and to my Navy A School I needed in order to go to BUD/S.

In 1994, I earned that coveted slot to BUD/S. I was on the threshold of realizing my life's dream, but instead of focusing and preparing for the ordeal waiting for me at Coronado, I cut loose in the weeks before we were to report in. When it came time to get to Coronado, a buddy and I drove his Mazda pickup across the country.

During one wild night in Arizona, I scaled an eight-foot-high fence and tried to balance atop it. Fine motor skills like balancing don't work so well when you're stumbling drunk. I pitched over and landed on my ankle. The next morning, it was so swollen I limped for the rest of our transcontinental journey.

By the time we got to Coronado, California, I was pretty beat-up. No worries. I'd be fine once we joined our class. I'd waited my entire life for this moment.

I checked in and limped across the quarterdeck, which attracted an instructor's attention. He grabbed me and demanded to know what happened. I told him I injured it getting out of the car. He laughed knowingly and gave me a look that clearly showed he thought I was full of it.

"Listen, you're not gonna make it very far in this career if you don't make training for war your life's sole focus."

I blew him off and hobbled away filled with indignation.

I know what the hell I'm doing. I'll show him.

If I'd listened to him, my life would have been much easier. But internalizing those pearls does not come easy to a teenager who thinks he's got a pretty tight grip on the ways of the world.

We were put up in some overflow barracks until the pipeline cleared and it became our turn to start the program. In the meantime, the class before ours, #199, had just entered Hell Week. At the time, I knew only a little bit about Hell Week and what it entailed. I figured whatever came my way, I'd handle. Then one night, I was ordered to escort a member of Class #199 back to his room in Building 602. He'd quit the program, and the navy required an escort for anyone who rang the bell during Hell Week. I went off to find him in the darkness.

He was waiting for me, a smaller guy like me, wrapped in a blanket. He was shivering so badly he seemed ready to fly apart. He'd put the blanket over his head like a hood, giving him a monastic look. He said little, so we made our way to his barracks in silence.

I walked alongside him, fit to burst wanting to get details on what I'd soon experience. Finally, I couldn't stand it anymore. As he reached his door and opened it, I blurted out, "So come on, man! What was it like?"

He turned to me and looked me in the eyes. His room's night-light cast an orange glow across his face. He skin was waxen; he looked hollowed out.

At length, he answered in a slow, earnest tone. "Dude, it was so cold I would have poured gasoline all over myself and lit a match, just so I could have been warm for a few seconds before I burned to death."

He stepped back without another word and slammed his door. For the first time, I wondered what I'd gotten myself into.

Chapter 13

Bagram Air Force Base, Afghanistan
September 2005

That night, as I lay on my cot thinking about what Charlie had said, I felt burned to the core. He wondered if I was one of those guys who become a SEAL to be cool. It felt like my entire adult life had been called into question. And as I lay there, revisiting the past in a way I'd never done before, I had to come to terms with the truth. Charlie was at least partially right. Digging through the ashes revealed a lot of painful truth.

I had joined for the cool guy factor. I had wanted to stand out, be different, do things that nobody else could do. I wanted to prove others wrong who had doubted me. I wanted to be distinctive. I needed that as part of my own identity.

Given all that had unfolded since those days, my reason for entry seemed superficial. I had no idea what combat was really like. It isn't cool. It is the furthest thing from it. When lives hang in the balance, the men won't follow the cool-guy showboaters. They'll follow the ones who are calm and capable of making the right decisions in crisis situations. To invest their trust, men in combat require a leader who gives of himself in return. I had not done that, and my "leadership" in this team reflected that.

I poked through the ashes all night, feeling suddenly rootless. If I'd joined for the wrong reasons, what value was all that I had given?

Maybe I joined for the wrong reasons, but part of me stayed in the navy for the right ones.

Basic Underwater Demolition/SEAL Class 200 reported to Coronado and started in January of 1995 with one hundred forty-eight men. Just nineteen of its original members graduated. I wasn't one of them. A broken arm and a bout with tendonitis got me rolled back into Class 202 and I graduated with that class in December.

Many people regard BUD/S as the toughest training in the military, but making it through BUD/S doesn't earn you your Trident. BUD/S training just gets you in the door. Once you graduate from BUD/S, you report to US Army Airborne School to learn how to parachute out of perfectly good airplanes. After BUD/S, jump school is almost like a vacation. The army instructors hated us for it, but we made the best of it. Once you complete Airborne School, you report to your first SEAL Team. This is where the crucible truly begins. Nobody on the team cares that you made it through BUD/S. They all did it. You are now a nobody and have to prove to the seasoned operators on the team that they can trust you and want to work with you.

In order to earn your Trident after reporting to the team, you had to successfully pass SEAL Tactical Training, or STT, which prepared you to handle the tactics and operational tempo of an actual SEAL platoon. BUD/S basically taught you how to be physically and mentally hard and how to be safe with weapons, demolitions, and dive equipment. If BUD/S was high school, STT was college. STT was a four-month course that taught you everything from advanced diving operations and long-range small boat maritime navigation to advanced demolition and land warfare tactics and operations. Although failing out of STT was rare, it did happen and we lost a few guys.

Once you successfully graduated from STT, you then were placed on a six-month probationary period where you were evaluated by other members of the team for how well they thought you would perform in a platoon. I cleaned a lot of platoon huts, painted, and stood a lot of watches during this time. The other thing you had to do during your probationary period was become an expert on everything related to life in the SEAL Teams as you prepared for the final hurdle to earn your Trident, your Trident Board, which consisted of an oral board where a table of senior subject-matter experts from the team grilled you on their respective areas of expertise. While you answered their questions, you were assembling and disassembling weapons, perform-ing first aid, making communications devices work, or maybe even just doing push-ups. It was stress-loaded multitasking at its best. Once you completed your oral board, you then had to take a written test covering all the subjects you had studied for the last six months. If you passed both the oral and the written board, had successfully completed your six-month probationary period without incident, and gotten at least ten para-chute jumps with one being a water jump, only then were you informed you would be getting your Trident.

On the morning that you received your Trident, the whole team would assemble, and the CO and the CMC would call your name and pin your Trident onto your uniform. They would then depart the premises and a line would form of all the seasoned Trident wearers on the team and one by one they would go by and punch your Trident in, to make sure it would stay. I still have a picture of me—grinning from ear to ear with my chest black and blue—holding up my bent and battered first Trident. I still have that first Trident and that day is one of the proudest of my life.

The teams no longer have Trident boards and it is no longer politically correct to allow older seasoned teammates to punch Tridents in as part of the official ceremony. I think this is sad, because the Trident boards were a huge rite of passage, a true test of mental and physical mettle. Not that it is incredibly easier to get a Trident now; the process is just different and I feel it lacks some of the prestige and sense of camaraderie.

I was sick at the thought of losing my Trident over a single bad moment in a valley whose name nobody back home would ever know, and whose location would matter not to anyone but a handful of men who had fought in it.

Ensign Redman has demonstrated a consistent pattern of bad decision making.

I thought again about my screaming match with Senior Chief Kerry during the NATO exercise. When it ended, what did I see in the eyes of my teammates?

Embarrassment.

This wasn't really about one moment in a valley, was it, Jay?

I had to face that fact.

I rubbed my aching temples. I felt like my head was going to explode from the pressure building inside of it. My life was being destroyed, and I had made myself vulnerable to these attacks with my own actions.

If I was allowed to continue to operate, stories of this deployment would circulate through the teams. If I go to my next platoon with my reputation in tatters, who will follow my lead?

I want to be a good operator and respected leader. It has been the driving focus of my entire adult life.

If I was sent to a Trident review board and they ruled against me, I would be sent back to the fleet, into the regular navy. After a stated period of time, I could return to the SEAL Teams and earn my way back as an operator, but few who've been cast out ever return. That's effectively permanent exile.

Sitting neatly on the wooden crossbar on the floor beside my bed, my holstered Sig Sauer P226 sat well oiled and cleaned. I leaned over and pulled it out. The grip felt like the handshake of an old friend. How many rounds had I put through this pistol? It had to be thousands on ranges all over the world. Long ago, it had become an extension of myself.

The short-barrel 9mm weapon had a fifteen-round magazine and a special phosphate-based, corrosion-resistant gunmetal gray finish that's applied only to P226s delivered to Naval Special Warfare units. An anchor was embossed on its stainless steel slide.

Overseas, our weapons are always kept loaded, even on the FOB. We believe in always being ready. I knew a round was already in the chamber, but I drew the slide back and took a look to make sure. We call this a press check, and it confirmed what I already knew. My gun was ready to go.

As I held the pistol, I thought of the great samurai warriors, who if disgraced would commit ritual suicide. Part of me willed my hand to raise the Sig and press it firmly to my temple.

My life is over. There's nothing left but an honorable exit.

I glanced over at the desk and saw a picture of my beautiful wife. Erica. The image of her face riveted my attention. Her easygoing smile, her eyes alight and lively, always quick to laugh or offer love and compassion.

What would this do to her? After all she'd sacrificed for me? Would my death snuff the life out of her gorgeous eyes?

With the bullet I put in my temple, I'd leave her the burden of my failed career and a ticket to a lifetime of grief. The kids would live under that cloud as well.

Where's your father?

He killed himself in Afghanistan.

A lifetime of answering with shame and bitterness. They would always know my career came first, to the point that I'd rather deprive them of a father than live with the consequences of my actions.

The last thought hit me like a sledgehammer. I dropped the magazine out, racked the slide, and cleared the chamber. I'd never been this lost before. It felt like an oppressive black hole. Clearly, I needed help. After stowing the Sig back in its holster, I slipped through my door and sought out the Special Operations chaplain.

I broke down and told him everything. It felt good to unburden myself, but it still did not help me find a path through this mess. We prayed, and I was reminded that taking your own life was the ultimate sin. Who are we to destroy the gift God has given us? When I left, I could barely stand the sense of shame I felt. Bigger than that, it reminded me of my view that suicide was the ultimate form of quitting. How had I allowed myself to get to this point?

I made my way back to my hooch. When I entered our living quarters, I walked by our message board and saw a note scrawled next to my name.

WHY DON'T YOU GO AHEAD AND KILL YOURSELF?

I stared at the words for I don't know how long. The hallway was empty. Nobody had been standing around, waiting to see my reaction. Slowly, I erased them until the board was wiped clean. Then I stepped inside my room and shut out the world once again.

I never learned who wrote that message. I have my suspicions, but the reality is it doesn't matter. The community will always be predatory, ready to pounce on any weaknesses. We have to be tough and thick-skinned to do our jobs, and part of the culture that has grown up around that would be considered heartless and cruel to outsiders. As a community, if we see weakness in a teammate, we zero in on it and hammer at it mercilessly. The operator either grows calloused quickly and toughens up or he is destroyed by it and leaves. Any weakness can cost lives in combat. It is another example of how warriors self-regulate who they allow to go into battle with them.

The rest of the team had already quit talking to me. Now they'd seen how I'd reacted to the adversity I faced and had just called me out on it. They were testing me, seeing if I would break. Truth was, I was already so broken that I had no idea how to put myself back together.

I awaited my fate. Days passed without a decision from on high. I spoke to Erica on the sat line and rarely anyone else. I hid out, felt sorry for myself, and counted the days left until we finally got to fly home. I silently pleaded that this would end soon. Yet I feared the outcome and dreaded the moment when I would learn they'd come to a decision.

When word finally came a few days later that I was to report to Captain Walsh's office, I had nothing left inside. I walked as if going to the gallows and stood before my chain of command.

Captain Walsh began, "Ensign Redman, I have found that you committed serious errors in judgment. Your conduct as a SEAL leader has been lacking."

So this it. This is how it ends. They are going to recommend I stand before a Trident review board.

I tried to stay stoic as these words sank in. Then Captain Walsh continued. "If anyone had been killed because of your actions, you would be going directly to a Trident review board. That said, you have done many good things and have performed well much of the time. You have shown that you have potential as a SEAL leader."

I tried not to get my hopes up. What was he saying?

"When we return to the States, you will sign a statement acknowledging that you have made multiple bad leadership decisions and a tactical error in combat that put yourself and your teammates' lives in jeopardy."

With dawning horror, I realized he was consigning my career to the scrap heap. When this went into my permanent officer record, I was done. I would never be promoted again, and the navy would show me the door. Upward or out. That's how the navy works.

The senior chief was going to destroy me after all.

"It will not go into your permanent record; instead, I will keep a copy in my safe. When you are assigned to your next platoon, the leadership will be briefed on your past and this letter. You will be placed on probation. During your next training and combat cycle, if you perform in an exemplary manner, I will shred this letter after consulting with your next CO."

I started to breathe again.

"If you do not perform in an exemplary manner, we will recommend your Trident be removed, and the letter will be placed in your permanent officer record."

There it was, the administrative equivalent of the sword of Damocles. If I ran into any issues in my next platoon, this deployment would come back to destroy me. I would live for the next eighteen months under this threat.

"You will not receive any awards for this deployment."

I thought of the decorations that typically followed from deployments as eventful as ours had been, but given everything that had happened, awards were of small consequence.

The captain paused, gauging my response so far. I tried to remain stoic. What he said next left me thunderstruck.

"When we get home in a few weeks, you will be sent to Ranger School. There, you will increase your understanding of ground operations and increase your tactical knowledge."

Ranger School? They were sending a SEAL to the army to learn how to fight? Years ago, SEAL officers sometimes attended Ranger School, but after 9/11 the demands of training and combat were so great that very few SEAL officers went anymore. The army hated us and always made things more difficult for SEALs.

Ranger School was two months of brutal deprivation and trial. It's all about leadership, and they teach it first by stripping away any status you've earned up to that point. You wear no rank and no one cares what you have done in your career. It's basically boot camp on steroids.

Captain Walsh dismissed me and I headed back to my hooch. Although I shouldn't have been, I was furious. Okay, so they didn't take my Trident, but what did they leave me? I'd been put on a choke-chain leash with zero margin for error. One personality conflict, one more chief with a grudge, and I'd be history.

I should have been grateful for the second chance. And the fact that my career, at least for the moment, had been spared. Instead, I railed in my head—and to Erica—that I'd been bulldozed by the senior chief. All I'd done was march to the sound of the guns. Now I was being smacked hard for only wanting to get into the fight and help my brother SEALs.

Part of me, a small part sparked by Charlie's comments, flared at those thoughts. *Wanting to get into the fight. Wanting to prove yourself—Jay, those are not the reasons to risk other men's lives.*

That new voice of humility was drowned out by the bitterness as I faced my reckoning with the army down in the forests and mountains of Georgia and the swamps of Florida. Once there, I'd have no connection with the kids, no connection with Erica. There would be no phone calls, no e-mails allowed. I would be cut off from the only people who had my back.

Those sixty days in the woodlands, mountains, and swamps were legendary for wrecking men who thought they were in superb physical shape.

What was this all for? To be taught things I'd spent the last decade already practicing?

After Ranger School, I'd be thrown right back into the next workup cycle for a SEAL Team deployment, which would mean twelve months of intensive training. Most of that would be away from home. Then I'd be sent into combat for another six or seven months.

I would hardly get to see my family for the next two years. It seemed unbelievably unfair, like they were trying to get me to ring the bell all over again.

I realized that even if I successfully completed Ranger School, I might never be able to convince the guys I was a solid operator and leader again. Part of me wondered if it was time to end my Special Operations career and start a new life. As we flew home a few weeks later, I had half a mind to do just that.

Erica was waiting for me in Norfolk. We landed late in the afternoon, stowed our gear, and met our families late that night in the SEAL Team high bay, a warehouse-sized bay filled with boats, gear, and homemade Welcome Home banners. I will never forget seeing her as I moved through the crowds of families surrounding their loved ones. She'd been working out and looked fantastic. I wrapped my arms around her and pulled her close. The feel of her finally against me again was enough to send a surge of emotion through me. She was the first person in the last three weeks who looked and acted genuinely glad to see me.

Erica had been the only one to stand with me through all this. Just before we left Bagram, the platoon gathered to write down what platoon they wanted to go into next and who they wanted to serve with, both fellow operators and leadership. I was last on the list. Nobody had wanted to serve under me. By now, I was used to the rain of blows coming my way, but it was one more humiliating reminder that my reputation had been shredded, even if the letter soon to be in Captain Walsh's safe hadn't.

"Let's get the hell out of here," I said.

We bolted from the team and drove off base, trying to leave all the tension and nastiness of the past month behind. Erica had gotten a babysitter since it was so late, so the kids were home in bed. I couldn't wait to get home and see them and soak up every moment I could within the closed ranks of my family.

We rolled up the driveway of our Virginia Beach home. It was a rich gray wooden two-story home with beautiful landscaping, and I marveled at the differences between our home here in America and the arid, dusty desolate homes in Afghanistan. I jumped from the car and blasted through the double glass doors and straight up the stairs to the kids' bedrooms. The babysitter must have thought I was insane. The kids were asleep, but I didn't care. As I got to the top of the stairs and reached the landing my heart pounded in my chest. I could feel all the stress of the last month start to lift and was ecstatic to see my children who knew nothing but unconditional love. I went into Phoenix's room first. He had a bunk bed and was asleep on the lower bunk. I climbed in and hugged him fiercely. Six years old, my man cub.

I crept into Angelica and Mackenzie's room. Three years old, my beautiful angel Angelica was on her side in her wooden trundle bed, tucked in tight under her blankets. Gently, I woke her up and stroked her blond hair. Her eyes opened and she saw me. I scooped her up and started to hug her. She hugged me back hard, then promptly fell back to sleep.

I went over to Mackenzie's crib in the corner of the room. My princess. The light from the hallway cast soft shadows on her beautiful baby face. I had been gone almost her entire life. Eleven months old now, she lay sleeping peacefully. At first, I didn't want to risk waking her. Then I couldn't help myself. I picked her up and held her tightly against my chest. She slowly woke and let out a cry of fear. As sleep drained from her eyes, she struggled to get away from me.

"It's Daddy, it's okay, Daddy's here," Erica said, moving in to help soothe her.

Mackenzie pulled away and regarded me as a stranger. She'd been only five months old when I'd last seen her. Shame and sadness filled me as I backed out of the room, watching my little girl writhe and cry at the sudden appearance of the strange man she did not recognize as her own father.

I walked downstairs and poured myself a stiff drink, listening as Erica softly talked her back to sleep. I sat down at my desk, feeling unbridled rage.

I looked at the calendar I kept atop my desk and flipped through it, counting the days. I had been gone for over 280 days of the last year. And for what? A shattered career and a daughter who didn't even know me.

And I was supposed to leave for Ranger School and be gone for two more months?

Right then, I hated the SEAL Teams with all my heart.

PART III

The Smelting

Chapter 14

Virginia Beach
January 2006

Six weeks of leave did nothing to improve my morale. I spent the holidays dwelling bitterly on what had happened. I drank heavily to drown my sorrows. Erica watched me spiral down, without ever saying a harsh word. She tried to cheer me up, but the truth was I wanted to dwell on it. I wanted to be bitter.

As far as the kids were concerned, I was there physically, but was so disconnected I might as well have been overseas. My mood left them puzzled and unsettled. I should have been focused on them and thankful that I was able to come home at all, unlike the eleven men we lost. Instead, as I had done in my plywood hooch while I waited for a verdict on my career, I obsessed over what had happened. Thanksgiving and Christmas came and went. I sleepwalked through both.

With all painful events in our lives that stem from our own faults and mistakes, it is a natural human response to build a fable that makes it easier to face. It allows us to tell others what happened without admitting our own shortcomings. It removes the responsibility for damage we have inflicted with our own actions. In those six weeks, that's exactly what I did. The more I obsessed over Afghanistan, the more I built that fable in my own mind. It became a wall around the empty hole in my chest. I'd already started this in Afghanistan, but once I was away from the team, that wall became the fortress that locked in the misery and protected me from the truth.

It was Senior Chief Kerry's fault. Our cancerous relationship had turned into a personal vendetta and I was living the nightmare of his petty vengeance. It flowed off my tongue and turned the spotlight off me. With every new day, I spun this web of self-deceit.

Shortly after the New Year, I checked in with my new team. I'd been assigned as the assistant officer in charge for One Troop, Alpha Platoon. Most of the task unit had already departed for individual training schools. The few men still around avoided me, a clear sign that my reputation continued to precede me. When I tried to interact with them, their eyes read "Stay the hell away."

My first day with Alpha Platoon, I was called into my new boss's office. Lieutenant John "J.P." Prince was about six feet tall and built like a brick. He greeted me warmly and offered me a seat next to my new platoon chief, Garth Johnson. As I sat down, I realized that Chief Johnson had been on that helo flight from Kandahar to Bagram after I'd been removed from combat.

There is just no escape, is there?

J.P. made introductions, then got to the point. "Red, I heard everything about what happened in Afghanistan. Chief knows all about it too."

I stole a glance at Chief Johnson. At forty-three, he was the oldest member of the task unit. Because of his age and silver hair, he'd been nicknamed "the Grizz."

J.P. continued. "Here's the deal. I don't care. Between Chief and I, you have a blank slate. Lead when called upon, follow when necessary. Despite what happened, I heard you've done a lot of great things also. Focus on the good, take things one evolution at a time, and this will be a great platoon.

"The guys may take a while to warm up to you. You know the deal. But you can win them over with time. I know you leave for Ranger School soon, so go kick that in the ass and come back and shine. Do you have any questions?"

I shook my head and was excused.

Wow. That could have gone a lot differently.

Maybe there was hope.

Then I walked into the platoon space, where all talk ceased as soon as I entered. The men eyed me warily until I passed through.

Dead man walking.

J.P. and Chief may have been giving me a blank slate, but I wasn't sure if I could ever win back the men I was supposed to lead.

Just before I departed for Ranger School, the senior leadership within the team rotated out. J.P. and the Grizz remained while a new crop of officers and senior enlisted joined the team. One morning, our new operations officer, Lieutenant Commander Hale Michaels, walked up and introduced himself. Hale was a big guy, about six foot three and two hundred twenty pounds with wavy brown hair. He was also a smart guy, having been selected for a prestigious Ivy League program through the navy before he came to our team.

As we chatted, he saw I was holding my orders to Ranger School.

"That's a tough school," he said. "Not too many guys volunteer for Ranger School these days. Why are you going?"

Michaels was a nice guy. I'd enjoyed our conversation, and it felt good to be treated like a fellow SEAL again. The question brought me down to earth. Our new ops officer wasn't treating me any differently despite what had happened in Afghanistan. He just hadn't been clued in yet.

For a split second I thought about telling the truth, but my pride got in the way.

So I lied through omission.

"Well, sir," I said, "I'm going to increase my tactical knowledge and understanding of joint operations."

Commander Michaels seemed impressed. "Outstanding!"

I walked away feeling pretty good about myself, as if I had regained a little of the respect I had lost. Except it was a lie. I had done nothing to earn it back. It didn't take him long to find out the truth. A day or so later, he sought me out and demanded, "Ensign Redman, why did you lie to me about the reason you were going to Ranger School?"

I stared at him like a deer in a Dodge Ram's headlights. I'd blown it again and had gotten off on the worst foot possible with my new chain of command. My lie would make its rounds through the leadership, up to the new CO. For a moment, I thought of the letter sitting in his safe, the sword of Damocles, just waiting to fall upon me.

"Well, sir," I stammered, "I really didn't want to air my dirty laundry."

Michaels stared at me for a moment, then said sternly, "Ensign, as the ops officer of this team, I need to know the facts. Period."

"Roger, sir," I replied.

"Remember that."

"Yes, sir."

He stalked off, leaving me kicking myself for being so stupid. Fortunately, I was not too far gone in my spiral of bitterness to learn the lesson from this incident. It is always better to be straight up with the truth, no matter how ugly it is. Trying to conceal it, avoid it, or omit some of it will only come back to haunt you in the future. A true leader understands this and has the confidence and self-possession to handle difficult truths about himself and his actions. A good leader will tell the truth regardless of the outcome.

I headed to Ranger School a few days later, feeling more under a cloud than ever. Saying good-bye to Erica and the kids was never easy. This time, as I

hugged and kissed them, my thoughts were dominated by how unfair this was to us. Later, I realized
I'd squandered much of the time we did have together
by spending it in embittered isolation.

Even when I was deployed, Erica and I had rarely
been out of contact for more than a week. Now, we
faced the prospect of not being able to talk for months.
Ranger School, like boot camp, cuts its students off
almost completely from the outside world. The thought
of not being able to stay connected through this made
my gut grind. Erica took it better than I did, but I could
tell she was suffering and trying not to be bitter toward
me or the teams for inflicting this on our family.

I showed up at Fort Benning, Georgia, on February
7, 2006. I may as well have stepped onto the frozen
tundra of Lambeau Field. Georgia is supposed to have
mild weather, right? No, the army's dirty little secret at
Benning is the sheer misery of Georgia winters there.
Students who attend Ranger School in the winter are
allowed to use white thread to sew on their Ranger
tab as a symbol of the cold they endured. I'd get that
opportunity in a couple of months when I graduated.

I had heard that the army instructors were not fans
of SEALs and gave them a lot of extra grief. It didn't
take long to find out this was true. Ranger School is a
tactical leadership school, and nobody teaches mission

planning better than the US Army. In Ranger School you learn the five-paragraph op order, which in Special Operations work is vital to master since we work with the army all the time.

After the towers fell, the pace of operations made it almost impossible to routinely send SEALs to Ranger School. There just wasn't time between deployments. So when I showed up, the instructors immediately keyed in on the lone sailor in the class and wanted to know why I was there.

It started at our first company formation. We'd been told to report in PT gear. All I had were my US Navy blue sweats. I stood out like a black sheep in the sea of US Army PT gear surrounding me. Of course, the Black Hats—the Ranger instructors—seized on this and started lobbing bombs my way.

The first thing we did was a gear inspection. Special Operations Forces have a lot of latitude in the sort of equipment and clothing we choose to wear under our uniforms. The SEAL Teams had issued me with an exceptionally nice Patagonia seven-layer system— basically ultra-high-tech clothing made of Polartec Thermal Pro fabric that is water-repellent, yet breathes and insulates heat. Wearing this gear on cold days in training and in the frigid mountains of Afghanistan kept me toasty warm. I had followed the list for Ranger

School and had been warned that I would not be allowed to have all my Patagonia gear. I had to leave it behind.

An army field jacket liner was also on the list. Liners function like an extra layer of insulation for soldiers and are very warm. My level five Patagonia fuzzy green fleece was the only thing remotely similar I had, so I brought it along hoping I'd be allowed to use it.

Bad move. The first time the Black Hats saw the fuzzy green fleece, they exploded in anger. "Look at the friggin' navy squid with the Gucci gear!"

I started the Benning Phase of Ranger School with the worst attitude I'd ever had. I went in filled with negativity, which the instructors only reinforced with their hazing. I let them beat me mentally. The cold wore me down until I hated everything.

On our first day, after we were sent running to the chow hall like raw recruits in basic, we were ordered to stand at attention and eat with only a spoon. We had to have most of our food finished before even getting the chance to sit down. I'd never shoveled food down my throat so fast before, and I paid for it. After we left the chow hall, I vomited all of it back up.

Sick, hungry, burning with resentment, I went into the first few days without my heart or mind engaged. The first week of Ranger School is nothing but a gut check. Long days with minimal sleep, exposure to the elements, and constant physical and mental evolutions to get those who don't want to be there to quit. I was definitely in the not-wanting-to-be-there category and did little to apply myself during the evolutions. Basically, I did as little as possible and didn't learn anything. I didn't talk to my classmates either. I certainly wasn't buying into the purpose of all this treatment. With a little perspective, I would have understood that they were using adversity to break us down to build us into a team. I'd seen it before in BUD/S. Teamwork, leadership within a circle of peers, and decision making under stressful conditions were the objectives of this first phase.

As a SEAL, I should have represented my community in the best manner possible by displaying leadership, a commitment to teamwork, and a willingness to overcome any obstacles. Instead, my actions showed me to be arrogant, ill-tempered, and unwilling to work with others. Many soldiers falsely believe that SEALs are like that, and my actions simply reinforced it. I failed to represent my community as anything but a stereotype.

On our third day in the field, the Black Hats ordered us out to a land navigation course. Arrogantly I thought nothing of the course—I had always excelled at land navigation and I'd taught it for two years as a training instructor. This would be the one easy part of this entire ordeal. I figured I'd glide through the course.

At 0300, we assembled in weather so cold the hose to my CamelBak water bladder froze solid. I don't know how cold it was, but I swore I saw a polar bear borrow one of my Ranger instructors' jackets. The instructors had allowed us to wear our black watch caps and jacket liners, but my green fuzzy Patagonia was doing little to take the edge off the subfreezing temperatures. I shivered and cursed steadily under my breath.

For each exercise, the students are graded at four levels, with a Major Plus being the highest and a Minor being the lowest. To get a Major Plus, we had to find six navigation points in a dense, swampy forest in a matter of only a few hours. I'd knock the five points down, then go for the sixth if there was still time. A Major Plus seemed a lock.

As we prepared to start the course, the instructors ordered us to remove our snivel gear. The fleece came off, as did everyone else's liners. I stood there jackhammering from the cold until the exercise finally began. In the predawn darkness, I moved through the trees and soggy ground, counting my paces and finding shadowy landmarks to help keep me on course. I wandered at a leisurely pace for the first two hours; absorbed in thought and fuming over the stupidity of the situation.

When I saw the first hints of sunlight breaking the horizon, I decided I'd better get serious and find the first point. That's when I ran into trouble. In the SEAL Teams we use the Silva Ranger compass for our land navigation. The army uses the Lensatic compass. The difference between the two turned out to be significant, and something for which I was not prepared. One mathematical error with the Lensatic compass and you'll never find your objective. I'd fooled around with a Lensatic compass a few years before, but I'd never used one in a field exercise.

Now it showed. The sun climbed higher into the morning sky and I hadn't even found the first point. I started to push, jogging through the swamp until I located it. I started to run and found the second and third points, but the exercise ended just as I found the fourth one.

When I walked up to the instructors and turned in my sheet, I knew I had flunked. The Black Hats chuckled with laughter. "Damned squid got lost! We should have given you a boat, swabbie!"

Another growled, "Not surprising. SEALs don't know how to navigate anyway."

I'd failed at something I once took great pride in.

"Not so good without your Gucci gear, are ya?" another sneered.

I lost it. All the pent-up fury frothed out of me. "Screw this course! And screw you! Kiss my ass!"

I stalked up to my company instructor and told him, "I'm out of here. I quit."

"Are you sure that's what you want to do?"

Without thinking, I said, "Yes."

I think he was glad to see me go. I'd contributed nothing, and my bad attitude clearly showed.

"Okay. Before you leave, you'll have to check in with the battalion commander and the sergeant major."

I was sent back to the barracks, where the army assigned me to a temporary holding company with the other quitters.

I sat on my bunk that night, wondering what to do next. I had thought Ranger School would be cake compared to BUD/S and the training we did every day in the teams. Although BUD/S is intensely hard, Ranger School demands a full mental and emotional commitment in order to succeed. I had given neither, and now I was paying the price.

Failure. Quitter.

You can get away with a lot of faults in the SEAL Teams, but quitters are never tolerated. From the moment I set foot in Bagram in September, my life in the teams had been compromised. Believing in something different, having any hope—a fool's delusions. Especially now.

Time for the next phase of my life.

I left the barracks and called Erica.

"Babe, I'm coming home."

She erupted in joy. "What? When?"

"I'm getting out of the navy," I said, voice devoid of expression.

A long pause followed. I could almost feel Erica weighing the statement. What did it mean? Financial uncertainty balanced against no more long good-byes.

"Jay. What's going on?"

Everything spilled out. I told her how I failed the land navigation exercise, how I had gotten angry and quit Ranger School, and how there was no hope of recovery. My career was done. Time to cut my losses and start over.

But what would that new life look like? I had no idea.

Erica listened quietly until I finished.

"Babe, you still there?" I asked when silence broke out between us.

"Still here."

"What are you thinking?" I asked, unsure of where she'd land on this. She was the mother of three children.

If nothing else, the military provided us with a steady paycheck and medical care for our children. What would her life look like when I got rid of the uniform? I hadn't considered that, or her for that matter. Or the kids. Part of me, a long-suppressed part, screamed that I was being selfish. But those screams were drowned out by my pain and bitterness.

"Babe?"

"Okay. I can't wait to see you," she replied. Her words struck me center mass.

"I can't wait to see you too," I managed.

"If this is what you want, you've got my full support."

"Okay, thank you," I said into the phone. "I'll be home in a few days. Then we'll figure out the future."

"We will."

"Love you, babe."

I hung up and wandered back to the barracks, where I spent a sleepless night staring at the rafters.

What the hell was I doing?

There's no salvaging this.

It all seemed so unfair. I'd done many successful things in my time in the navy. A lot. I waded through those memories, but they only spurred resentment, not pride. How could they do this to me after all the things I'd done? I'd never asked for anything. And now they were taking it all away.

Who's they?

I shoved that thought aside.

In one single moment I had just tanked my career. The sword of Damocles sitting in my former CO's safe would be pulled out and signed. It would be placed in my permanent record and wreck any hope I had of staying in the navy. I'd never be promoted. As an officer, if you don't get promoted, you get shown the door.

Either I quit, or the navy boots me out. At least if I do it on my own accord, I can do it somewhat on my own terms.

I'd tried my best to follow in the footsteps of my grandfathers. I thought of the Distinguished Flying Cross my dad's dad had earned over Europe while flying bombers. The DFC—his badge of honor that showed when the bullets and flak were thick and coming fast, he made the right calls.

I winced at the thought of what that said about me.

My father, honorably discharged from the army after serving as an officer in the Vietnam era.

My great-uncle had died fighting the Japanese. A pilot too, he had been thrown into the New Guinea campaign with little training and even worse equipment. Outnumbered, facing the best-trained and combat-experienced aviators of the era, my great-uncle and his brother aviators did not back down. He paid the ultimate price for that stubborn courage and devotion.

I remembered the framed letter of condolence sitting in my office at home, signed by President Roosevelt.

My sister served in the air force. My brother had been a marine. I was part of a family where service and dedication to country was as elemental as patriotism and church on Sunday.

Something else I'd gotten away from.

And what of me? What will future Redman generations say of me? I was the one screwup in the family pantheon of American warriors?

I thought of Phoenix, and guilt assailed me. How could I be his example? How could I show him the way to manhood when my own journey had been so flawed?

I searched for options. But I'd let my impetuous actions get the best of me, and there were none.

I wondered if I had made a mistake when I failed to pull the trigger in Afghanistan.

Come dawn, I had never felt so lost.

Chapter 15

Fort Benning, Georgia
February 2006

That morning, I walked over to the command sergeant major's office as if I were heading to the
electric chair. I'd been chasing my tail so long that my
brain had gone numb. No more thinking—it was just
time to consign this stage of my life to the dustbin. This
meeting would start that process.

I entered the office, and the sergeant major greeted
me with respect. The bitter part of me noted that this
was the first act of professional courtesy I'd received
from the army since I'd gotten here.

"Why do you want to quit?" he asked.

I recited the litany to him, starting with Afghanistan
and ending with the land nav course.

When I finished, he didn't try to talk me out of my decision, which came as a simultaneous relief and surprise. Instead, he led me into the colonel's office and introduced me.

"What's going on here, Ensign?" he asked. The colonel was a slight, wiry Asian American who exuded a sort of calm self-possession. I could tell from the outset that he was one of those guys who'd never get ruffled in a fight.

I had to pick the scab off and let the blood flow again. This time, I started with the lie I had managed to convince myself of. "Sir, I've been railroaded over some internal politics left over from my last deployment. Frankly, there is no way I can overcome that. And I just can't put myself through all this BS trying for something that is out of my reach. It is time for me to go back to my family and leave the military."

He listened attentively as I filled in the details. After I finished, he said, "Is there anyone you'd like to talk to?"

"Sir?"

"Your CO?" he asked.

"No." That thought was a horror.

"Anyone else from your team?"

"No one, sir."

The colonel deliberated for a moment, and I felt awkward in the silence. I just wanted to turn my back and go find a new path through life where Erica and the kids would be waiting at the end of every workday.

"Ensign, I have a good friend from your community," the colonel finally said, "a very respected SEAL. We served together at my last joint command."

"Sir, I really don't care to talk to anyone."

The colonel arched an eyebrow. "I'm just gonna give him a call. Captain Vince Peterson. Do you know him?"

You've got to be kidding me. This colonel is friends with the one SEAL on the planet who I respect above all others.

I had planned on the colonel basically saying, "Get lost, quitter," and I'd be on my way. Now I faced explaining to my mentor why I was train-wrecking my life.

"Sir, he's the reason why I became an officer."

The colonel nodded and fell silent again, seemingly lost in thought.

In 1998, I had considered two career paths, knowing I had to choose between them: become a SEAL officer, or continue on to higher-level operational and leadership opportunities as an enlisted SEAL. After long deliberation, I decided to try to follow in the footsteps of my father and grandfather and become an officer. I applied to the Seaman to Admiral program that year and was passed over. I sent my application in the following year and was picked up. Part of the process included having your team's leadership evaluate and support your desire to become an officer.

The chiefs at my team voted almost unanimously not to support my application. I'm sure some of my best impulsive actions contributed to their decision. They wrote that I would make a fine noncommissioned officer, but they did not think I had what it took to be an officer. Vince Peterson was my SEAL Team's commanding officer at the time. He went against his own chiefs and recommended me for the program, something that is almost never done. Usually, what the chiefs say is taken as gospel by the COs. When he endorsed my commissioning packet, Vince Peterson went far out on a limb for me. In 2001, he looked out for me again when he reminded me why I needed to stay in the program after the 9/11 attacks.

"Ensign? Want me to call him?" the colonel asked.

A swell of fear rose in me. What on earth would Vince Peterson think of what had become of me? What would he say when he learned that he'd stuck his neck out for a failure, a tactical screwup, a man whose bitterness had devoured his will to lead?

In my mind, I'd become a former US Navy SEAL last night. What was the point of talking to anyone? But I could not pass on speaking to Captain Peterson.

The thought suddenly struck me: What were the odds that this colonel would know the one man I'd be willing to talk to? Anyone else and I would have refused. But I would have followed Vince Peterson to hell driving a propane truck if he asked.

"Yes, sir. I'll talk to him."

The colonel picked up the phone and dialed a number from his address book.

"Hello, Vince," the colonel said.

I heard the tinny version of my mentor's voice come through the earpiece. The two chatted for a minute as the colonel explained the situation. I stood on the far side of his desk, hearing Captain Peterson's tone, but not his words.

At length, the colonel handed me the phone. I took it and put it to my ear.

"Hello, sir," I said.

"Red?" he asked.

"Yes, sir?"

"What are you doing, Red?"

I felt like a kid talking to his father after wrecking the family car. Although I am sure Captain Peterson had heard about my wayward Afghanistan deployment, I had yet to see him since I returned. I gave him the fable and told him how Senior Chief Kerry had screwed me.

Vince Peterson was the greatest natural leader I've ever known. He had a knack of expressing where the team needed to go with just a few words. He'd plant the seeds, let his men take ownership of the plan, then watch as everything went forward. When the plan succeeded, and it almost always did, he never took the credit. He gave it to everyone else.

In retrospect, I'm not proud that all I could manage was the fable. But at this point, I was still unable to face the truth myself, let alone admit it to the leader I respected above all others.

"Red, do you really think Ranger School is punishment?"

"It is, sir."

"Red, have you ever thought that maybe there is an opportunity here?"

"Sir?"

"You have a chance to learn something of value. If you're willing to take it."

I didn't know what to say to that. I'd not been trying to learn anything since Afghanistan. I'd been trying to defend and justify.

"You're getting ready to throw your career away, Red."

"I'm not sure I have a career left, sir."

"Red," he said firmly, "what are you going to do if you get out? If you come back, you'll be out of the navy in a month. How are you going to support your family?"

He let that sink in. I had no answer and stayed silent.

"Besides, do you really want to go through your life having ended your career this way? You can recover. You control your destiny and your future. You can earn back the respect of the guys if you give them something to respect, if your actions demand respect."

I hadn't looked at my situation from that angle.

"Red, get back in that course, finish it. Then come back with your head held high and show that you have the ability to lead."

I didn't know what to say at first. I never considered Ranger School as an opportunity to shine. I'd seen it as the concrete block tied to my leg, pulling me under.

"Okay, sir. I'll do it."

Vince Peterson had a way of pulling the best out of the people he led. I'd seen him do it countless times.

I hung up the phone thinking that only God could arrange for the one person who could get through to me to be on the other end of that line.

I looked up at the colonel. He was watching me expectantly.

"Colonel, can I return to my class?" I asked him.

He shook his head. "No. But I can roll you back and you can start with the next class next month."

Next month?

"Would I go home and come back?"

"No. You'll be placed into a holding company until next month's class begins."

I thought of Erica's face as she heard the news that I wasn't coming home after all. Worse, this sixty-day separation had just turned into ninety.

"Okay, sir, I'll do it," I said to the colonel. I just hoped Erica would forgive me.

The colonel explained to me that for the next thirty days, I'd have some basic duties around Fort Benning, but little else.

I thanked him and returned to the barracks, trepidation growing as I knew I'd have to call Erica. I'd already put her through enough lately, and I wasn't sure she would understand these abrupt course changes.

I was dreading her reaction, but I made the call.

It wasn't pretty. When I explained the meeting with the colonel and the talk with Vince Peterson, I could feel her disappointment boil over. I told her I was going back into the program.

Then came tears.

"Babe, I gotta do this."

"You're not coming home?"

"I've never quit anything. You know that. I can't end my career this way, as a quitter and a failure. I have to recover who I am. Who I know I have the ability to be."

A long, pregnant pause followed. I heard a heavy sigh on the other side of the line. Then I heard her voice, solid as stone, say, "I support you."

"There's one other thing," I said, knowing what would follow.

"What's that?"

"I can't return to my class. They're rolling me back into the next one."

"What does that mean, Jay?" she asked warily.

"It means I'll be here an extra month."

The tears turned to pure anger. Coming on top of all the angst and uncertainty I'd already dumped in her lap, this was just too much.

And yet, as livid as she grew, she never once questioned my decision. She never once came at me for my erratic decision making.

At last, the anger ebbed and she repeated, "I know you need to do this, Jay. I'm mad at you right now, but I'm behind you all the way. Go finish and come home."

This wife of mine, she never ceases to amaze me.

Chapter 16

Fort Benning, Georgia
March 2006

I bent down and picked up the cigarette butt laying in the grass at my feet. With a flick, the butt spun into the garbage bag I'd been dragging across the post with me.

Holding company. Seriously? I'm in Ranger School Jail.

I took a few steps forward and found another butt. Right then, I wanted to break every smoker's arm who couldn't find a trash can.

I looked down at the butt, half smoked then discarded in a hurry, probably by some soldier whose sergeant was screaming at him to get back to work. I felt the bitterness well up in me like bile.

The days crawled by. We were forbidden to leave the Ranger compound during the week. At night we were occasionally allowed to make calls, which was the sole saving grace. I was able to talk to Erica and the kids, and that kept my morale from teetering over the edge. Erica and the kids wrote me every day. And it made some of the other denizens of this army purgatory jealous.

One morning, as I filled my bag with litter, the bitterness flared again.

I've put in thirteen and a half years. I was a member of one of the most elite Special Operation units in modern history. Millions of dollars were spent preparing me, training me, outfitting me to handle the toughest battlefield tasks our nation can face. And my own brothers have reduced me to this.

I stopped and thought about that statement.

Where is the personal responsibility in it?

Vince Peterson's words came back to me. *You have an opportunity to learn here.*

If you're willing to take it.

I served with good men whom I respected. They turned their back on me.

Or did they?

What did all this say about me?

A door suddenly opened in my mind. The place it led to was a dark room that I had never entered. Inside

I could see the truth about myself through the facade of lies I had built. I stood at its threshold, not really wanting to walk through.

Sun Tzu once said, "If you know your enemies and you know yourself, you will never be defeated."

I didn't know myself. I was running blindly through life refusing to even acknowledge my weaknesses.

I have been an arrogant ass most of my career.

Clearly, I needed to come down to earth. Maybe trash detail did serve a purpose after all. I guess I needed to mentally flatline before I could reconstruct my potential for leadership.

Since I left Afghanistan I have lived a lie.

As I held that bag of trash, I finally faced the truth. I'd disgraced myself protecting my own ego. I'd lied, made up stories, and looked for any way to divert attention from my own faults. There is no room for a leader to be selfish, especially on the battlefield. Decisions must always be made for the good of the mission and the men. As a leader, you must always come last.

I'd done the reverse, then blamed everyone but myself.

I am not that man. What the hell happened to me?

Maybe I had always been that way and never had the self-awareness to realize it. That thought hurt like hell, but I didn't run from it. I stood my ground and embraced the cold hard truth.

Use this as an opportunity to learn. Learn who you really are and use it to make yourself a better person, a better warrior, a better leader.

I found another cigarette butt and flicked it into my bag. The bitterness over being forced into this sort of work evaporated. Far from a humiliating burden, it was giving me clarity I surely needed. For years, my attitude had hobbled relationships and endangered my career. I suddenly recalled a moment years before. I'd worked my tail off for months on a special project. When I had finished it, I knew I was going to receive a significant award for the effort. For whatever reason, it got downgraded to a lesser award.

What did you do after you found out?

I'd thrown a temper tantrum. I went off on one of our admin guys, who had congratulated me after I received it. Instead of being grateful for receiving any sort of acknowledgment, I'd thrown the award at him. I may as well have thrown it into the face of Captain Peterson, who was my CO at the time.

That incident stuck with my peers who'd witnessed it, and for years after when I ran into one of them, they'd remind me of it.

Jason Redman. Navy Achievement Medal Thrower. Vanguard of Leadership.

I scooped up a wrapper and sealed my trash bag. Done for the day, I tossed it in a Dumpster and walked to the barracks, burning with embarrassment at the memory. Why did I do that? Was I really that immature and impulsive?

Yeah. Apparently I was.

By the time I went to sleep that night, I felt like ten million pounds had been lifted off my shoulders. Although I didn't like some of the hard truths, the bitterness had waned. The sense of betrayal was gone. I wasn't sure what would follow, but I did know this: my path to learning how to be a good leader had just begun.

I can't say I looked forward to picking up trash the next morning, but I didn't start the day despising what would come next. I was ashamed that I had thought so highly of myself that I saw myself as above picking up trash. I realized that as a SEAL and a leader, it was my responsibility to set the example with everything I undertook. If I was picking up trash, I should be the absolute best at it—so good that by the time I left Benning, the State of Georgia would want to hire me to be its chief garbage collector. If there were an award for picking up trash, I should be striving to walk across that stage to receive it.

I laughed to myself at that and conjured an image of what that award would look like. My mood lightened, and this newfound perspective felt healthy.

I'd been an ass in the predeployment workup right from the get-go. I'd come back into the teams straight from college thinking that I knew everything. After spending the '90s honing my skills as an operator, I discovered all that I'd been trained to do had changed. The tactics had evolved; the techniques had become more advanced and nuanced. Frankly, the teams had passed me by. Instead of putting my head down and focusing on learning the new stuff one evolution at a time, I held on too tight and ate myself alive from the inside out as I made mistakes. I was more afraid of screwing up and looking bad than I was of asking for assistance and learning from the experienced operators around me. The farther behind I felt, the harder it was for me to fit into the team. And that just fed my bad attitude and heavy drinking.

Then I remembered our first mission in Afghanistan. My immaturity sure shone brightly on that operation. Instead of being pissed and bitter about not leading the assault force, I should have been focused on learning the job I'd been given.

A good leader doesn't pick and choose when he wants to lead.

As I thought about that, I remembered what happened when I'd been ordered to get our detainees out of the area. I hadn't asked anyone what kind of air support we'd have on the exfil. I'd assumed that the same Black Hawks that dropped us off for the mission would come and pick us up. I'd set up the extraction for the wrong type of helicopter. When our air expert, Senior Chief Mike Peters, stormed over and started changing everything, what did I do?

I felt threatened. I felt like he was undermining my leadership. I clashed with him as a result, and he told me to shut the hell up. That was exactly what he should have done.

What should I have done differently?

That question occupied a good chunk of one morning's trash duties. It was not an easy question for me at first. I found myself internally defensive again. But I knew better than to give in to that. You can't learn if you can't be honest with yourself. Gradually, I owned up.

Mike Peters was our walking encyclopedia of all things aviation related. Instead of butting heads with him for doing what he did best, I should have welcomed his arrival and asked for his help. I should have watched him and learned from him. At the time, I felt his arrival had weakened my own authority. But my insecurity was the only thing that caused that to happen.

A good leader knows his limitations and works to overcome them with knowledge, experience, and training. A good leader is not afraid to ask questions, seek counsel, or rely on others with greater expertise when necessary.

The only way a young leader grows is to be open to such teaching moments. I'd utterly failed on that front. Point taken. I resolved from here forward to rely on the subject-matter experts within our organization. Their input could only make me stronger.

Back in the barracks that afternoon, I began replaying my encounter with the general when I went up to his table at the chow hall in Afghanistan. I had convinced myself that this was a good example of leadership. The move was impulsive—that much I knew at the time. But the reasons behind it were flawed. I did it thinking that the team would see me willing to stand up to anyone on their behalf.

A teammate had dared me to go do something foolish. What was I—twelve?

The men didn't want crazy gestures. They wanted steady leadership. Their lives depended on the decisions their leaders made in combat. A leader who ignores his chain of command to confront a general does not engender confidence.

I lost my teammates with that stunt. Truth was, I probably lost them long before that moment. But it was the executioner's ax on what credibility I had left.

Toward the end of the month, as I grew nearer to the end of my time in Ranger Jail, I circled back to that day in the valley. It was time to lay what happened to rest. Sort out the mistakes, harvest the lessons learned, move forward with this knowledge, and bury the past.

I knew that I had not done what was best for the team. I knew I had made the wrong call. And in order to move on, I had to forgive myself for that. SEALs, along with most military professionals, are rigorous, dedicated individuals. Within the community, we have forged a culture of achievement. Perfection is our standard. It has to be that way, given the narrow margins we work with, in the most grueling conditions imaginable.

I could not change my decision. But I should have owned it in its aftermath. I should have listened to those with more experience, taken my lumps, and moved forward. That is how leaders grow.

I was so desperate to justify and defend my actions, I lost sight of what I was there to do. I was there to lead when necessary and to follow when called upon, but above all else to accomplish the mission as part of the team. Instead, in the aftermath, I'd made it all about me and the defense of my ego.

Yes, Senior Chief Kerry hated me. We loathed each other. But the truth? He was a damned good operator.

In a firefight, I would have wanted him there as a tactical leader.

In his own, abrasive way, he had attempted to mentor me. If I had put down my pride, I would have seen it, and I could have learned a lot from him. That never happened; I failed to manage our relationship and it poisoned the entire platoon. It also hurt my reputation with my teammates.

My self-deceit finally collapsed. Kerry had not done this to me; I'd done all this to myself. I was being punished less for the decision I'd made and more for the way I'd fiercely refused to take responsibility for it. The more I railed against those aligned against me, the more I deserved to be punished.

I wasn't betrayed by my teammates. I betrayed them with my selfishness.

It was time to grow up.

So where do I go from here?

My career was still in shambles. My reputation was still ruined inside the community.

In the final days of Ranger Jail, I deliberated for long hours. Internally, I'd taken ownership of my mistakes. But I still had no idea how I could recover my reputation.

I would do it just like J.P. had suggested: one evolution at a time.

What if I finished Ranger School strong and returned to the team with a fresh attitude? Maybe, if I demonstrated that I had learned and made the tough changes, I could overcome the reputation I'd earned and rebuild the respect and trust so vital between operators.

Maybe I would never win over some people. That would just be the legacy of my decisions. But others might be open-minded and willing to give me a second chance if they saw I was truly a changed and humble man focused only on the mission and the men.

Everyone encounters adversity in life. Sometimes it is small, sometimes life changing. How you handle it starts and ends with you. The measure of a person is not found in his or her past, but in how he or she overcomes adversity and builds the future. Outlook will always determine outcome. From here forward, my past would stay in the rearview mirror.

Ranger Jail came to an end, and the weekend before the new class was set to begin we were allowed a forty-eight-hour pass. I rented a car and met Erica and the kids in Atlanta. Gone was the brooding and moody post-Afghanistan me. The fire was back; I was excited and upbeat again. Erica was astonished by the transformation, but happy to see it. Her husband had finally come home.

Being with my family for those forty-eight hours completed my turnaround. With them, I felt whole again. Gone was the reckless arrogance, replaced by conscious humility. I was more self-aware than I'd ever been. I was motivated and relishing the challenges ahead. Most important, I was finally able to forgive myself.

On Saturday evening, I paced back and forth in our hotel room, Erica watching as I poured out the details of the internal journey I'd just gone through. When I finished, I laid out my plan for the months ahead. First objective: become the honor graduate of my Ranger class. If I could accomplish that, it would be a solid launch point to begin my journey back into the brotherhood.

Saying good-bye on Sunday was a tough moment. No serious words were exchanged, but I could just see it in Erica's eyes that she understood I needed to do this to recapture what I had lost. It would be a sacrifice for the both of us. When she headed back to Virginia that evening, I know she had to have been hurting. But she never complained.

Back at Benning, I spent my last night before we classed up getting my gear ready and my mind right. When I finished going over my packing list, I laid my fuzzy green Patagonia fleece on the top of my bag and laughed at the hate and discontent I knew it would bring starting tomorrow. I would take it in stride as an opportunity to stay humble and control my emotions.

I climbed up into my rack knowing tomorrow would be a kick in the teeth. It was the beginning of March and the temperature lingered in the thirties. This time, I would not let it affect me. I had been colder. I had been wetter. I had been more miserable. It was time to focus on my army brethren around me and help them. It was time to lead.

As I drifted off, staring up at the rafters as I'd done every night for a month now, my thoughts turned to my grandfathers and great-uncle. Their generation knew no quit. They transformed the world with their can-do spirit and steadfast resolve. Bad equipment, poor training, outnumbered by the enemy, it didn't matter. They pushed on and found a way to win.

I would too. No doubts now: my road ahead was crystal clear.

Chapter 17

Fort Benning, Georgia
March 2006

The next morning, I hit the ground running and never looked back. The company I joined was full of strangers. No matter. I did everything full bore, but I made sure to help everyone in my squad whenever I could. I was not going to be the disconnected selfish jerk I had been. This go-round, my heart was fully invested.

The Black Hats made my life hell, as usual, calling me squid, denigrating the SEAL Teams, and harassing me for my navy roots. This time around, it became my rocket fuel. I wolfed down food at the chow hall and managed not to throw it up. I had memorized the

Ranger creed, so as we did pull-ups, I recited it at the top of my lungs for the benefit of the Black Hats and my classmates.

During that first phase, we were to zip line across a lake, starting from a point about two hundred feet above the water. As we got within about ten feet of the surface, we were to let go of the T-bar and fall into the water. As I took my turn at this iteration, the Black Hats laid into me again. I stood on the platform as they shouted, "Sing us a song, Squid! Sing us a song!"

A month ago, I would have told them all to go to hell. This time, I took a long breath and belted out a lusty version of an off-color SEAL drinking song. When I finished, I looked over to see the Black Hats laughing.

We came to land navigation day that first week again. When the exercise started, I raced off into the boggy woods with single-minded focus. During the last week of Ranger Jail, I had gotten a fellow inmate to teach me how to use the Lensatic compass and I practiced my declination conversions until I could do them without thinking about it. I nailed the first point and never slowed down. I finished all six with thirty minutes to spare, earning a Major Plus.

The redemptive feel of that moment convinced me all things are possible. Few problems can't be overcome with tenacity and a strong work ethic.

The first week came and went in a blur. Ranger School is designed to grind you down. It wears at you without mercy, just like a long span of time in combat. You have to be mentally tough, physically capable of enduring misery while still leading and learning.

Our tasks in the first week culminated with a fourteen-mile ruck march. I had been a SEAL communicator for years in the '90s. I'd learned to carry a heavy ruck full of radios for days while on patrol. That turned out to be vastly different from road marching, something the navy doesn't do.

The army has elevated road marching to an art form. Soldiers can put on a heavy pack, get on a road, and move like Patton through Europe. A well-trained group of soldiers can maintain a fast walk for hours with sixty pounds of gear on their backs. I was not prepared for this, and to keep up with my class I had to start running.

Some of the guys couldn't hack it. Their feet covered in bleeding blisters, their shoulders aching, they fell out, puking by the roadside. I ran with a third of my weight slung in the ruck and never once looked down at those guys. By mile fourteen, my feet were trashed and my lungs burned. But I made it. The squid was still in the game.

After the road march, we moved to Camp Darby to begin field and leadership exercises. We remained on the move all day and well into the night. From 0430 to 0200, we marched, discussed, briefed, assaulted, and engaged simulated enemies. When we finally finished the last iteration of the day, the army had a knack for sticking us on a gravel lot. We called it "standing on the rocks." We'd be there for hours every night, waiting for the Black Hats to tell us to get some sleep. BUD/S had you moving at all times; if you weren't moving, typically you were getting "beat" doing push-ups or some form of physical remediation. At BUD/S there was no waiting around. In some respects, this part of Ranger School was the toughest for me. If I wasn't asleep, I wanted to be doing something.

In the morning we'd get our breakfast MRE, then go straight into twenty hours of continuous operations. Come midnight, we'd go stand on the rocks for a few hours. When we were finally released for the night, the Black Hats would give us our second MRE. Then we'd sleep for an hour or two. Every day was the same: we spent the day marching, assaulting, and sprinting through the Georgia forests on empty stomachs. By midnight, we were utterly famished. Some of my classmates lost over fifty pounds in Ranger school.

The point of all this was to make us stressed out, miserable, and physically beat down, all while being forced to make decisions in the heat of the moment. It was incredible training for the stresses of combat.

In addition, the Black Hats demanded perfection. I ended up with two Minor Minuses during the Darby Phase. The first came when one of the Black Hats discovered I had a lanyard on my gear unknotted. I deserved it. Lack of attention to little details can cost lives in combat.

The Black Hats hit me with a second Minor Minus when they discovered I didn't have a full CamelBak. After students had died in years past during the Darby grinder, the instructors made absolutely sure we stayed hydrated. During hand-to-hand training, I had drunk quite a bit of water without having an opportunity to refill my CamelBak. The instructors conducted spot checks and nailed me.

These were small setbacks. I flew through the end of the Benning Phase, with my eyes still fixed on being an honor grad. Ranger School relies heavily on peer evaluations within your squad. During the field exercises, everyone rotates through the leadership and technical slots, so by the end of the program, each student has had ample opportunity to learn every position from communicator to platoon sergeant to patrol leader. My peer evaluations were extremely high, which said a lot considering I didn't wear army green.

The feedback encouraged me to keep doing what I'd been doing. I focused on the tasks at hand, and encouraged and helped out the guys around me. I tried to lead by example and in the process, I began to make friends.

At Ranger School, just like in SEAL training, you always have somebody with you. You are never alone. At BUD/S that person is called your swim buddy; at Ranger School, your Ranger buddy. My Ranger buddy was Lance Brogan. Lance was about five foot ten and weighed about two hundred pounds. He had short (i.e., Ranger bald) dark hair. He was a father with two small children. He had great attention to detail and was a fantastic staff sergeant from an airborne infantry unit based out of Alaska. I enjoyed listening to his stories about jumping into the frozen tundra of Alaska during deep winter airborne drops. He told me once about a jump where it was thirty degrees below zero and when he finally got to the ground to take a leak, his urine froze before it hit the ground. He had done multiple combat deployments. He had a dry sense of humor but was quick to smile. Lance and I meshed from the outset. I convinced him from the beginning to let me call him my swim buddy, which drove the Black Hats crazy. The display of my SEAL heritage gave me a little victory, plus we both thought it was funny. Ultimately, it became our own way of showing the instructors that they could not beat us mentally.

One night, I told Lance how I ended up in Ranger School. That actually led to a running joke between us. Whenever we would be doing something that was really miserable, I would ask him, "Why am I here?" He would deadpan, "Because you screwed up." I would reply, "Oh yeah, that's right. I had forgotten." That interchange always lightened our mood in even the toughest moments.

At the end of our time at Camp Darby, we were released for eight hours. We poured into town for a good meal, haircuts, and a quick shopping trip to buy gear for the next phase. A pile of letters and packages of food waited for me from Erica and the kids. After I called her and talked to the family, I settled down to read every word while we all stuffed our faces.

The interlude ended all too soon. The class headed to Camp Merrill, located near Dahlonega, Georgia, for the start of Mountain Phase. For two weeks, we learned and refined climbing techniques. The Rangers had pioneered American mountain combat tactics in Sicily and Italy during World War II. Their experiences in the Mediterranean led to the famous assault up the sheer cliffs at Pointe du Hoc on D-day. Sixty years later, our gear was better, but the fundamentals remained the same.

We received a new set of instructors for this phase, and I discovered they had no issues with me for being a SEAL. I later learned one of them had a brother in my community, which may have been part of the reason the constant harassment ended. They still screamed at me like any other student, but late at night when I stood watch, a few of the Black Hats would come over and talk with me, warrior to warrior. They asked about my experiences in the teams and overseas. Those short conversations buoyed me and kept my spirits up. It was nice to be seen as a peer again. The hard work and dedication had made all the difference. No way would that have happened with the attitude I first brought to Georgia.

As good as things were going for me, the opposite was happening at home. Erica, now on month three of very limited contact with me, suddenly faced a flurry of hardships. Her car broke down. Several key appliances at the house went on the fritz. Animals got sick and needed immediate care at the vet. Then Mackenzie developed a series of ear infections, which grew so serious our doctor told Erica that she would need to have tubes surgically implanted to treat them.

While the surgery was routine, anytime you put a child under general anesthesia there are risks. The thought of our baby girl being exposed to these risks without me there was the final blow. I thought of her blond hair and big blue eyes and her quick smile. I thought of the story Erica had shared with me about Mackenzie trying to make her own bottle with formula. Erica walked into the kitchen and it looked like a formula bomb had gone off. Like it had snowed all over the kitchen. And now our little one was struggling with major ear infections, which I knew had to be putting major stress on Erica. She called the team's family support coordinator and vented all of her frustration. The teams take family issues very seriously, and the coordinator called our team's commanding officer, who was overseas at the time. He listened to the situation and promised to help out. Using a satphone, he called Erica to offer his assistance.

The next morning, I got called to see the Black Hats. I reported along with Lance, and they ordered us to drop and do a bunch of push-ups. I had no idea what was going on. I didn't think I had done anything wrong, but I was beginning to wonder.

I looked over at my swim buddy and asked, "What did you do?"

He fired back, "What the hell did you do?"

The instructors promptly told us to shut the hell up.

After they finished making us do PT, they told me that my commanding officer had called to let me know that my wife was having trouble at home. They gave me a phone and told me to call her.

I did, and for thirty minutes she vented everything that was falling down around her. I did what I could to console my wife, but nothing could really make up for my absence. Erica cried and I felt helpless and selfish. She was the one person who had my back, and my own actions had put us in this situation. Now, at the moment she needed me most, all I could do was tell her how much I loved and supported her through a telephone.

After we had to say our good-byes, I hung up the phone and felt sick. I thought of that moment when I returned home and Mackenzie wanted nothing to do with me, and now I was away again. The thought of my baby girl in surgery without me being there for her and Erica just destroyed me.

A couple of the older Black Hats approached and asked what was going on. When I told them the gist, they conferred a moment.

"Tell you what," one of them said. "We'll give your wife our cell numbers. When your daughter gets through surgery, we'll have her call us and we'll get word to you about how it went."

They didn't have to bend the rules like that for me. The gesture eased my mind and made me appreciate them even more. At least I could be connected somehow. I thanked them profusely.

The day of Mackenzie's surgery, my class embarked on a five-hundred-foot vertical assault exercise. Basically, it was Pointe du Hoc in Georgia. Though it was not straight up the whole way, there were some very hairy sections that could have caused serious injuries if we lost our grip and fell.

Lance and I did not have graded positions that day, which meant we carried about fifty pounds of gear. Two of the graded positions are communicator and FSO, or fire support officer, both of which require carrying radios, spare batteries, and an assortment of other gear that makes their packs about thirty pounds heavier. Halfway up, our FSO and radio man began to struggle as the additional weight exhausted them.

One of the Black Hats observed this and sarcastically remarked, "It is so good the rest of your classmates are looking out for your communicator and FSO by offering to help carry their rucks."

The guys in our squad above us pretended they hadn't heard the gibe. My swim buddy and I looked at each other with the same thought. Both of us were smoked. Climbing five hundred feet with all that gear had worn us down too. Did we have enough in our tank to do the right thing?

We looked back up and saw the rest of the squad ignoring our FSO and communicator. It is common during times of stress and adversity for men to look inward and focus on their own misery. As a leader, you cannot afford to do that. You have to be the one to drive and inspire those you lead, especially in the moments when the challenges are at their greatest. A good rule of thumb I learned is that if it sucks for you, it's time to get vocal and start motivating those around you.

Right then, one of the Black Hats appeared at the top of the cliff. He spotted me and shouted down, "Hey, Navy Boy! Your wife called and your daughter is out of surgery and everything went well."

I let out a victory whoop and felt a surge of energy. Lance capitalized on the moment and said, "Hey, man, let's go get those packs."

We clambered up to our two overloaded squadmates and swapped out with them. They were dumbfounded that we were going to carry their load, but frankly I didn't care about the extra weight after the good news.

My swim buddy and I made it to the top with the eighty-pound rucks. Our FSO and communicator arrived several minutes later, swapped out rucks with us, and collapsed beside us, grateful for the help. The moment reminded me again of the importance of team-work. That gesture not only went a long way in forging a bond with our FSO and communicator, but also earned us the respect of many of our other classmates and instructors.

Not long after that incident, our platoon was ordered to set an ambush for a simulated enemy force. We rotated into different roles again, and one of the younger students took over as our patrol leader. From start to finish, this young man screwed up the mission profile. His planning was faulty, his decision making was disastrous, the patrol route was a nightmare, and we botched the ambush. As the day wore on, the class grew increasingly angry with the mistakes. Debriefs are supposed to be candid, safe spots for constructive criticism designed to make squads and platoons stronger and more effective. But despite my best efforts to stay in control of my emotions, the long day of adversity, coupled with an empty stomach, got the best of me. I laid into the kid with a laundry list of his screwups. Our lead instructor for this patrol was a captain, who listened quietly as I pounded home all the errors I'd seen. I finished and the soldier looked like he'd been gut kicked.

After the debrief, the captain came over and pulled me aside. "Y'know, I've been watching you go through this training and listening to what the other instructors have to say about you. I've also read all your peer evaluations. You are doing a great job. You are a leader. You are ranked high, you are physically strong, and you seem to always be looking to help out the guys around you."

"Thank you, sir," I replied with surprise. I wasn't sure where this was going.

Then he continued, "You pull no punches about why you are here, or about the mistakes you made overseas. But after that last debrief, something dawned on me. I've seen it with other men. Have you ever thought that you may be here because your leadership regards you as a loose cannon?"

I stared at him, unable to answer.

"I would be willing to bet, if you look back over your career, there are numerous long periods of time when you were flawless, one of the top runners. Then you'd end up doing something erratic or unexpected that made your chain of command wonder if they could truly trust you."

His words felt like a sledgehammer. In an instant, a dozen episodes flashed through my mind. The thrown award. The fights and immature moments I'd had with teammates. The time when I was a new guy and I had a table thrown on top of me by a SEAL training instructor for mouthing off during a live fire exercise. My drinking. The charge down into the valley in Afghanistan.

He was right. I couldn't deny it.

"Ninety-five percent of the time, you're spot-on. You excel. It's what got you commissioned. But that other five percent is what gets you in trouble. Anyway, I would be willing to bet that is the real reason you are here."

Giving into my emotions and chewing out that kid was a five percent moment.

In the last year, the only reason guys had followed me was because they were curious to see what erratic thing I would do next. You can be the best operator on the team, but nobody will ever vest their trust in you if you are erratic.

To be a leader requires sound judgment, emotional control, and solid decision making. The best are never impulsive or unpredictable; they are the ones you can count on in the most demanding situations. They are rocks. And I'd never been that guy. I'd been the loose cannon.

In years past, my brothers had called me the "Social Hand Grenade" because they never knew what I'd do at a party or a bar. I needed to learn the discipline necessary to be consistent. The Ranger captain continued. "If you could learn to control those five percent moments, I have no doubt you could be a phenomenal leader."

I felt like a total moron. How did I not see this sooner?

The captain's words gave me sudden clarity and made me want to take a more objective look at myself.

There are three different components here: there is the perception of yourself, the perception others have of you, and then there's the way you really are. If those three aspects are out of alignment anywhere, you have a problem. I had lived with a false perception of myself for much of my career, and when it was tested, I collapsed. It had hindered me all the time. I'd never had a realistic appreciation of my strengths and weaknesses, which made it impossible for me to cultivate and amplify the former and find ways to minimize or fix the latter. In fact, I was so unaware that I'd been amplifying my weaknesses and crippling my strengths.

Senior Chief Kerry saw this in me from the outset. So did Captain Walsh. I took a breath and faced the truth: all my brothers had seen it. I'd lived in a self-inflating bubble of arrogance.

The captain saw the wheels turning in my head, and I think he was probably glad to see that his insight was having some effect. He slapped my shoulder. "Look, Jay, keep doing what you're doing. But from here on out, take a moment to evaluate what's going on. Think about the long-term effects of whatever decision you're making before you execute."

I glanced over at our young patrol leader. My job as a leader, and a member of a team, was to build his confidence and help him until he learned his role. I'd utterly blown it.

Lesson learned. I took the captain's every word to heart. Finally, I was beginning to develop the tools and knowledge to turn my life and my career around.

A few days later, we began the final stretch of Ranger School. Known as Florida Phase, it was composed of long movements in tropical woodland and swamps. We spent many patrols in calf-deep water. Our boots almost never dried out, and it was a constant battle of changing socks, applying foot powder, and giving your feet time to dry to prevent them from being utterly ruined. Having spent years in the jungles of South America, I knew how to take care of my feet. I did what I could to pass that on to my squadmates. But six weeks of lack of sleep and poor nutrition took their toll. Our decision making deteriorated. Everyone moved slower, groggy from sleep and physical misery. In the swamps, we had cases of hypothermia, which the instructors identified right away and made sure those men got dry clothes. A few years before, four students had died out in this swamp, so the Black Hats were careful to keep an eye on us for signs of life-threatening distress.

About a week into Florida Phase, we had our first maritime movement. The instructors felt that since I was a SEAL, I should be the patrol leader for this mission. For most of the students it was the first time they had done anything with the small boats, so just getting everything rigged for the mission in a timely fashion was a feat in itself. We were all functioning poorly, and I didn't crack the whip on the guys. I saw how much they were suffering and just didn't push them any further. We missed our start time as a result and ended up late through the entire mission profile.

The Black Hats failed me. I had yet to fail anything in the course, and in the past I would have beat myself up over it. Instead I took a deep breath and reviewed what went wrong. I learned my lesson. Sometimes the mission must take precedence over the needs of the men.

Several days later, I was tasked with being our company's sergeant major. My classmates were in the same mind-set as the last mission. This time, rather than taking it easy on them, I became Stalin incarnate. Sometimes you have to push the men beyond anything they think they can accomplish. The trick is to know when to do it, and when to show compassion. That's a delicate balance that the best leaders—men like Vince Peterson—innately know how to handle. For me, it was a learning process.

We weren't late again.

Several nights later, the Black Hats ordered us to assault a dug-in simulated enemy defensive network. A new patrol leader rotated in, and we began the longest swamp movement in Ranger School to get to our mission objective. We spent most of the day wading through chest-deep, brackish water.

We advanced to our final firing position where we planned to begin the assault on a series of trenches covered by a machine-gun nest. The ground was a little higher, but we had no cover or concealment. Right away, the machine gun opened up and revealed its devastating field of fire.

Our assault bogged down as the men went to ground. It didn't take a genius to see that we had to knock that gun out or we'd all get hit. I crawled forward with my swim buddy to get a better view of the machine-gun nest.

We were each given small sandbags wrapped in tape with a chem light attached. These functioned as simulated hand grenades. You would pull it out, crack the chem light so it glowed, then throw it. I was still at least seventy-five yards from this machine gun, which for those of you who have never thrown a grenade is an impossibly long throw.

I decided to give it a shot. I cracked the chem light and hurled the "grenade" as hard as I could. It sailed through the air, hit the ground, bounced, and rolled directly into the machine-gun nest. The weapon quit firing. In fact, I think everybody stopped firing. The instructors were so dumbfounded that one of them blew the whistle and stopped training.

"Who threw that grenade?" the Black Hat asked.

I raised my hand and rogered up.

"Fucking figures, the navy SEAL."

He gave me a Major Plus. In that moment, I managed to make the SEAL Teams look like the greatest warriors on the planet. Never mind that it was a one in a million throw—a lucky fluke after a long and grueling day. Still, we ended Florida Phase on a high note as a result.

Less than a week later, we climbed aboard buses for the ride back to Fort Benning. We had made it through Ranger School. The only thing left was graduation. In the end I didn't make Honor Grad—I didn't know this, but being a rollback disqualified me from being in contention for it. No matter, I had high marks in every phase. Even better, I found myself through that ninety-day crucible.

I'd learned a lot about army doctrine and mission planning, which would help me as a Special Operations leader. I'd also met some fantastic fellow warriors like my swim buddy, Lance Brogan. Lance had been great to work with and I learned a lot about leadership and holding people accountable from his example. As a hard-charging staff sergeant he did not tolerate shortcuts or laziness and despised guys in Ranger School who busted their butts when they were in graded positions but slacked off when not. He called many of them out throughout training, which earned him multiple enemies who did not appreciate it. Apparently the truth hurts. He had been a great support over the last two months and he was an outstanding example of leadership to all of us. I have the utmost respect for any man who has completed the training, and I know that men who go on to Ranger battalions are some of the best soldiers in the US Army.

Erica wanted to come down to the graduation, but it was just too much for her with the three kids and everything she was juggling at home. The last thing I wanted to do was add more stress. I told her stay home. I'd be there soon.

So I called my father. I knew Dad was proud when I graduated from SEAL training, but being a former army guy, I think he about bust a gut when I asked him to come down and pin my Ranger tab on. My dad is not a very emotional person, or at least he doesn't normally express his emotions aside from occasional frustration or anger. I'm not sure if my dad even said he was proud, but I could tell by the look in his eyes that he was. Dad still works for the army at Fort Bragg, and in his office there is not a single picture of me in my navy uniform. But the picture of us together at Benning proudly hangs on his wall.

As I flew home after graduation, it would have been easy to feel overwhelmed heading back to a task unit of men who had no clue about the personal journey I had just completed in Ranger School. To them, I was still Rambo Red.

I would change that opinion one training mission at a time. We called those exercises evolutions, so in my head every challenge I faced I took one evolution at a time. I'd apply all that I learned at Ranger School, lead when called upon and learn at every opportunity. I accepted I would make mistakes, but I would own them and drive forward. I would stay humble.

The SEAL creed states, "Earn your Trident every day." It was about time I did that. In the process, I would show my brothers that the days of my five percent moments were over.

*Photographs courtesy of the author
unless otherwise noted*

As a cornerback for the Lumberton High School football team, I made up with heart what I may have lacked in size or speed. Age sixteen, 1991.

Even at a young age, I was already showing a love and affinity for water. Age eleven, Magens Bay Beach, Saint Thomas, US Virgin Islands, 1986.

Attending my brother's USMC boot camp graduation. Age twenty-six, Parris Island Marine Corps Recruit Depot, South Carolina, 2001.

Erica and I having a date night a few months before my deployment, 2005.

Our wedding in the Shenandoah Valley, Virginia, July 2001.

Erica and I on our honeymoon. We took an amazing cruise through the Caribbean and stopped in Saint John to visit my oldest sister. July 2001.

The Redman clan in full force, years later, visiting the same spot where Erica and I were married for another wedding. Shenandoah Valley, Virginia, July 2006.

The ornament that started it all. Erica and I and the two-legged plutonium reactor walking on Virginia Beach. Erica bought this ornament but it almost didn't make it to our tree. Today it is one of dozens marking our amazing life together. Summer 2000.

The man cub and I hanging out at the beach. Virginia Beach, 2000.

One of the proudest days of my life. This picture was taken the day after I received my Trident. The bruises are from my older teammates ensuring it stayed on. 1996.

On the grinder at Basic Underwater Demolition/SEAL Training next to the "So you wanna be a frogman?" statue. Coronado, California, June 1995.

Showing off my camp during a week of survival training in the jungles of Panama. Two canteens of water, a knife, four waterproof matches (that didn't work), six feet of string, and a live chicken were all we had to survive on. That chicken never had a chance once I was finally able to start a fire three days later. To this day, it was the best meal I have ever eaten. 1998.

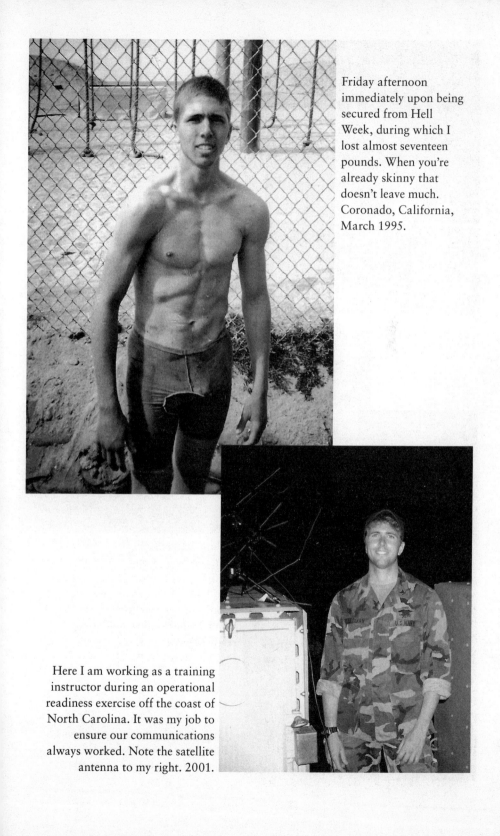

Friday afternoon immediately upon being secured from Hell Week, during which I lost almost seventeen pounds. When you're already skinny that doesn't leave much. Coronado, California, March 1995.

Here I am working as a training instructor during an operational readiness exercise off the coast of North Carolina. It was my job to ensure our communications always worked. Note the satellite antenna to my right. 2001.

We had modified grooming standards while deployed to Afghanistan. I sent this picture to Erica and the kids while I was there; they had never seen me with a beard. August 2005.

My graduation from US Army Ranger School. I think my dad, being former army, was more excited than I was. This was the beginning of my journey back to the teams, to which I would return humble and ready to lead.

This picture was taken a few weeks before I was severely wounded. Camp Fallujah, Iraq, August 2007.

Our platoon. Afghanistan, July 2005.

The structure in the background here is Tarnak Farms, Osama Bin Laden's old Afghanistan compound. Outside Kandahar, Afghanistan, September 2005.

Taking notes on a target outside Kandahar, Afghanistan. Note the female MP helping to search and watch the women and children. September 2005.

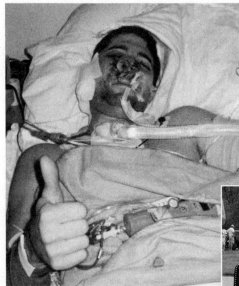

This picture was taken roughly ten hours after the firefight that almost ended my life. I had just come out of surgery. My chief pulled out his camera and, despite my drug haze, I threw the thumbs-up. Baghdad, Iraq, September 2007.

Seven months after my injuries, at my daughter's soccer game. This was my second arm external fixator and I was still trached. My eye would not be fixed for several more months and I was down to 120 from the 170 pounds I was before my wounds. Virginia Beach, 2008.

Around surgery twenty-six or so I brought in this picture of Brad Pitt and jokingly told the OR staff that this is what I used to look like. A nurse said to me, "That's Brad Pitt." So I told her, "I used to always get that." Chicago, 2009.

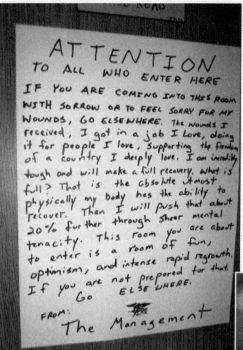

The Sign on the Door that went viral and earned my family and me an invitation to meet President Bush. Today it hangs in the wounded ward at Walter Reed National Military Medical Center, exactly where it belongs. October 2007.

An acrylic model of my skull that doctors made to help them figure out how to put Humpty Dumpty back together again. Note all the missing bone on the left side where my cheek and nose should be. Virginia 2011.

Courtesy of the Virginian-Pilot

The Sign on the Door and my detailed wooden Trident, which now hangs behind my bar, 2010.

Our first real family vacation since my injuries. Erica captured Angelica, Mackenzie, and me during this amazing sunset. Hawks Cay Resort, Florida, July 2012.

Angelica trying to be like Daddy. Virginia Beach, Virginia, 2009.

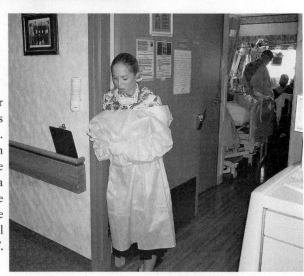

Erica putting on her yellow bacteria scrubs before entering my room. All visitors had to don these scrubs to reduce the risk of infections. Erica slept next to me in those scrubs in my room for five weeks. Bethesda Naval Hospital, October 2007.

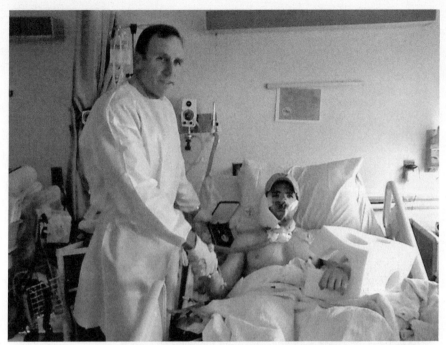

Vice Admiral Kernan presenting me with my Purple Heart, or as I like to call it, the Slow Movers Award. Bethesda Naval Hospital, September 2007.

My family and I enjoying a VIP tour of New York City, care of New York's finest, the FDNY. New York, New York, May 2010.

The dedication ceremony for the Sign on the Door at Bethesda National Medical Center, where it now stays among other wounded warriors. February 2009.

My family and I with Secretary of Defense Robert Gates at the Pentagon. I was incredibly honored to be invited. 2009.

President Bush signs the Sign on the Door in the Oval Office. The White House, October 2008.

Courtesy of the George W. Bush Library and Museum

As I was speaking to President Bush, I looked over to see my daughter Angelica dump her White House bag of goodies on the Presidential seal. A surreal moment for sure.

Courtesy of the George W. Bush Library and Museum

I worked with Phoenix for six weeks on mastering a firm handshake and looking people in the eye in preparation for him meeting the president. As this picture shows, I could not have been more proud of my young son.

Courtesy of the George W. Bush Library and Museum

Father, husband, brother, friend. Honoring fellow SEAL SOC Adam Brown at his funeral in Arkansas. This was one of more than fifty memorials and funerals I attended during my twenty-year career. 2010.

I am standing with Rob Marrow, Al Joliet, Shawn Daniels, and a member of the AC-130 gunship crew that called in fire on the night of our fateful mission. Rob and Al had just received their Silver Stars for that night.

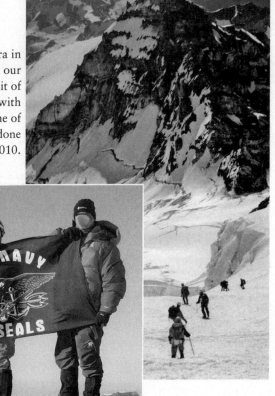

I am the closest to the camera in this shot as we make our descent from the summit of Mount Rainier. Climbing with bronchitis made this one of the harder things I have done in my life. July 2010.

My fellow SEALs Samuel Bryant and Dave Michaels and I on the summit of Mount Rainier. July 2010.

Looking across the snowfields on our way up to Camp Muir during a break on our ascent. July 2010.

My fellow wounded warriors MSG Spanky Gibson and SPC Kyle Carpenter and I kneel to honor our fallen warriors during the filming of the wounded warrior documentary *Still in the Fight*.

The Wounded Wear staff and volunteers in front of the Wounded Wear trailer at an event. July 2012. *Courtesy of RGB Studios*

PART IV

The Forging

Chapter 18

Nevada

Spring 2006

After Ranger School, I saw my family for all of about five days before heading out the door again. My SEAL Team's predeployment training had actually started in my last few weeks at Fort Benning, but J.P., our OIC, was kind enough to give me a few days at home before I flew out to join the unit in the desert outside Reno. I could tell Erica was not happy, but once again, she didn't give me grief about it. When I got to Nevada, it was clear that graduating from Ranger School had not earned me a spot at the table yet. The dark cloud of my record in Afghanistan remained. I hadn't expected anything less, but it still felt like diving back into an icy lake after I'd earned the respect of those around me at Ranger School. I stayed focused and reminded myself: one evolution at a time.

As we started working together in Nevada, it did not take me long to see the quality of the men in our platoon. Only seven men out of the entire thirty-seven-man task unit were new guys without a combat deployment under their belt. The experience level, combined with excellent leaders, ensured that our team meshed well and operated fluidly together. I'd been blessed with this assignment. Even though the men were less than thrilled to have me, the platoon was easily the best I'd served in during my entire career.

J.P. took me aside and told me that I would function as the mobility force commander when we deployed. This meant I had responsibility for all things related to our vehicles, plus our movement to and from target. The training in Nevada would prepare me for that slot.

We started at the most elemental level, rotating through each position inside our vehicles. We took turns being turret gunners, drivers, and vehicle commanders. From there, I started working at a higher level, planning routes to and from our simulated targets, holding security around them with our vehicles, and getting up to speed on maintenance issues with our specially designed Humvees.

On my first training evolution, I grew so paranoid about making a mistake that I tried too hard. That was exactly what I'd started doing in my other platoon, but this time I recognized it and relaxed. J.P. saw it too, and he offered me a sterling piece of advice when we'd finished on the range.

"Red, if the guys are squared away, you don't have to tell them what to do. They already know it. Trust them, and they'll take care of you."

I took that to heart. The platoon was filled with squared-away guys.

Over the succeeding days, I did more listening and learning than leading. We had subject-matter experts with years of experience that I could draw on for knowledge and advice. This time, I didn't waste any opportunity to grow and learn.

Once I relaxed and put the things I'd puzzled through in Ranger School into practice, I fell into a good groove at last. Staying loose allowed me to. It felt good to have that rhythm back.

The new attitude earned dividends. Toward the end of our mobility training, J.P. and the training leadership set up a complicated mobility scenario, which they gave to me to plan and execute. We started out on the mission, and our convoy immediately ran into trouble. Our simulated enemy harassed us with hit-and-run ambushes. As we fought through them, our instructors threw more tactical problems into the mix. They declared a vehicle had broken down. As we dealt with that, we got attacked again. Moments later, we received a radio report that a friendly Black Hawk had just crashed in our vicinity. We were the closest element to the wreck, so naturally we were ordered to go secure it and rescue the survivors.

For hours, this exercise continued, forcing me to abandon our preplanned playbook and make decisions on the fly. The simulated running battle lasted for several hours and tested my judgment to the utmost. When it ended, J.P. came up to me and said, "Great job, Red."

I wasn't out of the doghouse yet, but I was making progress. J.P. was a great role model and mentor. He worked with all of us junior officers to make sure we had opportunities to learn.

We completed our mobility training and headed down to the southern United States for land warfare training. By now, it was the dead of summer, and we arrived in the middle of a record heat wave. This gave us a chance to operate in conditions close to what we would face in Iraq.

As I worked closer with the guys in my squad, the wall between us began to crack. I still got the cold shoulder from a few, but I knew if I kept up the momentum,

I stood a good chance of breaking through with them as well.

Pat Donahue, whom we called "the Angry Irishman" for his often surly demeanor, impressed me from the first exercise out in the Nevada desert. He'd been a student at George Mason before the war, working at a Little Caesars pizza. He'd always dreamed of being a SEAL sniper. After the towers fell, he joined the navy at age twenty and threw himself into the pursuit of that dream.

Five years later, he was a deadly shot, a natural operator who excelled at being one of our platoon's point men. He'd no doubt heard all the talk about my Afghanistan misadventure, but he seemed willing to give me a fair shake, just like J.P. and our chief, Garth Johnson.

One day, during a land navigation exercise in hundred-degree heat, I saw the measure of the Angry Irishman. We maneuvered through rocks and gullies, over hills and through stands of trees with fifty pounds of gear, the sun searing our exposed flesh. By midafternoon, some of the men started falling out with heatstroke. Pat started to go down as well. I brought him water, but it was too late. He gutted out the end of the evolution, then our corpsman gave him IV fluids right there in the field.

After a short break, we rolled into a night evolution. I checked on Pat, figuring he'd be down for the evening. When I told him the squad was about to move out, he plucked the IV from his arm, strapped on his gear, and rejoined us.

Earn your Trident every day indeed.

Close-quarters combat training always gave me an adrenaline rush. When done right, a stack of operators moves like a ball of fire—smooth, quick, and violent. We used live ammunition in our exercises, blew doors with explosives, and shot our way through simulated enemy structures. Entering a building is among the most dangerous things a warrior can do in combat. Any single mistake can get people killed if there are hostiles waiting inside. A split-second's hesitation in a doorway is enough—as the marines and the army discovered during the second battle of Fallujah in 2004. During one close-quarters fight, a Seventh Cav fire team got hung up in a doorway just as they took fire from the street behind them—and from inside. The ambush and delay in the doorway cost the lives of four good men.

To avoid such moments, we trained for speed, decisiveness, and violence of action. Once inside a building, that speed becomes even more critical as the entry team splits up and clears each room. Give the enemy a moment to recover from your sudden arrival and you lose momentum, and that can lead to casualties.

The entry team also has to be very careful not to shoot one another by accident. Everyone starts from a common baseline of tactics, but as you get comfortable with the men around you, it becomes an intricate combat ballet. Only hundreds of evolutions ingrain the muscle memory required to do it properly.

A well-trained SEAL platoon can clear a house in a matter of seconds, with each member of the team knowing exactly what the other is going to do no matter what the situation. It is very similar to the orchestration on a football field where a quarterback and wide receiver develop a special chemistry together. That chemistry elevates their game and makes it possible to do incredible things, such as a receiver catching a ball without ever looking for it. He runs to a specific point, holds his hands out, never looking back, and trusts his quarterback to place the ball there.

Between evolutions in simulated buildings and urban areas, we honed our marksmanship with shooting drills. We practiced switching from our primary weapon to our sidearms in case we ran out of ammunition. We spent hours gaining the muscle memory needed for effective combat reloading. We worked our weapons one-handed to simulate being wounded in the arm. We trained to never stop, even if we were shot. Keep in the fight, no matter what. If we couldn't bring our rifles to bear, we would draw our pistols to keep sending rounds at the enemy.

I stayed in my groove, feeling the old confidence I used to possess returning. This time, it felt more mature and tempered. I stayed humble, and I learned all I could.

I'd always been a good shot, perhaps not the best in my platoons, but always competitive. During one marksmanship evolution, I scored a notable success when our instructor, a legendary SEAL sniper, took away our personal rifles and gave us stock M4 carbines with iron sights.

"You never know what may happen in combat. You could end up shooting a weapon that isn't yours."

He had us take a marksmanship qualification test this way. I placed second in the task unit; one of our snipers scored highest. I don't know if this changed any opinions of me, but I do know it felt good to excel again. Through every phase of training, J.P. entrusted me with more leadership opportunities. He watched me closely and coached me when I needed it. Instead of resisting his advice, I absorbed it. The more I absorbed, the more willing he was to give me more chances and responsibilities.

When I received my midterm counseling on leadership, I earned high marks. I was finally proving myself to my chain of command. Most of my teammates were coming around as well.

The process wasn't obvious. It wasn't like anyone came up to me and said, "Red, you've really turned things around, we'd like to welcome you back into the brotherhood." In a warrior community, such words would never be spoken. You are judged by your actions. When you get the job done, your teammates trust you. If you can't hack it, they apply direct and indirect pressure until you go away.

I noticed there was no pressure. And a little at a time, the rapport was growing between us. I redoubled my efforts to stay focused and humble. I would not have a five percent moment that wrecked all this progress.

The year blew by in a frenzy of activity. I spent Christmas and New Year's with the family, then hunkered down for one last sprint before we headed out the door for service in Iraq. It was during one of our final exercises that I ran afoul of Hale Michaels again, who had been promoted to be our task unit's executive officer.

Throughout our workup, I could still feel the effects of our first meeting when I lied to him about why I was going to Ranger School. He ignored me much of the time and rarely gave me feedback. Even this late in the training cycle, I sensed I was still in his doghouse.

Just before we were to deploy in 2007, we were scheduled to get a week of small boat operations. The chances of us utilizing boats in Iraq were probably as likely as Eskimos eating snow cones, but every team heading overseas has to be deemed proficient in a variety of skill sets, including maritime operations (MAROPS). As our departure date loomed, the MAROPS segment of our training got compressed from one week down to one twenty-four-hour cycle. Trying to cram everything we were supposed to do into a day set us up for some serious hiccups. Sure enough, as we prepared for a long-range maritime navigation exercise one night off the Virginia coast, we hit a snag.

Our leading petty officer and I were supposed to run the exercise together. When we got out to the launch point, the boats were already waiting for us in the water. As we checked things over, we discovered they'd been improperly rigged and didn't even have compasses, charts, or plotting boards. We would have to navigate by GPS, which is supposed to be our backup system. Part of the point of overwater navigation exercises is to learn how to use a map and compass so if the boat's GPS fails, the team can continue the mission effectively.

The LPO and I discussed what to do. It was too late to pull the boats out of the water, get the maps and compasses installed, then press on with the exercise. We'd simply run out of time. We decided to execute with what we had and make the most of the time available.

Right then, Hale Michaels appeared on the dock and announced he was going out with us. I thought to myself, *Great. Lucky me.* I knew we were going to get it. He checked things over and discovered the situation with the boats. When he came over and asked me what we were doing, I explained we'd run out of time to fix the problem. We were going to drive on and complete the course.

"Red, listen to me," he said. "Something worth doing is worth doing right. Bottom line: this should have been fixed before the boats were put in the water. Going out without the proper gear is not the right answer."

He was spot-on, of course. I owned the mistake, learned the lesson, and moved on. Still, I knew that I had more work to do to win over our XO.

By mid-March, the task unit was set to deploy in three waves. Our ADVON (advanced echelon) would go into Iraq first to coordinate with the current team there and get things set up for the rest of us. Our main body would follow next with all our gear. The third group would include all our stragglers—guys getting back from emergency leave, or getting off medical hold, or who had to finish school before they could deploy. I was the officer in charge of the second wave, and those final frantic weeks in Virginia had me running around in the typical predeployment paperwork maze.

Finally, a few days after our ADVON left, I took a last quick holiday with Erica. We planned to spend the weekend up in a remote mountain getaway close to where we got married.

On the drive up, I started to feel a pain in my right side. At first, I ignored it, not wanting to spoil our last weekend together. When the pain worsened, I asked Erica to drive. Sitting beside her in the passenger seat, I suddenly doubled over and could hardly move until the pain passed.

When we got to the hotel, I turned to Erica and said, "Babe, I'm sorry, I gotta lie down."

The pain grew more intense. Erica, by now thoroughly alarmed, called the local sheriff who was a friend of ours.

He told my wife, "I've got a friend who's an ER doc. Come on over to my place, and I'll have her take a look at Jay."

I staggered downstairs, and Erica helped me into the car. A few minutes later, we pulled up in front of the sheriff's partially constructed new house. Inside, we found him and the ER doc waiting to take a look at me. The sheriff had laid a door across two sawhorses and had me lie on top of them. He then moved two workshop lights around the table. It felt sort of like a battlefield medical exam.

After a thorough check over, the doc declared, "You've either got appendicitis or colitis. Either way, you need to get to a hospital."

I didn't want to get stuck in a hospital up here away from the kids if I had to have surgery.

I asked, "Do you think I can make it to Virginia Beach?"

The doc thought about it. "Yeah, you'll be able to make it back. Just go straight to the ER once you get there."

Our weekend retreat blown, we raced back to Virginia Beach, where I spent time in both the civilian hospital in town and Portsmouth Naval Hospital. At first, I was diagnosed with appendicitis, but the medical staff at Portsmouth discovered I had colitis after all. They put me on massive doses of pain meds and antibiotics and stuffed me in a hospital bed.

I confess, I made a lousy patient. I lay there, stressed out that our second wave was due to leave soon. I had to be on that flight. When a resident and an intern came into my room to check on me, I said to them, "Guys, I'm scheduled to deploy in a few days. You have to fix me so I can go with them."

The resident scoffed at me. "You aren't going anywhere."

The news felt like a baseball bat to the head.

"What you mean?" I demanded.

"You're not going anywhere. You're really sick."

For an instant, I had a vision of my brothers kicking in doors and fighting al-Qaida in the most violent place in Iraq—without me. I'd be lying here as they went to war.

Not acceptable.

The resident started to say something. I cut him off and said, "Go get me a real doctor!"

Shocked and rightfully offended, they beat a hasty retreat. Some time later, a captain, who was the senior doctor of this section of the hospital, stepped into my room. He laid it out bluntly.

"Lieutenant, we can't let you deploy right now. Your intestines are swollen and inflamed. We need to keep you on antibiotics and painkillers. We need to run tests to figure out what is wrong with you. It could be as simple as contracted infectious colitis, which I suspect, but we won't know until the tests are done and the swelling goes down. Once that occurs we need to do a colonoscopy."

"How soon can we do all that?" I asked.

"Six weeks. We have to make sure the swelling is gone before we do anything. If it's clear and all the tests come back negative, you will be cleared at that time to deploy."

The captain's reply leveled me.

After coming so far, now this?

I didn't know how to react, or even what to say.

He left me to wallow in misery. The physical pain was nothing compared to what I felt inside. I had fought my way back and slowly earned the trust of my teammates only to be left on the sidelines when it mattered most. I couldn't believe it. And then there was my career. I'd had a great workup, but that wouldn't be enough to salvage my future. I needed a good deployment to erase the stain of Afghanistan once and for all.

J.P. had already gone to Iraq with the ADVON. I called him from the hospital and told him my situation. Each day, I checked in with him to tell him my progress and find out what was going on over there.

As I lay in the hospital, my brothers already over there with the ADVON went into battle.

Their first mission was a turnover op with the platoon we were replacing. The old hands were going to show our platoon the area and help familiarize our guys with the local situation. They drew a tough first mission for that.

Our task unit was assigned to go after a key leader in the al-Keta cell. Our ADVON, along with the unit we were replacing, carried out the mission reinforced with a small contingent of Iraqi soldiers. Together, they rolled into al-Keta in the dead of night and surrounded a concrete compound. The entry team stacked up, poured inside the walls, and blew the door thought to be the main entrance to the house. It turned out to be the door to the prayer room, which afforded no access to the main house.

The assault element spun around and surged for the other exterior door. Inside the house, the initial explosive entry woke up four die-hard jihadists, who grabbed three AK-47s and a captured American M16 rifle.

As the assault team blew the second door and surged inside, the enemy opened fire. Petty Officer Joseph Clark Schwedler was one of the first into the room and was caught in a cross fire that killed him instantly. One Iraqi soldier behind him was also fatally hit. Jeff Clayton, another SEAL from our ADVON, was wounded outside the room when a bullet went through a window and struck him in the forearm.

One SEAL, Chief Dave Michaels, made it into the main room. The four insurgents turned their weapons on him. Shot repeatedly and wounded by at least one hand grenade thrown at him, Dave fell facedown on the floor beside Clark and the dead Iraqi soldier.

The rest of the entry team couldn't get inside. There was so much incoming fire and with no more comms from Clark and Dave, the only course of action was to back off and regroup. As they did, one of the insurgents bolted from the house, trying to make a break for it. He didn't get far before one of our snipers shot him dead.

That didn't keep the remaining three jihadists from celebrating. They shouted taunts at our platoon, screaming, "Allahu Akbar!"

Right then, Dave regained consciousness. Wounded over two dozen times and covered in blood, he was assumed dead by the insurgents. Among other places, he'd been shot in the stomach, the scapula, and the arm. As the enemy continued to celebrate, Dave saw that his rifle had been destroyed in the initial barrage of gunfire. So he drew his pistol and killed two of them. The third swung around and opened fire, hitting Dave several more times, including in the crotch. Dave kept pulling the trigger until his pistol ran out of ammo. Even as the enemy sprayed the room, Dave dropped the empty magazine and reloaded with one hand—just as we had practiced countless times before. He hit the last insurgent, who tumbled dead to the floor. In the silence that followed, Dave tried to use his radio to call the rest of the platoon, but it had been destroyed in the firefight. He crawled forward and grabbed Clark's.

"Come get me," he said into the handset. "They're all dead."

Despite twenty-seven wounds, Dave walked to the medevac bird that came to extract him.

Dave and Jeff were flown out of Iraq, first to Germany, and ultimately to Bethesda Naval Hospital in Maryland. They arrived just after Portsmouth released me. I was set for the colonoscopy in a few weeks, and if it came back with no issues, the captain had assured me I'd be able to deploy. In the meantime, the second wave departed without me, so I did what I could to help out. I stockpiled equipment and supplies J.P. and the other guys told me they needed. I'd haul it all over as soon as I could get cleared and catch a bird to Kuwait.

As soon as I was able, I headed up to Bethesda to link up with my wounded teammates. When I got there, Jeff told me that Dave had actually checked out that day. Despite all Dave's wounds, the insurgents had not hit anything vital. His scapula had been shattered, and he temporarily needed a colostomy bag. The one bullet that hit him in the crotch punctured his scrotum between his testicles, a one in a million shot that he had proudly displayed to everyone at the hospital, including the secretary of the navy when he came to visit.

I broke Jeff out of Bethesda and took him for some real food and drink. Over our meal together, he told me the full story of that night. I listened closely. We were dealing with a fierce and fanatically devoted enemy willing to fight to the last breath. I would be facing them soon too, if all the tests came back negative.

Jeff finished the story and we sat in silence for a minute, thinking about Clark Schwedler. I didn't know him personally, but I knew the caliber of man he was: selfless, fearless in battle. He represented the best of America.

Jeff broke the lull in our conversation. "All I want to do is get back out there."

I looked at his bandaged bullet wounds and empathized. It was all I wanted too.

We finished lunch and I dropped Jeff off at Bethesda, telling him to call me if he needed anything.

I left the hospital with renewed awe of men like Dave and Clark. Their courage and ferocity in the worst conditions imaginable epitomized the spirit and resolve in the SEAL Teams. That Dave was able to end the fight single-handedly, then walk to the waiting medevac bird astounded and humbled me.

If I'm ever in that situation, could I do the same?

The long drive back to Virginia Beach gave me plenty of time to think about that.

Chapter 19

Al Anbar Province, Iraq
May 2007

A month after I was hospitalized, I finally reached Iraq. The docs at Portsmouth had cleared me to deploy, and I went home and said good-bye to the family. A few days later, I flew from Baltimore to Kuwait, where I caught a flight to Fallujah.

Iraq that spring was a nation in transition, finally finding its footing after years of near civil war between the Shia and Sunni militias and terror groups. In Al Anbar Province, the open warfare that had characterized much of the past three years had given way to a persistent, determined insurgency centered on increasingly sophisticated cells. They excelled at planting roadside bombs, which became their most common (and effective) way of hitting coalition forces.

But those bombs came at a cost. The local population was starting to turn against the jihadists. Their depredations and callous treatment of villagers and city dwellers in the province had given rise to what became known as the Anbar Awakening. Gradually, the Sunnis were taking control of their own security, first by helping us, then by forming their own militias to drive the terrorists out.

It was a delicate time for the United States in Iraq. We needed to foster the Anbar Awakening while hammering at the heart of the remaining insurgent cells. It was a tricky mission—one mistake that resulted in civilian deaths could turn a town or village against us again and send it back into the arms of the terrorists.

That was what we were grappling with when I reached Fallujah and stepped off the bird. As we filed off, I saw J.P. waiting for me on the tarmac. He came forward and shook my hand warmly. J.P. had been in the SEAL Teams for almost twenty years. He had served over ten as a successful enlisted SEAL before being selected for a commission for his leadership and management. He grew up in the South and was a huge SEC football fan. He had a great personality and a calm, quiet demeanor regardless of the situation. He always looked mildly amused whether we were in a real-world firefight or one of the single guys was regaling him with last night's exploits. He had a good sense of humor and enjoyed practical jokes whether he was doing them or he watched them played out. He got along with and was respected by everybody. I was glad to see him and even happier to be serving under him and learning from him.

"Glad you're here, Red. We've got a lot of work to do."

"Right on. I'm definitely ready."

"Good. We need another mobility force commander."

It was go time.

When J.P. and I arrived at our compound, my teammates greeted me with backslaps and wisecracks about my rear end.

"Did you enjoy your colonoscopy?"

"I bet he asked for seconds!"

"Way to try to avoid the deployment, Redman."

"Don't worry; we got you a padded seat in your Humvee."

The humor was a good sign. If SEALs don't respect you, they will ignore you. They don't poke fun unless you've been accepted.

J.P. and Chief Johnson quickly got me up to speed. In the month since the platoon had been in Iraq, they'd conducted over twenty missions already. Keeping vampire hours, the team had been going after mid-level insurgent leaders throughout Al Anbar Province. The battle rhythm had been intense, a pace far different from what I'd experienced in Afghanistan, and it looked to only increase as our intel guys developed more targets for us.

With the team already functioning smoothly, I had a challenge on my hands. The task unit was progressing nicely on the battlefield learning curve. The daily schedule had been locked down, combat leadership positions had been filled, and guys were getting comfortable with how things ran. Combat trust had already been forged. Injecting me into that mix would cause some shuffling, and I would need to catch up quickly.

A few days later, J.P. invited me to join him on a meet-and-greet operation at an Iraqi police station in Fallujah. We rolled out in daylight, which was unusual. I rode in J.P.'s Humvee as he pointed out landmarks in Fallujah while we drove down Route Michigan, the main highway in the area. The streets were crowded with Iraqi pedestrians and vehicles. Our drivers maneuvered through the crowd aggressively, trying to keep the Iraqis from getting too close. If they did, or if our gunners suspected a threat, they would toss flash bangs overboard to warn the people to get back.

At the same time, Iraqi kids would chase after us, begging for candy. Our gunners would lob handfuls of goodies at them, and they'd scurry around scooping the treats up.

Block after block, it rained flash bangs and candy. Welcome to Iraq.

After a thirty-minute drive, we arrived at an Iraqi police compound. We spent about twenty minutes with the police commissioner; then after the meeting concluded, he offered to show us the station's detention facility. We approached the main cell block, and the smell assailed us long before we reached the barred windows and doors. Filth, human feces, and body odor combined to make a reek that could kill a rhinoceros.

The sight inside was even more shocking. The jail was perhaps seventy feet by fifty feet wide. Sweat-soaked and miserable, hundreds of prisoners sat clustered so close together I doubted they could lie down to sleep. I peered at them and their ragged clothes, faces smeared with grime and bare feet almost black with gunk. Their beards were scraggly and their hair greasy and long.

Some of the detainees fixed their eyes on the floor when we arrived. But there were dozens who stared intensely at us, cold hate in their eyes. I stared back, and I could tell that hate sustained them. They burned with it and the hope of someday escaping to exact revenge for such treatment.

So this is who we're up against.

I got an education that night. Those prisoners told us a lot about the demographics of the insurgency around Fallujah. They broke down into three main groups: the die-hard zealots, the loyal supporters, and the opportunists. The majority of men we would encounter, roughly seventy percent, were opportunists just looking for a way to support their families. With the economy all but nonfunctional, al-Qaida had become a prime employer. Each cell had a payroll of locals who received a few bucks a month to emplace roadside bombs. Without any other hope of feeding their families, men who otherwise would have held down honest jobs went to work killing Americans and their fellow Iraqis.

When we caught them, they invariably begged and pleaded for mercy. They didn't want to lose their families, and the thought of ending up in a place like this jail petrified them. They'd spill their guts to our intel guys and do anything they could to avoid detention.

The next tier, roughly twenty percent, were the loyal supporters who feared the Shia majority and the tyranny it had wrought on the Sunni population since the 2003 invasion. They were not jihadists, and they did not believe in al-Qaida's overall objectives. Instead, they forged an alliance with the jihadists to obtain skills, supplies, and weaponry. They would fight us— and fight hard—but they didn't want to die. When cornered, they would surrender, then push every button they could short of provoking lethal force. They'd start fistfights with our men, resist detention, swear and curse the United States. But in the end, they loved life more than their cause, which meant a hellhole like the one I'd just seen would be their fate when they fell into coalition hands.

If the twenty percenters formed the skeleton of the insurgency, the remaining group, the ten percenters, formed the heart and brain. These guys were the committed jihadists. They would fight to the death almost every time. They would convince young men, women, and sometimes even children to sacrifice themselves in suicide attacks. They even used mentally retarded and handicapped civilians as suicide bombers, and they had managed to kill a key police commissioner elsewhere in Iraq with that tactic.

They were the bomb makers and the high-level leaders. Their dedicated and loyal bodyguards were cut from the same fabric and had been given extra tactical training. The enemy our task unit encountered when Clark was killed were probably such bodyguards. At the very least, they were ten percenters.

As we departed the Iraqi police compound I watched the sun slip below the desert sands on the horizon. I thought of the upcoming missions and the enemy we would encounter. I saw once again the prisoners' eyes burning holes into my soul, and I recognized there was no room for selfishness this deployment. Whatever happened would happen. I must focus on mission accomplishment and whatever task I was assigned. There was no doubt that my life—and, more important, the lives of the men I would be leading—depended on it.

The following night I was assigned to shadow the existing mobility force commander, a fellow junior officer named Chris Cramer who was a former enlisted mustang like J.P. and me. Chris was a big guy, not tall but built like a brick, probably weighing about two hundred thirty pounds. He came from the South and had a great sense of humor. We got along well, and he was eager to get me up to speed so he could shift over to the assault element.

Chris sketched out the situation around Fallujah for me. The city had been the nexus for the insurgency in Al Anbar Province since 2003. In 2004, there were two major battles for control of the city. The second one saw the US Marines, First Cavalry and First Infantry

Division, clear the entire urban area one house at a time.

All the fighting and destruction in Fallujah had not brought peace in the end. Instead, the enemy, like all good disciples of war, had adapted. They grew more cagey and sophisticated. They recognized that facing us on our terms simply got them killed. So they turned to suicide bomb attacks using people on foot or in vehicles. They planted roadside bombs by the hundreds, changing tactics frequently, which caused US forces to constantly refine and redevelop our own counter IED tactics.

By 2007, the level of sophistication these cells around Fallujah had achieved was daunting. They used infrared triggers and remote-detonated bombs with cell phones. Some had pressure plates that would detonate when we drove over them. The Iranians also began to supply the Iraqi insurgency with EFP (explosively formed penetrator) technology. These were the deadliest bombs the United States faced during the war. They destroyed their targets by sending a jet of molten, liquefied metal into the crew compartment of a vehicle.

During this deployment, one of our sister task units operating out of Baghdad was hit by an EFP ambush attack in Sadr City. It cost the lives of three teammates: SO1 Jason Lewis, CTI1 Steven Daugherty, and MC1

Robert McRill. Another brother SEAL and friend lost a leg from that attack.

Some of these roadside bombs were command detonated—meaning somebody was watching the target area and initiated the device. Others were not, relying instead on the pressure plate or IR trigger to explode as soon as something made contact. Unfortunately, all too often it was innocent local Iraqi citizens who set off these devices. Figuring out the best way to mitigate the roadside bomb threat was the mobility force commander's most important responsibility and required working closely with our explosive ordnance disposal (EOD) technicians. Staying on top of which roads had been swept, which were clear, which were considered dangerous—all of which was fluid and constantly evolving—demanded intensive study and staff work. Once the threats were known, we had to develop the best route into and out of our objective area.

The task was made immeasurably more difficult by the Iraqi road network. Global positioning systems, aerial photographs, and paper maps rarely agreed with one another. Dirt roads marked on one map sometimes did not exist anymore. New roads or tracks did not appear on older imagery. Sometimes the roads were still there but had been blocked off by either the local authorities or the insurgents themselves, making their use impossible.

Few of the roads were named, and signage was non-existent. We had to rely on navigation software, landmarks, and vigilant navigation when we rolled beyond our compound. It was a complex, ever-evolving dynamic that made just getting to where we wanted to go exceptionally difficult.

More often than not, if we drove to a target, it was deep beyond normal areas where coalition forces worked. This was both good and bad for us. It was good because if coalition forces did not typically drive on those roads, then usually there was less chance of seeing IEDs. It was bad because if there was substantially less traffic on those roads, then al-Qaida or insurgent forces could emplace them defensively to stop anyone from coming into their area.

Two missions later, J.P. told me I would run as the mobility force commander. Chris Cramer would ride in the seat behind me to offer advice and take over if there were any problems. It was our own internal turnover op.

We were assigned a kill-or-capture mission in the heart of downtown Fallujah. The Jolan District had long been a hotbed of insurgent activity. Located in the northwest corner of Fallujah along the Euphrates River, it had been the scene of some of the heaviest fighting in

2004. Three years later, coalition forces still routinely got attacked when going into the district, and a mosque in the center of Jolan Park served as a center for insurgent operations.

With Chris's advice, I planned our route into the objective through Jolan's rabbit warren of streets, blind alleys, and narrow thoroughfares. The place was an ambusher's paradise with dozens of natural choke points. Chris pointed out for me the worst spots where coalition units had been hit, and I worked up a way around them. When we finished, Chris approved the route and we uploaded it into our navigation systems.

The mobility force commander always rode in the lead vehicle's front right seat. Although an IED can strike anywhere in a convoy of vehicles, typically the lead vehicle is hit first. The fear I felt before every mission never fully went away. As with many aspects of a highly dangerous job, you learned to compartmentalize your fear, joke about it, and continue on with the mission.

I settled into my seat, put on my headset, and had all the vehicle commanders check in. They came over the radio one by one. Everyone was good to go.

Chris slapped me on the shoulder and said, "All right, bro, you got this. Let's do the deal."

We sped down Route Michigan and into the city, our Humvees blacked out so we presented a less obvious target. The world through our night-vision goggles was bathed in a pale green glow. Lights burned in scattered windows, but darkness dominated the landscape. Fallujah had a curfew at night, which meant the only vehicles out were supposed to be either friendlies or hostile. Reality wasn't so cut-and-dry, as Iraqi civilians often ignored the curfew. We encountered them speeding around town, and we would have to make split-second decisions on whether or not they posed a threat.

As we moved into Fallujah I watched our progress on Falcon View. This system is one of those remarkable innovations that makes the American military such an incredible force on the battlefield. Falcon View displayed a computerized, real-time map of our route onto a flat screen mounted in front of the Humvee's dashboard. It took some getting used to, as the system updated from the satellite a few seconds behind real time. To make sure you made the right turns on the way to your objective, you had to think several seconds ahead, comparing what was on the computer screen with what you could see in the road ahead.

I was balancing that as we made our turn off Michigan toward the Jolan District. Heaps of rubble, houses, cleared fields, and run-down buildings soon surrounded us. Despite the destruction, there were still decent-looking houses in Fallujah.

I listened over the radio to the chatter of our turret gunners as they called out movement and picked up fields of fire as we moved deeper into the urban sprawl. We had nine vehicles that night, and our gunners maintained extreme vigilance. Jolan was Fallujah's most dangerous neighborhood.

Suddenly, as we made our turn, my navigation system blinked out and went blank for a few seconds. When it reset, it showed us still going straight.

"What the hell?"

We were supposed to make another turn in a couple of blocks, but I was still distracted by that Falcon View malfunction.

Chris saw what was happening and said, "Sometimes the nav systems will just glitch out. Stay at least two ahead of your turns."

I looked back at the road and realized I had missed our turn.

I reported the situation to J.P., who as our ground force commander was riding a few rigs behind mine.

"Are we on course?" he asked.

I studied the screen. "No, we're off by a couple of blocks. Chris is helping me. We're sorting it out."

It looked to me like we could box around and get back on our original route. Chris concurred. We made our turn and the street narrowed. The ruins gave way to a series of three- and four-story buildings that made it seem like we'd just entered a canyon. Our gunners grew nervous.

Over the radio, one of the gunners calmly came across. "I don't think we want to be here."

Somebody else piped in. "Dorothy, we're not in Kansas anymore."

I knew by the nervous joking we were in a bad spot. Chris leaned over the seat and looked at the tall ominous buildings around us.

We'd been channeled right into a beautiful ambush point. Quickly, I gave our driver new directions that took us out of the dense urban cityscape—and directly in front of a structure that Americans took to calling Blackwater Bridge.

Staring at it through my night-vision goggles, I felt a chill run down my back. In the spring of 2004, insurgents walked up to an SUV carrying four Blackwater military contractors and shot them through the doors before they could defend themselves. They dragged the bodies out of the vehicle and defiled them. As locals celebrated, the jihadists strung the corpses up on the structure of the bridge. The incident triggered the first battle of Fallujah and laid the seeds for the full-scale invasion of the city later that year.

"Red, get us outta here," J.P. called over the radio.

I studied Falcon View, trying to find the best way out of this. It was like staring at one of those maze games, where you have to find the only route through to the exit. Except this was no game. The enemy lurking nearby had surely been alerted to our presence by now.

Chris said, "Hey, bro, three-point turn and let's get the hell out of here."

I passed the word to the vehicle commanders and like a choreographed dance, all nine Humvees executed the tight turnaround. The rear vehicles held their position as the lead vehicles turned around and drove past to pick up the lead again. Once reconstituted into our original formation, I navigated us into the city again, our gunners scanning the rooftops. This time, I focused on Chris's advice and made sure that the lag on the navigation system didn't cause any more issues.

We were back on our planned route and reached our objective. The neighborhood was not as tight as where we had gotten turned around by Blackwater Bridge. Most houses were two stories and were large compounds with tall walls and gates. The assault team dropped off to enter the compound while I took our Humvees and set up a cordon around the block. Once everyone was set, the assault team went after the men inside the building.

Around us, our gunners spotted movement on the rooftops. A head appeared then ducked out of sight.

"Second story, movement, northeast!" one of the gunners called.

Feeling eyes on us in the darkness put me on edge. But once again, I watched the reaction of the guys around me. They remained calm, quietly coming across the radio to identify potential threats. The enemy chose to observe and did not attack that night. Meanwhile, our assault team scooped up the bad guy we were after and completed the raid.

We sped back through the city until we reached Route Michigan. Less than a half mile from the front gate, Chris pointed out some unearthed dirt beside the road where insurgents had laid a roadside bomb. Fortunately, we'd discovered it, but the sheer audacity of that move served as a reminder that there was no safe place beyond the wire. Vigilance would be the only thing that kept us alive.

When we debriefed, I was kicking myself for what had happened. My first mission out and I had an issue. I felt the intensity of the microscope pointed my way. Would they consign me to a desk?

We walked through everything that happened, step-by-step. When it came to the missed turn, I heard a lot of grumbling. But then Chris stepped in and deflected it away from me.

"Hey, it happened. The Falcon View fritzed out for a second, which caused us to miss the turn. Red was making the best calls he could to try to get us back on course. It took a minute, but we got out of there and back on track."

I heard one of the guys say, "Well, it couldn't have happened in a worse spot."

I couldn't argue with that.

As we concluded the debrief and walked out, J.P. walked up to me. "Hey, bro, these things are going to happen," he told me. "Be prepared for them and just make sure to learn from it."

I took that to heart. This was one of those moments in combat that the Prussian military analyst Carl von Clausewitz called "the fog of war." Until you encounter it, there's really no way to know it was even a potential problem. That would never happen to me again. I'd memorize the route into our objective so if I did lose Falcon View again, I'd still know exactly where we were based on the landmarks around us.

When I checked the mission board the following night, I saw that I'd been slotted to run as the mobility force commander again.

Seems like the snag from last night is behind us.

Those first few missions working mobility demonstrated that Iraq was vastly different from Afghanistan. The people were different, the terrain was obviously different, and the tactics we used had to flex to accommodate. Running as the mobility force commander in Fallujah's urban sprawl and in the rural areas of Al Anbar presented an intense challenge that Afghanistan did little to prepare me for, so I focused on learning everything I could from each mission. I asked questions, relied on the experience of those around me, and worked harder than at any other time in my life.

It paid off. I had conducted about seven missions now as mobility. Thankfully we had avoided IEDs and had no major problems navigating to our targets. The assault teams had wrapped up over a dozen midlevel leaders in the first few weeks I was there.

Team guys never stop talking smack. Even on missions. The playful banter and jabs went back and forth through the vehicles and over the radios. It is how men in combat relieve stress. I'd been the target of many spikes and one-liners. Now I started to join in and get a few jabs in myself.

The natural progression from mobility element was to join the assault element, as Chris had. One morning, as we wrapped up the debrief for the last mission, J.P. came up to me.

"Red, tomorrow we are doing a joint mission with the marines. They will be running mobility for us, so you will be running in the assault. You'll be the acting SSE commander but I want you to shadow the assault force commander. If you do well, you'll start rotating back and forth with Chris for assault force commander and mobility force commander."

The AFC was in charge of everything that occurred on the target. It was the most difficult and complex leadership position a junior officer can be given in a SEAL platoon. The fact I was getting a chance at the job spoke volumes of the trust I had earned.

I thought of Vince Peterson's words that day in Ranger School.

You can earn back the respect of the guys if you give them something to respect.

The next mission with the marines would be a tricky one. Two Iraqi brothers living in a small town south of Fallujah had been identified as key members of a cell dedicated to laying roadside bombs. The marines wanted them off the streets, so our intel built a target package around them. With an average of about a hundred roadside bomb encounters a day in our area, knocking out these cells remained one of our highest priorities.

We left the base in unarmored seven-ton trucks driven by the marines. They were a far departure from our modified armored Special Operations Humvees, and I felt both cramped and exposed in the back as we rode to the target area. The initial plan called for us to drive into the village. At the last minute J.P. and the marine commander decided to be more stealthy. The vehicles stopped about one kilometer from the village and we dismounted. I was glad to be out of the vehicles. Although we were not safe from IEDs in our own Humvees, I felt especially vulnerable in those marine bomb magnets. My respect for the marines who patrolled in those things doubled that night.

I conducted my last-minute equipment checks and watched as my warrior brothers did the same, silently in the dark Iraqi night. Through hand signals we ensured everyone was ready to go and began our patrol to the target.

Pat, the Angry Irishman, punched me in the chest and whispered, "Let's get some."

He moved up to be one of the point men as part of our reconnoiter, or recce, element. We spread into our tactical formations about ten yards apart from one another and began to maneuver toward the town across the arid desert landscape. It was eerily quiet as we walked across the open Iraqi desert. The town, surrounded by a sea of empty desert on all sides, was the only thing that dotted the horizon as we slowly closed the distance from nine hundred yards out. We moved silently, like predators on the hunt.

Several dogs approached the recce element. Feral dogs wandered everywhere in Iraq, and while some of them might be dangerous, their biggest danger was alerting others to our presence with their barking. The ones that got too loud we put down with suppressed MP5 submachine guns.

Pfooft. Pfooft.

The Heckler & Kochs sounded like somebody spitting air through a blow-dart gun. No way anyone in town heard them. The element of surprise had been preserved.

As we moved closer to the town we paused briefly to observe the nearby compounds for any signs of movement. Nothing. We proceeded slowly to reduce our noise signature until we'd entered the heart of the village. At that point, speed became essential. We picked up our pace, knees bent, weapons at the ready. Hearts pounding, we shifted formation and began the final surge to our target houses.

As we ran, my teammates picked up and rotated overlapping fields of fire, which allowed us to cover every inch of the urban playground. We still held the element of surprise and no enemy fighters had appeared and fired on us, but our guns were up at the ready, covering all sides, fingers on the triggers, ready to engage at the first sign of an enemy attack. If we got ambushed, we would not be surprised and could respond in kind in a heartbeat.

Cover high. Cover low. Left high. Left low. Scan right building. Scan left building. Cover down the alley. Check rooftops. Check the windows. Weapon always at the ready.

We had the choreography of this combat ballet down cold. We'd trained so thoroughly together that we could read one another's movements like a unique language only our team could understand. Our senses were on their highest alert—vision, hearing, and even smell. The closer we got to our objectives, the more on the razor's edge we felt. It made every element of life more lush and vivid, more deeply felt than anything you can imagine, like a high very few things on this planet could ever match.

Hemingway once said, "There is no hunting like the hunting of man, and those who have hunted armed men long enough and liked it never care for anything else thereafter." I know balancing on that edge can become just as addictive.

The first entry team peeled off and stacked up on their objective. One of our guys mistakenly went with them, which left us down one man. There was no time to grab him as he silently faded into the darkness of an alleyway behind the other train.

My entry team kept going. Our house was the second one in line, a few dozen meters up the street. Our upper bodies swung like tank turrets as we moved and scanned for threats, ready for whatever menace might pop out as we made our final approach.

We reached the door to the second house and stacked up without missing a beat. No words, no unnecessary movements. Our security team stepped out to cover the front of the house as our breacher moved up and placed his explosive charge on the door. That done, we waited for the third team to reach their objective so we could hit all three targets simultaneously.

The seconds ticked by. The final entry team reached the farthest house. All in place. Ready. I listened as the three AFCs checked in and said they were in position. I then heard J.P.'s calm voice come across the command net.

"Three . . . Two . . . One . . . Execute . . . Execute . . . Execute."

On the third execute, all three explosions blew almost in unison. Before the debris stopped flying, we poured into the house.

*Main room clear. Stairs ahead to a landing that prob-
ably opens onto the roof. Kitchen next to the stairs.*

All clear so far. The rolling ball of fire swept through
the rest of the house.

*An alcove opened up from a small hallway in back
to our right. Bedroom doors on other side of the hall.
Coming out. Keep moving. Fall back into the train.
Weapon up, finger just outside the trigger guard,
ready at a second's notice to shoot in case some-
thing should happen. Give the squeeze. Make entry.
Identify threats. Clear right. Clear left. All clear.
Next room.*

As we rolled through the target I identified hiding
places and items I knew we would want to take with us
for evidence but pushed the thoughts to the back of my
mind.

We'll do the thorough search later.

We swung into the bedrooms and came face-to-face
with several Iraqi men. Before they could react, we had
them facedown on the floor and zip-cuffed. We'd identify who was who once the target was secure.

"People sleeping in the courtyard," I heard somebody call across the radio.

Al Joliet and I rushed to the back door near the
kitchen. The three houses we hit all abutted this com-
munal open space. About ten meters away, I saw a bed
with two figures in it: a man and a woman. The Iraqis

often slept outside at night because it was cooler than their stifling concrete-walled rooms.

Leaning next to the bed was an AK. The man in bed sat up but had yet to reach for it. Do we shoot? The problem was the other target building with one of the other teams was directly behind him in the line of fire. We rushed instead, fear and intimidation our weapons. He saw us and knew he'd die. His hands went up. We kicked the AK clear, then cuffed him and his wife. A quick look at his face and I recognized him right away. He was one of the two brothers the marines wanted so badly.

With the inhabitants secured, we began a thorough search of the three houses. In the alcove of ours, we found empty rocket-propelled grenade warheads and a bunch of automobile alternators. The brothers had been cracking open the RPG warheads to extract their explosives in order to make larger and more powerful roadside bombs. The alternators served as the source for the wires they ran from the bombs to the detonators.

Elsewhere in the compound, the search uncovered initiators, more copper wire, weapons, and other bomb-making equipment. We had these guys cold. We also discovered that one of the brothers had been a Ba'athist officer in the Republican Guard before the war.

We finished up our search and consolidated all the evidence. I then marshaled the detainees and assigned a handler to each one for the ride back to Camp Fallujah and the detention facility there, hoping that we would not see them on the streets again. Unfortunately, all too often the Iraqi courts that processed them simply turned them loose. Now we knew what the cops back home had to deal with every day in their own cities.

After the debrief, several guys, including J.P., came up and said, "Good job out there." I knew I might never win over all the guys. I just needed to stay humble and focused. Keep doing what I was doing, and not sweat what I could not control.

Later that morning, I finished my after-action report and headed to bed as the Middle Eastern sun broke the horizon and the morning furnace kicked on. I crawled into bed on a high I hadn't felt in a long time.

Chapter 20

After that first successful mission on the assault team, I had earned a spot in the mix and harmonized with the task unit's battle rhythm. Our platoons rotated back and forth between running the mobility force or running the assault force. Eric Darby was J.P.'s counterpart in our sister platoon. Eric was an academy grad. He was about five foot ten and a hundred seventy pounds. He had black hair and sported a large red dog tattoo on his back, which earned him the nickname "Red Dog." Eric could be somewhat standoffish until you got to know him. Once he opened up he had a pretty good sense of humor. When Eric's platoon functioned as the mobility element, we went in as the assault force. Every week, we'd switch off, and we'd have the mobility duties again while Eric's guys kicked in doors. I'd switch off from mobility commander to having an entry team depending on the week and what our platoon was doing. I began to relax and stop worrying about my reputation, getting comfortable once again in operating and making the right calls.

There was no shortage of work. More often than not, our missions were a success. Sometimes, we ran into dry holes, meaning the intel was not totally accurate or the bad guy we were after was not there, but most of the time we were able to find the men we were after.

Over the next few weeks we conducted dozens of missions and we brought down several important cell leaders, including one very influential al-Qaida financier. Our intel guys had told us to expect suicide vests and a fight to the death with his security detail. We prepped for this mission twice, planning to air assault into the objective area aboard helicopters. Each time, the mission got scrubbed for one reason or another. It was tough to ramp up mentally for the danger we expected. So every time it was canceled it took a while to come down. Thankfully, the third time proved to be the charm. We got the go order and climbed into the birds, adrenaline pumping. We fully expected a major fight on our hands, and when we got boots on the ground after a short flight, I was as amped as I'd ever been.

Fortunately there were no suicide vests, and they surrendered as soon as our assault element stormed inside. We identified the financier and hauled him off to face justice. Such successes seemed almost anticlimactic. We struck so suddenly and with so much force that nobody had the time or the fortitude to fight back. It was a great way to dismantle our enemies' networks without firing a shot.

The pace was intense, and the missions started to blend together in a Groundhog Day sort of way. Some stuck out, like our DUSTWUN rescue attempts. DUSTWUN stands for duty status whereabouts unknown, the modern military's acronym for MIA. A few weeks before our task unit had deployed, the insurgents had captured a marine and a US Army soldier.

No effort was spared to try to find and save these two Americans. So when we received intel that they were being held in an abandoned building deep in the rural areas of Al Anbar, our command did not waste any time sending us in after them. For me, there was no more important mission than this one. As we prepped and headed for the helos, I felt a surge of pride and honor to be out there with the rest of the team, entrusted with this sacred task. Getting those men back to their families gave our job special meaning.

As we boarded the Black Hawks, Charlie Wingate's words came back to me.

Red, I have to tell you, I've always kind of wondered about you. I guess the biggest question I've had about you is why you joined the teams.

I may have lost my way years ago, but through God, and a willingness to work hard and learn my strengths and weaknesses, I had earned my way back into the brotherhood. There was no doubt in my mind this was the reason. I may not have known it at age eighteen. But I did now. There was no higher calling in the military than to be called upon to rescue fellow American military members or citizens. It is what makes our country the superpower it is. If you are an American citizen and anything ever happens to you, rest assured, this country will do everything in its power and send some of the best trained forces in the world to try to bring you home safely and administer justice to those who do us harm. This is what it means to be a part of an elite unit: to bear that responsibility and to lead men who have this unique yet deadly capability. I understood that now, and that was all that mattered.

After a short flight we hit the target hard and fast. It was a compound of multiple buildings with a large quarry nearby with water at the bottom. The main building was nothing but piles of brick and twisted metal. We quickly cleared that, searching for any signs of our missing Americans. Upon completion of the main building, the assault teams broke up to search different sectors of the compound. I took my team to a cluster of buildings that we quickly blew through. Nothing. It looked like nobody had been here in a while. One last building remained in our sector. My team and I found it virtually empty. A few piles of debris lay here and there, and a wooden pallet lay on the ground. One of the guys wondered out loud about spider holes or some sort of underground cellar. I started thinking the same thing. What if there was a trapdoor in the floor concealed under one of these piles of random crap?

Our EOD guy was down in the quarry doing a thorough search of the bottom. Pat Donahue and I searched all around the pallet with our SureFire flashlights, looking for any signs of a booby trap. When we didn't see anything suspicious, I told my team to go get behind the external concrete wall of the building. I was almost positive there was nothing there, but I wasn't about to risk my teammates' lives. After they left, I made one final careful search. I thought about calling our EOD guy. So far, there didn't seem to be cause to pull him out of the quarry. But my mind was still going a hundred miles an hour. Sometimes, the enemy directly targeted Special Operations teams by feeding false information to our intel networks. When a task unit would show up, the building they entered would turn out to be wired to blow. Was this a trap?

Finally, the pallet was the only thing left in the outbuilding to check. I circled it carefully and still didn't see any warning signs.

Stop being a Mary and lift the pallet.

"Okay, I'm going to flip it," I called to my teammates.

I got on my knees, grabbed the pallet, and lifted it up.

Something metallic caught my eye underneath.

Fuck me, a 155 shell!

In that instant, I thought I was a dead man. My life didn't flash in front of me—I had no time to think of family. I didn't even have time to think.

But nothing happened. It turned out to be an empty shell casing and posed no threat. I started breathing again and tried to get my heart to start beating again.

I may need a new pair of pants after this mission.

Right then, a black scorpion scampered out from inside the shell. The thing was huge, eight inches of poisonous, stinging, pissed-off wildlife. That definitely jump-started my heart. I leaped up and stomped on it.

I called all clear and rejoined the squad. As we walked to link up with the rest of the team I told Pat how I'd almost passed out when I saw the 155 shell and then the scorpion.

He of course laughed and made fun of me.

"Big sissy."

Unfortunately, the mission was a dry hole. The platoon found no sign of our missing American brothers that night. Dispirited, we flew back to Camp Fallujah, hoping we'd have better luck next time.

The al-Qaida cell in Karmah continued to cause a lot of trouble around the province. That network needed to be stopped if the Anbar Awakening was going to succeed.

We'd learned that a rural village on the outskirts of Karmah served as a hideout for some of the cell's members. The plan ambitiously called for us to take the entire village down and search every one of the thirty structures there. We wanted to neutralize that element of the cell, then return to Karmah and go after the main network.

To pull this off, we needed every member of our task unit as well as every SEAL who was part of the

Combined Joint Special Operations Task Force. Also, we brought a squad of Iraqi police and a platoon of Iraqi Army Special Forces troops—some seventy men total—along with gunship support and a company of helicopters for transport on the mission.

We divided the village up like a pie. Each part of the pie was a different phase of the mission. Each pie slice was broken into sectors of buildings and each assault team was given a sector to clear and search. Once each sector of the slice was secure, all the assault teams would move together to the next slice and tackle their individual sections. It was highly complex and required a lot of coordination between assault teams and J.P., our GFC, to ensure there would be no blue-on-blue or friendly-fire incidents.

That night, we climbed into the helos and raced low across the desert to the village. I was leading one of the assault elements and had thoroughly studied the entire village. I knew every building compound, courtyard, and bush backward and forward, thanks to the overhead imagery we'd been given. Pat was my point man for the op. As always, I was glad to have him. The Angry Irishman seemed to have his own internal GPS.

The birds touched down, and we streamed out. We hadn't gone far when gunfire broke out. An insurgent standing guard spotted us coming from his house. He grabbed an AK-47 and bolted into a nearby tree line, where he opened up on us. He died a few seconds later from a gunshot to the forehead, a round delivered by one of our snipers.

Element of surprise lost, it was game on now. We hit the village moving counterclockwise through our pie slices. Each element had access to air support if we needed it, and I thought we sure might. People moved around everywhere, and sporadic shots rang out.

Pat quickly led us to our section of buildings and we stacked on the door. There was a window between me and the door so I broke it and threw a flash-bang grenade into the room. A second after it detonated, we poured into the house. I swung into the hall and rounded a corner—right into a two-year-old child. He stood in a doorway, stunned and terrified, crying for his mother. I looked down at him and thought of my own kids.

How terrified would they be if something like this happened in the dead of night?

I buried the thought and slipped past the boy to encounter his mother in the next room, screaming in fear, her face streaked with tears.

Her husband had been building bombs in their house. We captured him and put him in zip cuffs after discovering his cache and equipment. We secured several other detainees, separated the civilians we would leave behind, and kept going. As we went from house to house, we found more bad guys, and lots of hiding spots for weapons and ammo. We discovered fake walls and hidden trapdoors filled with rifles, Russian-made assault vests, battle gear, explosives, and other bomb-making components. In one house, we encountered a complete IED waiting to be planted.

The men we captured were sullen, angry, and confrontational—the twenty percenter type. They knew exactly how far they could push us before we resorted to lethal force, and they'd go right up to that line before backing off.

In another assault team, one of our teammates, Frank Collins, encountered this firsthand. As he tried to zip-cuff a particularly defiant Iraqi, the man tried to punch him in the face. He slammed his fist into Frank's night-vision goggles, which dug into both of his cheeks and left deep, bloody gashes. Frank could have justifiably shot the man at that point, but he chose to drop the Iraqi on his face and finish zip-cuffing him. I have no doubt that Iraqi regretted throwing that punch. We finished toward dawn. The search had netted useful intelligence, and we'd captured several known bad guys and a bunch of other fighters. It was as complicated an operation as any of us had ever been a part of. It felt amazing to have played a role in something so complex and successful.

After the debrief, I headed to breakfast with the guys on another postmission high. Six weeks into the deployment and everything was clicking. Perhaps this was why I let my guard down and relaxed a little too much. I stopped keeping a close eye on my strengths and weaknesses. Let me tell you, I paid for that mistake.

Chapter 21

Al Anbar Province, Iraq
June 2007

We had been tasked with a capture/kill mission in downtown Fallujah and it was my turn in the saddle as mobility force commander. It was after midnight. Remember when your mother said nothing good ever happens after midnight?

She was right.

As we rolled into Fallujah a vehicle appeared in the distance ahead of us. With the curfew in place we doubted it was a civilian rig, but we couldn't be sure. Worst-case scenario, we were facing a suicide bomber in a vehicle. The marines had occasionally run into such attacks around Fallujah, and they were almost always devastating. The Fallujah car bomb factories were constantly looking for opportunities to attack coalition forces. With Special Operations Forces' high rate of success, we were priority number one with the insurgency.

We stopped and watched the vehicle. About five hundred meters away, it halted too, and several other vehicles stacked up behind it. We knew from the premission briefing that the marines were out patrolling in Fallujah that night, so I was pretty confident that we were looking at a marine convoy traveling with its lights on. In moments where two friendly forces came in visual contact, it was standard operating procedure to utilize a challenge and reply system to ensure they were indeed friendly. The enemy would watch our convoys, learn our challenge and reply code, and sometimes try to duplicate it in order to get close enough to trigger a suicide bomb. As a result, the procedure we used changed at irregular intervals.

Part of my duties as mobility force commander included checking our team's incoming message traffic to ensure we were using the most up-to-date procedures. On our last mission, the night before, I'd checked and found they had not been changed, but I hadn't looked since.

We walked through the authentication procedure and received no reply from the vehicles ahead. We tried again. Nothing. We waited, and by now I'm sure our gunners were caressing their triggers as they spoiled for a fight.

On every mission, we carried a high-powered, Class Four visible laser that we dubbed the "Green Beam." Unlike most of our lasers that could only be seen by other humans wearing night-vision goggles, the Green Beam could be seen with the naked eye.

We lased the vehicles ahead with the Green Beam. This was standard and represented the next step in an escalation of force. Eric was the GFC for this operation and I let him know what was happening. Holding the Green Beam, I kept it pinned on the set of headlights ahead of us. We sat and waited, engines idling. Still no response.

This was odd. I sat there, puzzling over what to do next. Should I move to the next level of escalation? Right then, the lead vehicle signaled us with regular white light. This was correct procedure, but it should have happened with our earlier authentication sequence.

Okay. They were friendlies. The vehicles came toward us, and we recognized them as marine Humvees when they got closer. A minute later, they turned off Route Michigan, bound for the marine FOB not far from us.

Situation resolved, we both went on our way, and I didn't think anything of it. We hit our target inside the city and returned.

J.P. was waiting for me after we secured our rigs. "Hey, Red, Paul wants to see you." Lieutenant Commander Paul Erickson was our task unit commander.

Hmmm. What for? I wondered.

I racked my brain. Had I done something wrong? I couldn't think of anything.

Together, J.P. and I went to see Commander Erickson. When we stepped into his office, I knew right away he was not happy. In fact, he looked thoroughly pissed off. Sitting in the office next to him was Eric Darby. I had no idea what was going on, but I could tell I was about to get chewed out for something.

"What the hell happened tonight?" he demanded.

"Sir?" I asked.

The commander told me that a marine colonel in charge of the battle space we were in that night had been out on patrol and had called him in a white-hot rage. Apparently, the challenge and reply procedures had just changed earlier that day.

We had not used the correct ones, which irritated the colonel. Then when I escalated with the Green Beam on his unit, the colonel erupted in anger. In his mind this was the equivalent of opening fire on his men.

As Commander Erickson breathed fire at me, a cold bead of sweat rolled down my back. I knew exactly what had happened. Either the message traffic hadn't been updated or we hadn't been pushed the changes before we rolled out. Either way, I had not seen them. The bottom line: I had screwed up. No wonder the colonel was pissed off.

Commander Erickson continued to read me the riot act. J.P. and Eric were not happy either.

I thought of all the progress I had made this deployment and the trust I had earned back with the guys.

Did I just throw that all away?

I should have defused the situation by acknowledging my error, apologizing, and taking my lumps. Learn from it, and move on—just like all the other lessons I'd embraced since Afghanistan. Instead, I reacted to the harsh criticism with the same defensiveness that had been my Achilles' heel for years.

"Sir, I checked the traffic last night and saw no changes," I retorted. "We had no idea the procedures changed!"

I could see my reaction displeased them. I continued anyway, "We could not tell they were a friendly convoy. And in the darkness they looked like Iraqis violating curfew."

Paul barked back, "That's irrelevant, Red. You were briefed marines were operating in Fallujah tonight, and you should have had our operations officer double-check the procedures during the mission deconfliction before you guys went out. The point is you lit them up with a Class Four laser. Somebody could have been hurt."

Class Four lasers like the Green Beam can damage eyesight.

I looked over at J.P. and Eric. Both were watching me intently, looking even more pissed off. For a moment, I had flashbacks to Afghanistan. The same thing was happening. All the progress I'd made was coming unraveled over something like this?

A stab of fear went through me. My career had been hanging in the balance. A mistake could kill it off, no matter how well I'd been performing up to this moment. I'd been thorough and deliberate with my decisions. I'd turned that around. At least I thought I had. Was this a five percent moment? No. This was bad communication. If the recognition procedures had changed, why wasn't that information pushed down to us? I spoke up and said so. I got even more defensive. The scene grew confrontational.

Eric Darby suddenly injected, "Look, Jay, you made a bad call."

I rounded on him, ready to defend myself. Before I could, he leveled the boom. "Frankly, I don't know if I want to go out with you again."

There it was. The nightmare of Afghanistan all over again. His words sent me reeling. A moment later, the task unit commander dismissed me. By then, I'd grown quiet. What could I say after Eric's comment?

I walked back to my hooch and reflected on what had just happened. For a second I stood on a mental precipice, looking down at that void that I'd fallen into after my last mission in Afghanistan.

No. I refuse to go there. Not this time.

What's the takeaway? How can I fix this?

Don't let the reaction to the mistake destroy your relationship with your teammates.

I let one of my own weaknesses beat me again.

Humble yourself.

Later that day, I went to go eat at the chow hall. I grabbed my meal and saw Al, Eric, Chief Johnson, and J.P. eating together at a table.

"You guys mind if I join you?" I asked.

J.P. nodded. I sat down. The guys seemed friendly. Eric, on the other hand, did not look too happy to see me. I took a deep breath.

Here it goes.

"Look, I know I'm under the gun here. Everyone's watching me ready for me to fail. My career is at stake, and I'll admit, we've had some great successes and I let my guard down. I made a mistake and I should have owned it. Instead I got paranoid and fought back. I apologize for the way I reacted. I messed up."

Al spoke up first. "Hey, man, just keep doing what you're doing."

J.P. echoed that. "Look, Red, you're doing a great job but you suck at taking criticism. Someone offers you advice after you make a mistake and you take it personally. We're trying to help you grow, make you a better leader. You got this. We all mess up. Just happens. Learn to absorb the lessons, take the heat, and move on."

"I got it," I said.

Eric nodded at their comments, but I could tell he wasn't sold on my apology yet.

When I returned to our compound, I went straight to Commander Erickson's office.

"Paul, do you have a minute?"

He called me in.

I repeated everything I had stated to the guys about stressing out and worrying about messing up and being under the gun. It was no excuse and I'd keep my mouth shut next time.

"Red, you're kicking ass. Keep doing what you're doing and stop worrying about the past. You just have to learn to take criticism better. Great leaders know when they make mistakes, own them, then learn from them."

"You're right. It is one of my biggest weaknesses. I know it but I let my guard down amid our successes. I'll stay on top of it."

"All right, Red, keep doing what you're doing. Now get the hell out of here."

I walked out of Paul's office and breathed a sigh of relief.

Disaster averted.

Stay humble and don't lose sight again.

I thought once again of Sun Tzu's words, *If you know your enemy and you know yourself, you will never be beaten.*

Sun Tzu forgot to mention, to know yourself means to pay attention to what you're doing at ALL times.

Duly noted, Mr. Tzu.

"Hey, Red!!" one of the guys called to me as he walked into the platoon space.

"Why don't you go lase some marines and then come lose some of your combat pay at the poker table?"

I couldn't help but laugh as I watched him grinning like a banshee waiting for my reaction.

I could see the guys took the mishap in stride better than I did.

No mission tonight, so the platoon poker game was on. As usual, I was an easy mark. I lost another twenty bucks before we all turned in. Call it another weakness.

Chapter 22

Al Anbar Province, Iraq
Northeast Fallujah
Rural area of Karmah
June 2007

Over the next few weeks we conducted multiple missions and aside from the guys making fun of me every time we did a friendly vehicle deconfliction, it seemed the Green Beam incident was behind us. I noticed Eric still seemed somewhat standoffish, but I figured if I stayed focused, eventually he would come around. If not, at least I knew I was doing the right thing.

In late June, we were tasked with going back into Karmah. As we sat through the brief, it became clear we were about to step back into the lion's den. Our intel analysts explained in depth that one of the key enemy leaders we'd been tracking all spring frequented the compound we'd be hitting that night. He traveled with a well-armed, well-organized security detail that could have a few men wearing suicide vests.

Karmah was the thorn in our side that we could not seem to pull out. The place had become an insurgent refuge in 2004 after the second battle of Fallujah. From this little desert town of about fifteen hundred, bombs were built, and weapons and ammunition were smuggled to cells all over Al Anbar Province. Some of the ammo they delivered was stamped with the Nazi swastika, evidence that after the Iraqis lost the fight in 1942—despite German assistance—the people in Al Anbar Province squirreled away guns and bullets for another rainy day. The network laid roadside bombs, sniped at marines, and launched suicide attacks in Fallujah. They had blown up local governmental officials, hit the gates of nearby bases with cars full of explosives, and frequently tortured people they discovered working for the coalition. Any citizen of Karmah who tried to stand against al-Qaida died. The fate of the town's police chief, who had been blown up by three hundred pounds of explosives wired to his car, had served as the warning to everyone else. Al-Qaida owned Karmah.

Tonight, we wanted to drive a stake through the heart of the Karmah cell.

An hour after midnight found us patrolling through the hundred-degree desert heat toward a small village on the outskirts of Karmah. Desert surrounded us in this rural area in the middle of Al Anbar Province. Farmers' fields dotted the landscape and we had to navigate around them as they were crisscrossed with irrigation ditches to water their crops. As we patrolled we would occasionally pass by palm tree groves or an occasional squat level concrete compound, which we would give a wide berth to avoid waking dogs or human occupants.

Iraq this time of year is a twenty-four-hour blast furnace. We moved slowly, the Angry Irishman out front with the recce element as usual. Five hundred meters from our objective, the hairs on the back of my neck suddenly stood straight up. Something was about to happen.

My radio crackled. Our AC-130 gunship spotted movement all over our objective area. I moved up to Pat to relay the information to him. He was loping along like a ghost—even right beside him I couldn't hear him. His boots seemed to skim across the powdery desert floor. I placed my hand on his shoulder, and he almost jumped out of his skin. A quick flick of his eyes revealed his annoyance. "Red, damn it, will you quit doing that!"

He was right. I gave him an update and told him to monitor the air frequencies due to all the movement on target. "Already there," he replied. I should have known. Pat knew what he was doing better than most. I backed off to my proper spot with the rest of my element. *Let him do his job.* I had to relax and trust him to do it.

Lucky for us, it was an unusually black night. That made us almost invisible to any sentries standing watch on the objective. Pat along with the other members of the recce element led our fifty-man task unit through the darkness toward our predetermined split point. Once there, the team broke into three assault elements. I was the assault force commander for the second one.

We separated from the other two elements and pushed another hundred meters down a road toward the building my guys would take down. Meanwhile, reports came in from our aircraft overhead that the target area had grown still. Whoever had been moving around had gone inside.

We reached our set point and waited for the rest of the platoon to get into position as well. Through our night-vision goggles, we could see the house we'd been assigned to secure. It was an ominous, one-story concrete structure with Middle Eastern windows and a small tiled porch leading to the doorway. There was also an alcove and another porch that wrapped around back. Hundred feet by a hundred feet—a big house to be sure. It looked like a giant Amazon.com box turned upside down.

Beside the house, somebody had parked a black four-door sedan. Black was unusual in Iraq; the dominant car color was white. I took note of the sedan, thinking it could mean our target was indeed inside.

Off to our left about fifty meters ahead was another smaller house. To the right was a large open field, and a dirt road ran directly in between the homes and fields. There were several compounds around us, but they were separated by hundreds of yards for the most part, with palm trees littering the area between the compounds. We'd have to slip around the small house on our way to the objective, and if anyone was inside, things could get dicey.

We shifted into our assault formation for the final bound. Pat stepped off first, and the rest of us followed. As we passed the small house, Pat spotted something and suddenly held up his fist. The element froze.

Two men were sleeping on cots placed outside against the small house. They were partially hidden in the shadows, which was why we hadn't seen them earlier.

We'd have to deal with them silently.

I passed the word to our interpreter to have two of our Iraqi Police partners drop off and wrap up the two sleeping beauties and hold them until we were target secure. The Iraqis conferred, then two of them split off to get the job done. I had seventeen men with me that night, including the Iraqis assigned to us. I made a mental note to align my head-count total to fifteen, then I gave Pat the signal to move up to our final set point.

We reached a small pump shack about thirty meters from the main house and paused. This would serve as our set point to the front door. I checked in with J.P. and let him know we were set.

As I waited for his call, I saw one of my men, Shawn Daniels, pointing to the left of the black sedan. Shawn was one of our junior team leaders with a huge personality. He had a family member who was also a SEAL so he grew up around the SEAL Teams. He was about six feet tall and about two hundred pounds, with blond hair and blue eyes. He looked like the SEAL most people imagine. Cocky and arrogant when I first met him prior to our platoon, he was also loud and funny, always cracking jokes and making fun of everyone who crossed his path. When he showed up in our platoon, it was his second platoon and he was maybe twenty-one. By the time we reached the end of our deployment, the immaturity and arrogance was gone, replaced by a quiet confidence and desire to lead. Not to say he didn't make wisecracks and make fun of people, he was just subtler about it, especially and, most important, around those he did not know.

Tonight he was running as our team leader and a second later, his voice came over the radio. "We have about a dozen people sleeping outside on the ground to the left of the car. The entry team will make for the door, and I need the next four to wrap up our sleepers." Shawn had it covered. We would hit the house and the civilians outside simultaneously.

The first assault team checked in. They were ready to go. I keyed my handset and whispered, "Assault team two, set."

"Assault team three, set."

I switched freqs and told my guys to stand by. We'd be going in any second.

J.P. came back up on the command net. "Stand by . . . Execute . . . Execute . . . Execute."

I watched as the train rose from their crouched positions and began their final silent run to the target. Knees flexed, weapons at the ready, covering every threat at once. We descended on the target building like a machine.

Part of the element peeled off to hold external security. Four more swung left to wrap up the sleepers—mainly women and children from the looks of it. The rest of us followed Pat and Shawn to the front door.

No need to blow it. The door was open, as if they were expecting company.

We poured inside silently. I swung right, moving through the entryway and into another room. All clear.

I stepped into the main hallway a moment later and joined the back of the assault train. Together, we flowed into another large room. This one had windows on the left, doors on the right, and a stairwell going up to the roof set into the far wall. We split off and I stacked on the first set of doors. Meanwhile, Pat and Shawn went up the stairs.

Chief Johnson fell in behind me and gave me the squeeze to signal he was ready. Garth was the oldest guy in the platoon. He had been in the navy for over twenty years. He was on the helo with me when I flew back in disgrace from the valley in Southern Afghanistan. I felt a moment of irony as we flowed into the house. Chief was six feet tall and about two hundred pounds. He had gray hair and a pleasant, weathered face. He had done a lot in his career. He was an avid hunter, and when he took time off, he frequently traveled for big-game hunts and dreamed of one day going to Africa to hunt. I got along with him well, but many of the guys didn't, as he had a tendency to obsess over small administrative details that many guys felt were not as important as combat and readiness to fight the enemy. While there was a time and place for it, many of our guys felt that he spent too much time focused on the wrong things.

We entered the room. It was empty, but there were multiple closet doors on the far wall. I took the first closet door and flung it open. Empty. Chief and I moved to the next one. Empty. One more to go.

Crack! Crack! Crack!

I froze. That was the sound of one of our M4s. Seconds later, a grenade exploded outside. Pat and Shawn started yelling. Another grenade went off. Then a PKM machine gun went cyclic.

I looked at Chief. The machine gun was above us on the roof.

More shots, shouts, and screams welled around us. I keyed my handset and called J.P. "Troops in contact! Troops in contact!" I called across the command net.

The Grizz and I cleared our last closet then moved toward Pat, who was holding security now at the base of the stairs. Shawn was with him, and when he saw me, he shouted, "Multiple men on the rooftop!"

Pat added, "Caught them off guard."

Shawn said, "One shot at us with a pistol and hit me in the chest. Pat smoked him. I'm okay."

I looked him over. No blood. Thank God. Not many people survive a point-blank gunshot to the chest from a Russian pistol.

Pat finished by telling me what we'd already heard. "They have a machine gun up there, so we fell back."

Cade Williams came up on the radio. Cade was an extremely quiet guy. I could probably write everything he ever said in our platoon on one page. He was a big guy, about six foot two and two hundred thirty pounds. He loved guns and loved being a sniper. Cade was also supersmart when it came to computers. We all joked he was hacking Chinese mainframes in his spare time. Tonight he was my assault team's primary communicator. He'd been part of the element that had gone to secure the sleepers.

"Red, guys on the roof threw grenades down on us. I'm hit, and the terp is hurt bad. We've pulled him onto the porch."

In the background, I could hear the interpreter moaning. Before I could acknowledge, a sudden rash of gunfire broke out again. Bullets struck the outside wall of the house and stitched back and forth. They couldn't have come from the machine gun on the roof. Somebody was shooting at us from another position.

Our EOD specialist, Lieutenant Ernie Rodriguez, called over the radio, "Contact rear! Multiple shooters engaging us from a small building!"

Ernie was part of our external security team. He and his men traded shots with this new threat. The firefight swelled into a cacophony of overlapping sounds. Men all around me tried to give status reports as more explosions shook the building. The PKM on the roof went cyclic again. It was total chaos.

My mind raced, trying to keep up with all the things happening around us. But right then, all the years of training took over. A long breath, and things slowed down in my head.

I keyed the handset and called, "Cade, give me a SITREP."

"Red, I'm okay. Hit in the leg and ear. I'm bleeding a lot but nothing serious. But we're taking heavy fire from that building behind us. Do you want me to call in a fire mission?"

"Stand by," I told him.

Just then several of our Iraqi Police came in with a gaggle of screaming women and kids in tow. Somehow, even as the fighting escalated, they managed to get the women and children out of the line of fire and into the house. Miraculously, none of them had suffered any wounds. It was an odd moment, protecting the families of the men who were trying to kill us.

Wes Morrow, who had been with me in Afghanistan, came in with them. He was an experienced SEAL sniper who'd long ago earned tremendous respect among his peers.

"What can I do?" he asked.

"Do something with these women and children."

J.P. had been blowing up my radio the last thirty seconds. I took a step back to collect my thoughts.

"J.P., it's a mess over here. Cade is hit but is okay. Our terp is badly wounded. I'm waiting for a status report on him. It's raining grenades. We are taking fire from a house behind us, and we have a machine gunner on the roof."

Wes and the Iraqi cops began moving the women and children into the main room. For a second, I thought of Erica and the kids and wondered how anyone could put their families in the line of fire like the husbands and fathers on the roof had. But they were willing to kill their own sons, wives, and daughters to net an American casualty.

We were facing ten percenters.

J.P. snapped me out of that thought. "Red, we are going to call in a fire mission on the house behind you using the helos. Do you have a full head count?"

"J.P., stand by."

I counted all the men around me, then moved to the front door. Outside by the pump house, I could see Dale Erlich shooting at the machine gunner above us on the roof. Off to the right, one of our newer guys, Sam Maddox, was using his machine gun to try to suppress the enemy in the house behind us. I added them to my mental tally. Several more of my men were also outside nearby, firing away at either the house behind us or at the rooftop. I slipped outside and stayed close to the wall as I moved on to continue my head count.

On the backside of the house, there was an overhang that afforded protection from the insurgents on the roof. Huddled beneath it, I found several of our Iraqi cops. Without night vision, they couldn't see who was shooting at us, so they had taken cover. I added them to my mental tally.

We had two more police back at the small house we encountered on our way into the objective. I added up the numbers, paused, then did it again.

I was one Iraqi cop short.

The machine gun above us rattled off a long burst again as I edged along the wall in search of the rest of my guys. Several explosions—all sounding like they had come from above—quickly followed. I rounded the porch just as bullets smacked against the wall nearby. More incoming from the house behind us.

Using a corner for cover, I leaned out to take a look at the situation. My other three SEALs, including my medic, Brad Larkin, were out there, standing totally exposed in the open, raking the house behind us with their weapons. Shoulder to shoulder, guns blazing, they reminded me of the shootout at the OK Corral.

"What are you doing?" I shouted over the din. "Get behind that wall and get some cover!"

They looked back, startled by my sudden arrival. They'd been sucked into the moment and were so focused they hadn't considered their own safety. The lightbulb went on, and they moved to cover.

"We need grenades!" one called to me. "Do you have any?"

I handed him one of mine. He pulled the pin, stepped out, and lobbed it onto the roof. The blast sent a fierce shiver through the building. The machine gun kept firing. They must have some sort of protected nest up there.

I turned to Brad Larkin and said, "Go get our terp and set up a casualty collection point in the front room. When you have his status, let me know."

"Got it!" Brad headed to the front room.

J.P. came up on the radio. "Red, what's your status?"

"J.P., still getting a head count. I'm down an Iraqi. Stand by."

I called Lieutenant Rodriguez. "Rod, where are you?"

He came back amid gunfire. "Red, I'm holding the front corner closest to the door."

"Roger that. Do you have an Iraqi with you?"

"Negative, man. I'm the only one on this side."

Just then, Brad Larkin, our medic, came up on the radio.

"Red, the terp is stable. He took some big frag to his shoulder and neck. We've stopped the bleeding, but he is definitely going into shock. He's moaning in Arabic. The cops are telling me he's calling for his mother."

"Brad, can you move him?"

"I think so. Chief is with me. Just give me a heads-up before we move."

"Roger, you have time."

Where was our missing Iraqi cop?

Before any air attack can be executed, all friendly troops have to be accounted for, lest the aircraft accidentally hit one of our guys. I'd learned that lesson the hard way in Afghanistan. The clock was ticking. The longer it took to get the helos on target, the more risk we ran of further casualties.

I ran back inside. No sign of the missing cop. Nobody knew where he'd gone.

We tried to contact the two Iraqis guarding the detainees at the small house, but we could not raise them on the radio.

The more I thought about it, the more I suspected our missing man had simply hung back with the two assigned to the small house. We had to confirm that.

Everyone in my element was fully engaged. We needed that fire mission. I knew what I had to do, but I sure didn't like it.

I yelled to Dale Erlich, "Cover me!"

He poured fire at the enemy as I bolted from the cover of the house and sprinted across the open ground. I hit the dirt road we came in on and ran flat out toward the small house, the firefight raging behind me.

I prayed my men could keep those machine gunners down. I ran on through the open space kill zone, feeling like my gear weighed ten thousand pounds. It was the longest moment of my life. But I got to the building. Sure enough, our missing Iraqi policeman was there.

I raced back for the house as the machine gun and grenade battle continued.

"J.P., I've got a full head count. Cleared hot."

"Roger that. Stand by. Helos inbound."

I yelled out to the guys, "Helos inbound!"

Thirty seconds later I watched as two Navy MH-60s armed with miniguns spewed 7.62 rounds into the building behind our house.

BRRRRRRAAAAAAPPPPPPP!

The minigun is a devastating six-barreled cyclic machine gun that can fire almost six thousand rounds per minute. I watched as the 60s made multiple passes. I couldn't imagine being on the business end as I watched it turn the small building behind the house into a pile of dust and debris.

No more fire came from the building.

Okay. Shooters to the rear eliminated. What next?

We had to get our wounded to safety. To do that safely, we'd need to kill the insurgents on the rooftop.

I paused to report the situation to J.P. and told him we were going to try to clear the roof.

"Roger that. Let me know when you guys are secure."

I could still hear the gunner on the roof shooting sporadically.

Pat was still holding security at the base of the stairs that led to the roof. Our only option was to charge up those stairs and attempt to engage the gunner before he engaged us. I said as much to the guys.

"Screw that, I'm not walking into that machine gun," I heard Pat say.

He was right. There was no way we could get up on the roof without an extraordinary amount of risk to our own people.

I stepped back from the stairs as my comrades continued to cover the stairwell. I thought about the situation.

We couldn't assault up the stairs. Pitching grenades onto the roof hadn't worked. We'd been pouring fire onto them since the fight began, and that hadn't suppressed them either. They'd turned that roof into a minifortress, and we had no way to kill them.

Well, except with the AC-130 gunship orbiting overhead.

"Okay, game over. We gotta drop this house," I said.

I turned to my guys and told them we'd need to move to the small house down the road. We'd link up with the Iraqi cops there, then call in the AC-130. We'd have to fight our way out from under that machine gun, carrying our wounded across sixty meters of open ground.

Wes asked, "What about the women and children?"

If we'd been the Russian army in Afghanistan, we'd just blow them up with their husbands and fathers on the roof. But that was not the American way.

"We'll have to take them with us," I said. They would slow us down and add to the complexity and risk of the movement, but there was no other option.

I called J.P. and told him what we were going to attempt.

"Roger that, Red. The gunship's waiting to be cleared hot."

One of the older Iraqi women looked to be the family's authority figure without the men around. I took her aside and waved over an Iraqi cop who spoke a little English. I had him translate what we needed to do.

She understood. As we got ready, she picked up a young child and told the others in her family to follow her.

I went to the door and shouted to our external security, "Crush the rooftop!"

They poured everything they had on the space above us. The PKM went silent. We needed to move.

"Let's go!" I yelled and bolted through the doorway. The rest of the team followed me, carrying our wounded and shepherding the women and children. Every few meters, we'd stop, shoot back at the rooftop, and then move again. We leapfrogged across the open space. Palm trees to our left, the road and open field to our right, firing and maneuvering the entire way back to the smaller house where we had first encountered our sleeping beauties. Our external security collapsed back with us. The women and children screamed in terror, but they kept running with us.

It seemed to last a lifetime, but it could not have been more than a quarter of a minute when we reached the safety of the small house down the road. I made sure we had everyone: seventeen SEALs and Iraqi police, plus eleven women and children.

I radioed J.P. "We're out of the target area. Full head count. Cleared hot."

A moment later, the heavens spit fire as our AC-130 opened up. Twenty-five millimeter shells tore into the house. Bits of masonry cartwheeled from the impacts.

The PKM team on the roof sent a long burst in response.

How did they survive that fusillade?

The gunship made another orbit and switched to their 40mm guns. The big shells slammed into the roof and detonated secondary explosions. For several seconds, the area was strobed by red-orange flashes as flames shot up from the rooftop. Either the gunship had hit more grenades stashed on the roof, or there were suicide vests up there like intel said we could expect.

More shells rained down, and it looked like the roof collapsed, killing everyone on it. By the time the

AC-130 ceased firing, the house appeared to be little more than a broken concrete husk.

We linked up with assault teams one and three and set up a landing zone for the helos. We left the civilians standing at the T in the road, watching as mothers and children wailed in anguish. They'd just seen their home destroyed and all their possessions blown to pieces. Their men had endangered them by throwing hand grenades down into the court-yard where they'd been sleeping. Now those same men—husbands, fathers, uncles, maybe even a son or two—lay dead in the rubble of their home. They'd witnessed all of it.

No matter how committed to the jihad they were, I couldn't imagine what they had just been through. War is a vicious, terrible thing, and often the most vulnerable suffer the most.

I turned and walked to the helo as Shawn gave me the signal for a full head count. I sat on the helo, feeling both exhilarated and numb. I had finally slapped the dragon. Now that I had, I couldn't believe I'd wanted that experience as desperately as I once did. I finally understood.

Every decision, every second in battle hangs on a knife's edge. A wrong call and men can die. To be a leader means to project confidence in chaos, stay calm, and base your decisions off one premise: the mission first balanced against the lives of the men. There is no room for selfishness.

As soon as we landed, I helped our terp and Cade into the waiting trucks. Chief Johnson realized he had taken a piece of shrapnel in the leg also and climbed aboard. J.P. and I went along with our wounded to the battalion aid station at Camp Fallujah, where Cade was patched up and returned to duty.

Our interpreter had taken the worst of it. He would live, but his operating days were probably over. Chief was released, and the three of us rolled back to our compound. We missed the debrief while at the aid station but discussed everything that had happened on the drive back. As we wrapped up our discussion, Chief Johnson slapped my shoulder. "Great job tonight, Red."

J.P. added, "Yeah, man, way to handle all that. That was a chaotic night."

There was an understatement.

We made it back to the compound and headed into the platoon space to write up the mission after-action reports. Only a few of the men were still up. A couple clustered around a television at the far end of the room, watching a movie. Al was typing on one of the computers.

J.P. asked him, "How did the debrief go?"

Al ticked off the lessons learned for us. When he finished, he looked at me and said, "All the guys said you kicked ass tonight, Red. Great job, bro."

It felt good to hear the compliments, but I made sure to stay humble. This was one victory. It didn't catapult me to superleader. There were far too many men who had figured it out and set the example long before me.

I sat down at my computer and began to knock out the paperwork. As I banged it out, J.P. came back in.

"Hey, bro, Hale Michaels said stop by when you get a chance."

Ever since I had lied to Michaels about why I was going to Ranger School, we had never gotten to friendly terms. Cordial maybe. Professional definitely. After the small boat navigation screwup at the end of our training cycle, I'd given up hope that I'd be able to change his opinion of me.

I got up and headed across the compound and rapped at the open plywood door.

"Hey, sir, you wanted to see me?"

He seemed pleased to see me. "Red, sit down, brother. Tell me about the fight. We were watching it through the overhead."

I spent the next hour walking him through the firefight. After I was done, he got up and slapped me on the back.

"Great job tonight. I've been watching you and keeping track through J.P. You've been doing a good job, but tonight was really outstanding. Keep it up."

As I left his office and walked through the dark, I dwelled on this turn of fortune. From outcast to leader. It was the most painful road I'd ever traveled, but it had culminated on the battlefield that night in redemption I never thought would be attainable. I had earned my brothers' respect. I swore to myself that I would never let it slip from my grasp again.

The sun was rising. Back home I knew Erica would still be awake, so I headed into the tactical operations center to call her. I couldn't tell her anything of the mission; just hearing her voice was enough to send my spirits even higher. We talked about the kids, and she gave me the latest on their antics. By the time we said our good-byes, the adrenaline rush from earlier in the evening had worn off, and I was starting to crash.

Time to call it a night. Or day, seeing as it was not yet breakfast time for the rest of the military. As I headed to my hooch I walked by another office and caught sight of Eric Darby on the phone inside.

Frankly, I don't know if I want to go out with you again.

He looked up from the phone and saw me. We made eye contact for just a second, then he nodded at me before turning away. No words were spoken, but I knew what he meant.

For the first time in almost two years, I felt like a part of the brotherhood again.

Chapter 23

Al Anbar Province, Iraq
September 2007

"Hey, Red?"

I looked up from the computer at my desk in our team's planning space to see J.P. standing next to my chair.

"How's progress coming?"

I was awash in paperwork. We had another week's worth of missions, then we'd roll into turnover ops with the incoming unit set to replace us. After that, we'd be going home. Already, our battle rhythm had slackened, and more of our days were spent knocking out all the admin stuff required to get us back to the States. Much of the team's gear had already been packed. We kept a minimal amount at hand for the last few missions.

I gave J.P. an update. There were awards to finish writing up, evals to complete, a few other odds and ends that added hours to my day.

When I finished, J.P. said, "We've still got a couple of targets worked up. We'll run a few more, including the turnover ops, before we leave."

"Roger that."

"We're going to have you run as the ground force commander on the next one."

For a second, what this meant failed to register.

"Really?"

J.P. nodded. "Yeah. I spoke to Eric and Paul and we all agree. You're ready for it. Besides, this will help get you up to speed to be a platoon commander."

I thought about the last four months. The lessons I'd learned. The battles we'd fought. We'd broken up several IED-laying cells and put a huge dent in the Karmah group's operational abilities. The deployment had been a huge success, and everyone was riding high from it.

I thought of my identification procedure error. After that, I had read all the message traffic and double-checked with operations to make sure I was on top of any changes. After that first mission as the mobility commander, I never relied exclusively on the GPS again. That lesson paid off in August when we went after a target in a village west of Fallujah. For some reason, there was a dead spot on the route in that town that caused our nav system to stop working. This time, we didn't stray off course. Like a game of chess, I stayed at least five or six moves ahead. Without our navigation system I got us to the target area without incident.

That one had felt really good and had validated all the extra work.

At length, I finally answered, "That's awesome. Thanks for the opportunity."

"You earned it, bro."

He turned to leave.

I had done it. My career was back on track at last. I knew some in our community would always hate me for my mistakes, but I had earned back the trust of the men I served and fought with.

Since 2004 I'd been an officer. Within our community, rank does not automatically make you a leader. Your character makes you a leader. Your actions make you a leader. Rank is almost irrelevant. After years of selfish focus on myself, I'd finally understood what it meant to lead men of this caliber, and what was required of a man in order to be a part of this most elite of all fraternities. The letter in the safe would be destroyed. For an instant, the horizon ahead had no boundaries.

But first, I had to get through our platoon's customs declarations. And the evals. And the award citations for the men. I returned to the admin morass and lost track of time.

A few afternoons later, we gathered for the 1600 briefing. The mood was light. Everyone was looking forward to going home. As we went through our movement update, our chiefs announced that our first wave would depart in eight days. The second bird would go out a week later, and the final one was scheduled for early October. I'd be on that last one since I got into the country late.

I was looking forward to going home, and I'd be there in time to get to my sister's wedding. Erica had already purchased plane tickets for the family. A few days after I got back, we'd be airborne for the Virgin Islands.

J.P. continued with the brief. We were starting to work on our turnover ops with the new task unit slated to replace us. They would be in-country in the next few days. The planning for those joint missions was well under way. In the meantime, we still had a couple of target packages for missions remaining. One of those I would be running as our GFC.

We broke for dinner, and most of us returned to the admin bog. I sat at my desk until about ten that night. Around me, the planning space began to bustle with activity. When I looked up to see what sparked the commotion, I could see surprise and excitement on my brothers' faces.

We'd just received intel that one of the high-ranking al-Qaida leaders in Al Anbar Province would be in the rural area of Karmah tonight—in the same place where we got into the big firefight in June. We'd been tracking him for months, but he was elusive. Every time we thought we had him, his trail would go cold.

The information our analysts had developed suggested he'd be in town for only a couple of hours. This made him what we called a "time-sensitive target." I looked over the target package and talked to J.P. Due to the late hour, I wasn't sure it would make it through the approval process fast enough to launch and get the guy before he left. J.P. agreed. He said he'd stay in the operations center just in case, but he didn't think we'd be spun up for it.

I decided I'd follow the schedule I'd already laid out for the evening. I took a break and went over to the gym to work out. Many of the other guys were doing the same thing. Nobody thought we'd get this mission.

I'd been lifting for about twenty minutes when one of our intelligence analysts came into the gym. "Looks like we're a go for tonight's mission. Guys are starting mission planning now."

We were flabbergasted. We dropped everything and streamed back to the team area. I was surprised at the approval with such a quick turnaround but apparently our general wanted this bad guy taken out. It was close to midnight. We needed to be wheels up in one hour to make the window. Guys were in a frenzy pulling gear, making preparations, talking among themselves.

He would be well defended. We were in for a fight.

J.P. came over to me and said, "Red, sorry, bro. I know I told you you'd run as the GFC for the next mission, but this is not the mission for on-the-job training."

"No apology needed. I understand."

"Listen, I'll be running as the GFC tonight. You'll be the assault force commander on the main target."

I'd be leading the team designated with killing or capturing one the most important al-Qaida leaders in the province.

"Sounds good."

We didn't have time to insert off the target and patrol silently to it as we had in most of our other air assault operations. By the time we did that, our quarry would be gone. This forced us to abandon the element of surprise. We'd have to land directly on the objective, or land on the X as we called it.

Almost every assault I had been on, Pat, the Angry Irishman, had been my point man. Pat was scheduled to be on the first flight for home, which would be leaving in a few days. J.P., Eric, and the chiefs had decided that the Irishman had taken far more than his fair share of risk. He would be a sniper assigned to our heli-borne aerial reaction force. He'd be overhead covering us, not leading the way into the lion's den.

We didn't need a point man, in any case, since we were landing directly on the X, so we identified the rest of our team and moved on to other details.

Tonight Al Joliet would be running as my team leader. Al was a rock solid leader, operator, and without a doubt the best joint tactical air controller in our task unit. He had also become a good friend. I was glad to have him. Together, we worked up a plan that traded the element of surprise for speed, violence of action, and overwhelming force. I listened carefully to Al and the other team members and all their input. Two years ago, in Afghanistan, I doubt I would have listened. After the hasty plan and brief, I went to get my personal gear. As I was strapping it on, I kept getting a bad feeling. It came in waves, like my spidey sense was trying to tell me something.

You're missing something.

I put my body armor on. Front and back were level four plates that could stop multiple rounds from a 7.62 gun. We also had optional level four side plates.

Take your side plates.

The thought came to me in an instant. I wore my side plates only if I was running as mobility force commander and we were rolling into an IED-intensive area. I never wore them on assaults because they added weight and restricted movement. I traded protection for speed and freedom of movement.

Take your side plates.

It felt like I was on autopilot. I pulled the plates out of my gear locker and slipped them into my vest. I checked my pistol. Loaded, ready to go. Grenades. Check. Flash bangs. Check. Chem lights. Check. Loaded mags. Check. NVGs with extra batteries. Check.

I sprayed a little extra lube on my rifle, slapped a thirty-round magazine into it, and slammed the bolt home. I closed the dust cap and slung my single point sling over my head and shoulder.

It was go time.

We had pushed hard and the team was ready and assembled less than two hours after the go order arrived.

It was now close to 0100. Three army Black Hawks arrived to carry us to the target area. As usual, we flew with no seats. Tonight, the entire team was about fifty men while my team, with our Iraqi partners, had a total of fourteen.

Al and I watched our assault element load up, then we climbed aboard and sat in the doorway, strapping into the helo by a lanyard so any sudden maneuvers wouldn't pitch us overboard.

The other assault element, commanded by Chris Cramer, loaded into the second UH-60. Chris's assault team was tasked with external security. J.P. and our command element, along with Pat and the members of our aerial reaction force, filled the third helo.

We took off and headed for Karmah, not far from where we had been engaged in the big June firefight. Landing on the X required precision, speed, and supreme force. The helicopters would be heard from miles away. Those inside the target building would know we were coming for them. Our only chance would be to get inside fast. To do it, we'd told our helo pilots to put us down directly outside the compound's open gate. A field would be our birds' X. Our breacher and initial entry team sat in the left side door of the bird, and the pilots were supposed to put them down facing the door to the main building. Al and I were on the right side. We'd go in last, as the assault team command element usually does.

We roared over the desert, Karmah sprawling out in front of us. A few lights were on in the town, but for the most part it looked like the people were asleep. The birds stayed low, skimming the earth at max power to make it harder for anyone on the ground to take a shot at us.

Our target came into sight. Ours was the lead bird in the formation; the second assault element was flying just off to one side and behind us. J.P.'s element formed rear security.

Our pilots swung the Black Hawks toward the compound. As they came in and flared, I realized the pilots had made a mistake. They landed facing the wrong direction. This put Al and me in front of the door instead of our breaching and entry team. There was no time to correct the error.

The Black Hawk's wheels hadn't even fully touched the ground and Al was out and racing toward the door. I followed him and could hear the rest of team pouring out of the helo behind me. We couldn't slow down and wait to form up on the ground. It was up to us to get in first now.

Al and I reached the door and prepared to face the maelstrom.

Chapter 24

Al Karmah Area
September 2007

I yanked the door open and stepped forward, flash bang in hand as the rest of the team stacked up behind me. With one fluid move, I activated it and threw it beyond the threshold. A second later, its thundering detonation shook the building.

I watched Al glide through the door in his assault crouch. I flowed behind him, moving the opposite way. As I stepped through the doorway, I braced myself for the weapons fire and the bullets I fully expected to encounter the second we made entry. Nothing happened. We were inside a large, fifty-by-sixty-foot room that seemed empty. The rest of the element swept in and cleared the rest of the building.

I keyed my radio's handset and called J.P. "Target secure. There's nothing here."

It was a dry hole.

Bad intel? Or were we just too late? I didn't know. I was disappointed that we did not get our guy, but thankful we didn't get ambushed.

The adrenaline and fear drained away. My assault team gathered on the main building's porch and waited for orders. Meanwhile Chris's element had cleared and searched the rest of the compound. In the courtyard, they'd found several buried weapons caches, including RPG launchers and ammo. They found more guns and ammo stashed in the compound's main outer ten-foot wall, which caused a flurry of digging and prying in hopes of further discoveries.

J.P. told us to stand by on the porch as that work was completed.

Our interpreter brought me some leaflets he had found inside and translated them. Anti-American, jihadist propaganda. No surprise. This whole town was one big al-Qaida fan club.

The ammunition and weapons the second assault team found began to stack up in the courtyard. Since there was too much of it to carry out with us, the EOD team decided to stuff it all in the trunk of a vehicle also found in the compound and detonate it in place.

J.P. walked onto the porch.

"Hey, brother, we've got movement about a hundred meters north."

The AC-130 gunship circling overhead had seen seven or eight men bolt from a nearby house. They ran into an overgrown thicket at the crest of a gentle sloping hill and went to ground. We had seen this before many times.

On one of our last missions, several men had squirted off a target and ran out into a field and hid in it. One of the other assault teams walked them down and wrapped them up. When asked what they were doing, one of the men replied he was out for a run. The guys laughed at him—he was barefoot. They thought they were hiding from us, but our eye in the sky watched their every action through a thermal imaging system.

"Red, leave your Iraqis here since they don't have night vision. Take the rest of your team with your terp and go walk these guys down."

"Roger that."

I passed along the order to Al who got the guys up and ready. Within a minute, we'd formed up and started patrolling toward the thicket. We moved north at first, then sideslipped the road to weave around another small hill. As we came out from around it we were standing in front of the dense thicket. It was about a hundred yards wide. I was in constant comms with the gunship, and the crew informed me, "Go straight; the guys are in there. At least five or six that we can tell."

We got on line with about five yards between each man. I was in the middle, with our terp on my immediate left. Beyond him we had two new guys and our EOD specialist completing our line to the west. Al was on my right shoulder with Shawn Daniels, then our medic, Brad Larkin, and Rob Marrow forming our east flank.

I gave the word, and we walked north into the thicket. The brush was unusually dense, and we soon ran into trouble. Dead leaves and branches carpeted the ground, and every step we took made so much noise that whoever was in front of us now knew we were there.

We pushed a few more meters. The tangle of small trees, vines, and bushes negated our night vision. We couldn't see more than a couple of feet in front of us. I started to have second thoughts about this approach.

"You're twenty yards from them," the AC-130 crew told me.

The foliage ahead formed a solid wall. How were we going to find these guys safely? I knew we were in a bad spot. We'd be blind, sitting ducks if they opened up on us.

The gunship relayed again. "You need to turn to the northeast. If you keep going straight, you're gonna miss them."

The hair on the back of my neck stood straight up. That hadn't happened since just before the June firefight.

I called back, "Can you see any weapons?"

"Negative. They are just lying there not moving."

I passed the word on our inner freq that we were turning to the northeast. I slid over and told our terp who wasn't on comms. We started to push forward, each step cracking twigs and crushing dead leaves. It was unnerving.

The gunship called again.

"You're right on top of them. Less than ten feet."

I could feel my heart pounding in my chest.

Our terp, Slyder, came up to me.

"I don't see the guys to my left anymore."

"What?"

I stepped over to the left and listened. The night grew still. No sounds of boots crushing twigs to give any indication that the rest of the element was trudging our way.

I called on the radio to our new guys. No response. I tried again. Nothing. I called the EOD specialist and got nothing.

"Where the hell did they go?" I asked Al as he slid up to me.

Al tried to raise them also. Our bad spot just got worse.

At last, one of our new guys came up on our net. He apologized and said he'd been on the wrong frequency and got separated. They must not have made our turn.

They'd moved out of the thicket and onto a road on the west side. We were now on opposite sides of the underbrush, out of visual contact, with potential enemies hiding between us. It was a terrible tactical situation and put us in a position for a possible blue-on-blue incident. If I had ever learned anything from Senior Chief Kerry, it was never to have two elements moving at once.

We had to fix this immediately.

The AC-130 radioed us again to tell us they still saw no signs of movement or weapons from inside the thicket.

Al said, "Rob's at the edge of the thicket on the eastern side. There's an open field beyond it."

We had to reunite the element before we did anything else. I radioed our new guys and EOD and told them to move up to the northwest corner of the thicket and then hold their position. Al and I would take our group and move to them.

Al, Slyder, Shawn, Brad, Rob, and I moved north while the AC-130 gave us regular updates on what the squirters were doing. They were doing nothing but hiding. The gunship reported again that they didn't appear to be armed.

We reached the edge of the thicket. Brad made it out first to join Rob. Shawn and Al followed them. Slyder and I popped out last. We regrouped in the northeast corner. Across from us, but out of our field of vision, the separate section reached the northwest corner. They paused and reported in. Now came the tricky part. We needed to link up in the darkness, then get back on line facing south this time. We'd enter the thicket from the north and see if we could get these guys.

I keyed the handset I kept just below my left shoulder and explained what we were going to do. I told the separated element to hold fast and reiterated that we would move to them in order to reunite the element. Everyone understood.

I glanced over at Al and started to move. Slyder followed me with Al behind him. We slowly headed across the open space on the north side of the thicket. Behind Al, Brad, Shawn, and Rob pulled rear security and kept pace with us.

We walked right into a kill zone.

As we moved past, Brad and Rob saw an enemy fighter lying at their feet. They raised their weapons and promptly killed him. With shots fired, all hell broke loose. Forty-five feet away, the rest of the squirters opened up on us with a PKM machine gun they'd somehow concealed from the AC-130 overhead. They weren't squirters at all. We later found out they were the backbone of the al-Qaida commander's personal security detail. They'd dug fighting positions out in the thicket in preparation for the meeting that their boss attended—not at the main compound we'd hit, but at the house a hundred meters away that sat just west of the thicket.

Al, Rob, and Brad pivoted, each dropping to one knee as they began shooting into the thicket.

Fearing a blue-on-blue incident with the guys on the northwest corner, I shouted, "Cease fire!"

I looked into the thicket and saw at least five muzzle flashes blazing away. No way could we cease fire.

I yelled out again, "We got guys on the northwest corner! Make sure you know what you are shooting at!"

I hoped that our angle of fire was not toward them. Thankfully, our EOD guy that night was Louis Vincenzo, a super squared-away leader with four combat deployments under his belt. He also recognized the bad situation and when one of the new guys started to fire, Louis shut him down and sucked him back to a point of cover. He was tactically smart enough to recognize they were out of this fight. At least for the time being.

Bullets sprayed around us. We were trapped in the kill zone in the middle of an open field. The only way to win this fight was to kill the enemy before they killed us. Firepower was the key. I leveled my rifle at the muzzle flash closest to me and pulled the trigger.

Just then, Brad Larkin cried out. He'd been hit in the leg. The large 7.62-by-54mm bullet ripped through Brad's tibia and fibula and split his leg apart in such a way that the broken pieces of bone speared into the ground and anchored him into place.

Hell was erupting around me and I kept pulling my trigger. The situation was desperate. All we could do was fight back and pray.

The PKM gunner swung his weapon my way. Bullets smacked the ground around me, kicking up bits of dirt and rocks that pinged off my gear. Another burst, and a flurry of rounds streaked past on either side of me. Then he found the range and caught me in the arm. I staggered forward, rolling over onto my back. It felt like an eight-hundred-pound gorilla had just hit me in the funny bone. The nerve impulse rocketed up my arm and slammed me in the base of the skull.

As I lay wounded, Al, Shawn, and our terp spotted an old tractor tire laying in the dirt several meters behind us. They made a break for it while Rob rushed forward to get Brad, who was lying in the dirt, unable to move.

Another PKM opened fire, stitching the ground around my two brothers. A long burst, and Rob was hit by three bullets, twice in the leg, and once in the right arm. Ignoring his wounds, Rob reached Brad, broke him free, and dragged him back to the tire.

Al radioed me. "Brad and Rob are hit."

I keyed my radio and called J.P. "Troops in contact! Troops in contact! I have three wounded including me!"

The machine guns were still blazing away at us, and they walked their barrels right and left, crisscrossing our position with hundreds of 7.62mm bullets.

I recognized if I didn't get a tourniquet on what I thought was the stump of my left arm I was going to bleed out. I looked back to Al and the rest of my team behind the tire.

Right then, Al saw me get to my feet and try to run back to join them. Al told me this later, but I have no recollection of standing up after I was hit the first time. The PKM gunner spotted me moving and laid on his trigger. According to Al, I'd taken only a step or two when my head whipsawed forward and my body spun around to the left. I fell limp to the ground. The team thought I'd been killed.

When I started talking to him and Shawn a couple of minutes later, they were astonished I was still alive. The machine gunner kept up a steady fire on the tire, and around me. Had he been equipped with night vision, I have no doubt he would have killed most, if not all, of us. Without the technology, he shot blindly, aiming by sound and by our muzzle flashes.

Al recognized the dire situation we were in and called in an immediate fire mission. The AC-130 crew turned it down the first two times before finally making Al acknowledge that if anything happened to us, it was Al's fault, not the gunship's. The first 25mm shells hit the thicket behind the enemy. I lay less than fifty feet from the enemy machine gun that had engaged me. I drifted in and out of consciousness the entire time, awake in a fog of confusion one minute, out cold the next.

Al next risked his life to save me. During a lull in fire he rose from behind the tire and charged over to me. Shawn laid down cover fire as Al ran into the teeth of that PKM. Bullets cracked and whined around him, but he reached me and dragged me back behind the tire where he put a tourniquet on my mangled arm. I remember nothing of this and didn't know Al had even moved me to the tire until months after the firefight.

During the firefight and after I had been moved back to the tire, Brad called out that he was getting ready to throw a grenade. I had been lying in what appeared to be an unconscious state when I suddenly sat up and yelled at Brad.

"Don't throw that grenade! It's gonna bounce back from that vegetation and kill us all!!"

Apparently even in my disoriented state, I still remembered my tactical lessons from working in the jungle years ago. Never throw grenades into vegetation. They have a tendency to bounce back, and their blast does not distinguish between friend or foe. The guys were dumbfounded as I sat up to offer this tactical lesson when they thought I was dead. To this day I don't remember doing this.

Seconds later the fire picked up again and didn't slacken. Al went back to work directing the AC-130's incoming. He walked the 25mm rounds into the enemy's ambush line, taking out the PKM gunner at last. Once it appeared the fire had been suppressed, Al coordinated the linkup with J.P. and the other assault team.

The medevac bird arrived a few minutes later, and the guys helped us aboard. Once we were airborne and out of harm's way, the remainder of the task unit fell back to the original target compound to wait for extract. But the fight wasn't over. The gunship detected more movement in the thicket.

Enough was enough. Al called in 105mm howitzer fire from the AC-130 and turned the thicket into a smoking crater.

Months later, when J.P. visited me at home, I learned that the al-Qaida commander had fled the house when he heard our birds coming in at the start of the mission. He left part of his personal security detail behind to fight a battle he had no stomach for himself. They were the loyal ten percenters, and they died to the last man after inflicting three casualties on us.

Months later, another SEAL team ran the al-Qaida commander to ground and killed him.

Justice served.

PART V

The Reforging

Chapter 25

Landstuhl, Germany
September 2007

"How you feeling?"

I was in another hospital room, another ICU. I knew I was in Germany, but I didn't remember the flight that got me here. It was disorienting to realize I'd traveled to a different country without having any knowledge of the journey. A pad and pencil rested on my chest. With my one good hand, I scribbled a response. I had double vision, and I was loopy from the Dilaudid; it was a combination that made my handwriting a mess. It took forever to get the words on the paper.

Still on the right side of the earth.

The nurse said something to me but I didn't hear her. She worked her way around to the other side of the bed. I drifted in and out in that drug-infused twilight.

I wrote on my pad.

I feel like all these tubes are pulling to the right. So annoying.

"Let me see what I can do."

I had a veritable snake's nest of tubes running from my body to various machines. I had no idea what they were all for. They hamstrung what little movement I had left so thoroughly that it felt like I'd been imprisoned by them.

"You need anything else?"

I'm good, thanks.

Time was so strange when on Dilaudid. It seemed like the nurse had been in my room for hours, but apparently only a minute or two had passed. I couldn't tell if it was night or day. I drifted back off.

At some point, doctors came to talk to me. I awoke to learn they planned another surgery to clean my wounds. Iraqi soil had been ground into my body, and the threat of infection was very high as a result. I was also slightly anemic, which meant I would need a blood transfusion during the surgery.

I floated on the Dilaudid waves again. When I woke up again, I saw Tony Morales standing in the room. He'd been assigned to escort me back to the States and made sure I got everything I needed.

"The drugs treating you okay?" he asked.

I scratched at my pad.

Yeah, man. I feel like I've been missing out all my life.

He laughed.

"You talk to the docs yet?"

Yeah. Good news. They said all the facial damage was just superficial. Some plastic surgery and I'll be back to my pretty self.

"You were never that pretty. Plastic surgery would definitely be an improvement," Tony said, laughing.

I am worried about my kids.

Tony took that note and stared at it for a long moment. Eventually, he chose not to say anything, just nodding his understanding instead. Our conversation fell off, and soon I drifted into the drug-sleep again. When my eyes opened, Tony was gone.

As I lay there thinking, a nurse came in to check my vitals. As she worked, she made small talk.

"Do you have a family?"

Yes. Three kids. Son—8. Two daughters—4 and 2.
I just wish they wouldn't have to see me like this.

The nurse looked at the note. "They aren't going to care. You're their dad."

I just hope I don't scare them too much.

I reached up and felt the feeding tube stuck in what was left of my nose.

"Have you spoken with your family yet?" she asked.

Not yet.

I thought that over, then added:

I want to talk to my dad before I go into surgery.
Is that okay?

My father is one of the most godly men I know. I needed faith and his prayers in that moment. For some reason, I developed a bad feeling about this operation. How many guys get to Landstuhl, only to die on the table during surgery? I had no idea, but the thought of that happening left me concerned enough to smother the sense of humor I'd been using to keep my spirits up.

I wrote a note for my dad. The nurse agreed to read it to him over the phone, then put the handset to my ear so I could hear his response. It took forever to carve each word into the paper, thanks to the drugs and my intermittent double vision. When I finished, the nurse took the page and dialed the phone. After she introduced herself, I listened as she read the note to my father.

Dad: it's your son. I am sure Erica has talked with you, but if not—I got shot up a couple of nights ago. I am pretty messed up right now. I can't talk because my jaw's wired shut. I am having a blood transfusion and will have another surgery before I fly to Bethesda tomorrow. I am going to have the nurse hold the phone to my ear so I can hear you pray for me. Don't worry. I am a fighter and will come out of this okay.

When she finished, the nurse placed the phone to my ear, and I listened to my father's prayer. "Lord, give my son peace and strength through these difficult times. May Your grace and Your angels protect him through these upcoming surgeries and the flight home."

The nurse took the phone back and said good-bye for me. A few minutes later the staff wheeled me out to be prepped for surgery. Just before I went into the OR, somebody put a clipboard in front of me. On it was a legal document of some sort. A voice nearby explained that this was a release form showing that I understood that European blood banks didn't test for hepatitis type C.

So a transfusion may be the only way to save my life, and yet because of it, I could end up with hepatitis? Awesome.

What option did I have? The docs had already told me I needed blood. I signed the document.

The anesthesiologist arrived to start pumping more drugs into my system. I wondered if I'd make it out of this surgery alive. Soon the drugs ensured that I didn't care either way. My eyes closed, and I tumbled into darkness.

"Good news! We were able to get you American blood. No threat of hep C with that."

I awoke from the twilight drug-fog long enough to feel relief at that news. I blinked my eyes clear for a minute and saw I was back in my private room. Lights were dim. The place was quiet, except for the beeps of the machines that monitored my body.

The nurse in the room with me asked, "Can I get you anything?"

The pad lay on my chest, pencil attached to it. I reached for them, my arm feeling like a thousand pounds.

I'd like a bourbon and Coke.

She laughed. "I don't think I can help you with that."

It hurts to swallow. Is that normal?

"Yes. Don't worry about that."

I am really thirsty.

The nurse told me I was not allowed to have any water until the swelling went down and the doctors could examine the extent of damage to my jaw and mouth. The thirst grew more intense, and I tried in vain to get my mind off it.

At last, Tony came into the room to see how I was doing. Thirst forgotten, I hung on every word as he told me he'd been in touch with Al, J.P., and a few other members of the team. That prompted a short conversation about the firefight.

We are lucky. God loves warriors.

Tony nodded in agreement.

He stood silently with me for a while, until he asked, "Want to call home?"

I closed my eyes. It was time.

Yes.

Tony walked over to the nightstand and lifted the receiver. I watched him punch in the numbers and waited with growing trepidation as the phone on the other end of the line began to ring. When Erica picked up, I could hear her voice, tinny and distant, say hello.

After Tony introduced himself, he explained that he would read the notes I wrote, then hold the phone to my ear so I could hear her response.

I gave him my first note.

"Are you serious?" he asked me, raising an eyebrow.

I manage a slight nod.

"Okay."

Tony read into the phone, "Hi, babe. I got all shot up, but my wang is okay."

I heard her laughing through tears as Tony put the handset in my ear. She told me no one knew my mental state, and she had been terrified I'd suffered brain damage. My feeble attempt at humor had confirmed for her that I was okay.

She said, "I love you. I love you. I love— You." Her voice colored every word with relief and emotion. It seemed almost like a mantra as she repeated them.

Will this love still be there when you see me? I thought.

I love you too.

"I'll be waiting at Bethesda for you tomorrow night," she said.

A stab of fear hit me.

I wrote quickly. Tony read it. "I don't want the kids to see me like this. Don't bring them until after I've had some plastic surgery."

"Whatever you want, babe. Anything."

This cumbersome method of communication quickly wore me out. Erica and I said a few more things to each other, then said our good-byes. Seconds after Tony hung up the phone for me, I fell back into a deep sleep.

The next morning, a nurse came into my room and told me that it was the day I would fly back to the States. She loaded me onto a gurney and wheeled me downstairs to a loading area. Rob and Brad were there, and this was the first time we'd been reunited since the medics pulled us off the helo. They parked the three of us together as we awaited a bus that would take us to the airfield.

It did wonders for my morale to be out in the morning air with my two teammates. We talked about the firefight and what happened. I chimed in whenever I could with the pad and pencil, silently swearing that I'd never take speaking for granted again.

Getting separated threw a wrench into everything.

The guys agreed, and that set us to dissecting the early stages of the fight.

I heard Al is taking it kind of hard.

Brad and Rob talked about what they saw Al do that night. He was flat-out amazing: fearless, professional, calm in the midst of the storm. The three of us owed our lives to him; I hoped Al would get the Navy Cross I had recommended for him.

The conversation ebbed a bit. In silence, I regarded them. Days before, we were all healthy, supremely fit human beings. Now we all lay on gurneys unable to move much, our bodies full of holes. I felt a rush of sadness. How did we come to this?

I could sense the guys were thinking the same things, and I knew that wallowing was not going to help us. So I scratched a few words on my pad and handed the note over to Brad.

We're all on the road to recovery. Cool scars. Cool stories.

"Chicks do dig scars," Rob said, laughing.

Maybe superficial ones. But what of real scars? What would Erica think?

The bus arrived. Orderlies came over to help us aboard, one at a time. As they rolled me toward the waiting doors, one of the nurses brushed against me. I scratched out a note and handed it to her.

You copping a feel?

They slid my gurney into a specially designed rack for litter cases in the back of the bus. Up front, walking wounded filled the remaining seats. This was a part of our war effort rarely seen.

The bus drove us over to the airfield and parked on the tarmac not far from the gigantic C-17 transport that would fly us home. We waited. And waited. The bus grew hot in the German late-summer sun. The pain I felt grew steadily worse as the temperature rose. One glance at Rob and Brad, and I knew they were starting to suffer as well.

After an hour, the orderlies pulled the walking wounded off the bus. Out my window, I could see them sitting in a spot of shade a short distance away. I couldn't help but envy them as the rest of us litter cases continued to bake inside the bus.

I couldn't talk to the guys around me. I couldn't sleep in the heat. Covered in sweat and increasingly dehydrated, I saw the same pain and discomfort stamped on the men around me.

Two and half hours later, we finally boarded the C-17. The walking wounded streamed up the ramp to find a seat. The orderlies came for us litter cases. As they reached me, my mood shifted from slow-burning anger to a lighthearted happiness. I was one step closer to home, thank God. As they carried me into the plane, I had a mental image of a drogue chute attached to the end of my gurney so I could be slid off

the ramp like an aerial resupply mission. I wrote to
the orderly:

Are we jumping when we get to Bethesda?
Sending us out as a bundle drop?

The orderly read it and laughed.

They stuck our gurneys on racks secured to the
C-17's cargo deck. Three deep and stretching perhaps
twenty feet inside the bay, there were at least twelve
of us unable to sit up. In some ways, it was like being
inside a submarine's crew quarters.

We had one nurse to tend to all of us on the flight.
After she hastily introduced herself and gave me some
meds, I saw little of her.

The engines spooled up. The C-17 lumbered down
the runway and waddled aloft. I was only dimly aware
of getting airborne, since I was high as a kite on a fresh
dose of painkillers. I slipped into light sleep, but I
awoke minutes later coughing and choking as my trach
tube had clogged up.

Where's the nurse?

My field of view was impossibly small since I couldn't
raise my head to look around or even turn it much in
any direction.

I'm choking here!

Whenever I coughed, the trach tube brushed against my throat, triggering a gag reflex. It made me want to throw up. I'd been warned many times of the danger that presented since my jaw was wired shut. If I vomited, I risked aspirating it and dying, just like Jimi Hendrix did. To guard against that, the nursing staff had made sure I had a special pair of scissors with me at all times. Should I throw up, they'd cut the wires and free my jaw. That was not without consequences though. If we used the scissors, I'd have to endure another surgery to wire it shut and start over. That would have been an absolute last resort.

Tony saw my distress and came over to check on me. He discovered that they'd forgotten to send the scissors with me. I mustered the strength to write:

Smart!!

He shook his head in frustration, then went to find the nurse. She was occupied with some of the other wounded men and told him she would get to me when she could. I lay in my rack, fearing another choking incident as the trach tube grew more sloppy. Each breath became a labor. Several times, I was racked by coughing fits.

Don't throw up. Don't throw up.

Tony talked to the nurse again. At last, she came over and took care of my trach. Exhausted, I fell asleep, only to wake up coughing and choking again. Tony had to talk to her several more times to get her to come back and help. This went on through the entire flight, leaving me frustrated and frightened. Being this dependent on other people was utterly foreign to me. I hated it.

The C-17 landed at Andrews Air Force Base on a Sunday evening. The orderlies separated me from Rob and Brad before I could say good-bye to them. I had no idea where they were going, or when I'd see them next. Being taken from my brothers only unsettled me more.

They loaded me aboard another blue military bus for the last leg to Bethesda. Soon we turned onto a freeway, and I watched headlights streaming by in the darkness beyond my window. Days ago, I was in a firefight in Iraq. Now I was home in the entire splendor that was the United States of America. Most people here have no clue how good we have it.

The thought provided no comfort. Every minute, the bus carried me closer to my reunion with Erica. The horror stories I'd heard played through my mind. The operator, badly burned, whose fiancée showed up at a military hospital, saw his face, and without a word pulled off her engagement ring and left it beside his bed.

The wives who came to Bethesda with their lawyers, divorce papers already filled out, asking their husbands to sign as they lay in bed with broken, unhealed bodies.

The kids who fled from the sight of what their father had become.

For decades, Bethesda has been the backdrop for countless scenes like that. Everyone says looks don't matter. Everyone says the heart, the soul, the spirit are all that count in a marriage. Chemistry. Connection. That's what keeps a union sound.

For most, that is never tested. How often does a man lose his face here at home? How often does a father lose a leg, or an arm, or suffer burns across his body while making a living for his family? A hundred years ago, that sort of thing was much more common. Now, not so much.

But in the community of warriors, we'd seen the fallout too many times.

The beautiful wife sees her future lying immobile in a hospital bed, and reality sinks in. Sure, she may put up a brave front for a little while. Then it crumbles, and she flees as surely as some of the children do.

During the Vietnam War, the wards at Walter Reed were full of men recovering from amputations, burns, and gunshot wounds. They grew accustomed to such wives and would jeer them as they left with the divorce papers in hand. Signed, of course.

My career and erratic behavior had put Erica through hell for years. She had always handled every curveball with love and unconditional support. She had more capacity for both than anyone I'd ever known. But I could tell the roller coaster after Afghanistan had worn her down.

We'd never been the lovey-dovey couple. We lived our love, we showed it. We shared it with small acts of kindness and consideration throughout the grind of daily life. It was always there, running in the background, even if we didn't acknowledge it often. When we did, it was a special occasion and the words remained sparse.

But is that enough now?

I've known many couples who have discovered there are limits to how long their relationship could survive in the face of adversity. Some marriages survived longer than others, but there was always a breaking point. That's why the vast majority of marriages within our community failed. Love is not eternal. It is finite— and can be run into the ground.

Marriages crash and burn all the time over things far less challenging than battle wounds. I'd seen them flushed over finances, affairs, division of the household responsibilities, or lack of emotional investment. Fights born from an unstable foundation or fundamental compatibility tanked more than a few. Couples raged over seemingly trivial things, but those fights etched away the core until there was critical failure and the whole thing collapsed.

Perhaps if it was true love, couples would stand by each other. The idealist within me always believed that, I supposed. The tests that God and life deliver reveal the depth of a couple's commitment. The strength of the bond is either proven—or broken.

My face didn't feel like my own. With my nose gone, tubes sticking out of my body, jaw wired shut—I had to look pretty ragged. At least I imagined I did. I had yet to see myself in a mirror.

Everyone thinks they've got the kind of love that can endure rough times. Few actually do. I guess I am about to learn the true measure of our love.

The physical reality of my wounds would be tough enough. There's a deeper level too. The way I looked now reflected a new reality. I may have been the one who got shot, but for my family—for Erica—the life we'd known was slain on that battlefield. I had to be honest about that.

Nobody signs up for that kind of sudden change. In a heartbeat, life gets redefined. How it looks gets yanked from our control. A world turned upside down.

How would Erica handle it?

When we got to Bethesda the bus lurched to a halt. Doors opened, and voices barked orders. The orderlies offloaded the remaining wounded men. They lifted my gurney out of the bus, unfolded its wheels, and pushed me through a pair of double doors. Once inside, they took me to a room full of doctors and nurses. They poked, prodded, and examined me as I lay there, helpless and feeling like a slab of meat. I drew within myself and tried to ignore what was happening around me.

Erica. Think of her and the kids.

In a sudden rush, all the things that I had missed over the years filled my head. Mackenzie's ear surgery, countless ups and downs with Phoenix and Angelica. I'd missed the basics of running a household together too. There was no equitable split there. I was hardly home for much of the time. Erica handled the domestic side of things, raising our children virtually single-handedly while managing her own Bengal cat–breeding business at the same time. She did it all alone just so I could go do what I loved doing.

I had constantly laid all my burdens on her and she had never wavered. But everyone has a breaking point. Would this be it?

Our relationship was never work. It was just elemental. Like breathing.

I remembered standing in her doorway after my crazed flight through the storm to her home in that old Jeep of mine.

I could still hear her saying, "The only way I am moving to Virginia Beach is with a ring on my finger."

My failed *Jerry Maguire* moment. My horrible proposal.

I crossed the threshold, thinking I'd better fix that and propose properly.

It was one of countless moments that, when put together, added up to the amazing life and family we had built. I thought of that first Christmas ornament, the shark with our picture in its mouth, and how we now had a Christmas tree full of ornaments of our own memories.

How I came up with a better proposal became another one of those moments. Months after my initial inept proposal, I had surprised her at a waterside restaurant in town. The place returned to me now, and in my mind I saw its dark hardwood floors, thick ivory-colored tablecloths, and the spectacular view of

Lynnhaven Inlet. We sat by one of the tall windows overlooking the water. The bamboo blinds were rolled up, and the golden light from the evening's sunset had set the water afire. Erica wore one of her little black dresses. I was in jeans and a button-down shirt.

The waiter brought us a bottle of wine. Frog's Leap merlot. I couldn't think of anything more appropriate. I knew nothing about wine. Coors Light maybe, wine not so much. I only knew I was a frogman and I was getting ready to make the leap, so it seemed the perfect choice. We toasted, ordered, and chatted, enjoying being together.

When we finished eating, the waiter brought Erica a bouquet of multicolored roses, no two alike. I was rarely ever that emotional, but after my failed initial proposal I felt the need to set the bar high to show Erica what she truly meant to me deep down inside. So I'd researched the symbolism behind each color and had that printed on a card. I sat across from her, pulled a rose out of the bouquet, and read to her.

A yellow rose, symbolizing friendship. I handed it to her and pulled the next one out. Orange. Desire. I read the card and gave her the rose. One after another I did this until the bouquet had only one left. It was a deep red, beautiful rose. I pulled it out and attached to the stem by a string was a platinum diamond ring.

I got down on one knee and said, "Erica, this last rose represents love. Like I told you on your front porch in Louisville, I want to spend my life with you. Marry me."

When Erica said yes, the entire restaurant erupted in applause.

Then I heard a voice that shattered the memory. "Lieutenant, your wife is here."

I know. And I am not ready to face her yet. I'm a mess.

I haven't had a shower in days. Dried blood glued strands of my hair together. I stank from the long flight and from lying in that sunbaked bus on the tarmac in Landstuhl. I couldn't even remember the last time I was able to brush my teeth.

What was left of them.

I had never known fear this primal before. I didn't know what to do. My heart raced like I was about to go through a door on a capture/kill mission. I scrawled a note to the nurse and asked her if she could clean me up a little and make me more presentable for my wife.

She found a sponge and tried to scrub off some of the dried blood that was crusted and caked to my skin and hair. I closed my eyes to compose my thoughts and tried to build myself up for what was about to happen.

I don't know if I can do this alone. Without her, where will I be?

The nurse finished the once-over. "There you go, Lieutenant. All set."

All set. I have tubes running into what's left of my nose. I have a tracheotomy. I am too weak to even sit up. All set for what??

I took a breath and prepared myself.

OK. I am ready.

Just after midnight, Erica stepped through the doorway. She never slowed as she rushed to my side.

And then, she was there, her face above me. Her doe eyes, deep brown, full and watery, were like a balm to my soul. She eased down and kissed me tenderly around all the tubes. Her lips felt soft and I tasted the salt of her tears.

"We're gonna be all right, babe. We'll get through this together."

I was so ashamed for doubting her. She was the rock I'd always known. In that moment I knew we were going to be okay.

Chapter 26

Bethesda Naval Hospital
September 2007

I awoke before dawn the next morning from a fitful sleep, fueled by the painkillers. It took a minute to remember where I was and what had happened. Then in a rush, the reality of my condition returned.

Erica lay asleep in a recliner that the staff had pulled next to my bed. She made it clear to them that she was not leaving my side. I watched her sleep for a few minutes. My heart rate slowed. The unsettled feeling I had drained away. The sight of her with me brought me comfort and peace.

We would need help getting through this ordeal. Fortunately, our families stepped up to take care of the kids while Erica remained with me. We wanted to make sure that in the weeks ahead their daily routines were impacted as little as possible. They would still go to school and soccer practice, and each evening good food would be waiting on the table for them. In time, when I was ready, they would see me again.

At 0400, my room suddenly filled with doctors and nurses. This was part of the routine I came to find out. Military hospitals start their days early, which ensured patients never sleep all the way through the night. By the time everyone squeezed inside, there had to be a dozen medical specialists there to see me. They introduced themselves as the team assembled to oversee my recovery. Their names went in one ear and out the other on this first morning. Still dazed from the journey home and heavily medicated, nothing stuck with me for long.

That was until my eyes turned to a navy commander in khakis standing beside my bed. Perhaps six foot two, thin and muscular. Balding. He wore a Trident on his chest.

He said, "Hi, Jay, I'm Dan Valaik. I'm the head of orthopedics here. I'll be taking care of you."

The sight of the Trident on this doctor's chest left me dumbfounded. I raised my right hand unsteadily to point at it.

"Yeah, I was a team guy before I became a doctor."

I fumbled around until I found the notepad and pen. He waited patiently as I wrote:

Nothing more to say. I know I'm in good hands.

What were the odds that a member of the brotherhood would be taking care of me? I felt nothing but relief at the sight of that Trident.

Dr. Valaik began to talk to Erica and me about the road ahead. I was grateful to hear we would start right away. I scrawled a note and passed it to the doc.

Let's get a plan going!

Dr. Valaik and the rest of the team understood my eagerness. The sooner I was out of that bed, the better we'd all be. And so, they carefully laid out the basic strategy. It would come in phases. The first phase was cleaning and stabilization of the wounds. During the second phase, they would begin the reconstruction of my arm and face. The last phase would be cosmetic work.

I was already partly through the stabilization phase. Despite the fact that I couldn't walk or even sit up yet, I wanted to move on to reconstruction as soon as possible. The quicker I got through that, the quicker I could return to the teams and continue my career.

In the immediate future, the next big step for me would be a series of tests, CT scans, and x-rays to determine the extent of the wounds to my face and arm. From that data, the team would build a more detailed and robust game plan. In the meantime, they had already scheduled several surgeries to further clean and stabilize my wounds.

That first morning at Bethesda passed in a blur. People came and went, and I barely took note through the drug-fog and exhaustion. My dad and stepmom appeared in the room at some point. Erica never left my side, that I know for certain. More docs buzzed in and out, along with a steady parade of nurses. My brother and sister showed up in the mix somewhere that day as well. Between those visits, the orderlies took me away so more tests could be run. The whirlwind continued until well after dark.

A full blood workup revealed a serious issue that first morning. I tested positive for a very nasty bacteria native only to the Middle East. The staff at Bethesda had encountered it many times since 9/11. They filled me full of powerful IV antibiotics and took measures to prevent me from spreading it to other people. For weeks after, those who came into my room were required to wear special yellow scrubs and masks.

They put me on blood thinners to minimize the threat of clots developing that might cause a stroke or an aneurysm. Twice a day, a nurse came in and injected that stuff directly into my stomach. Now that was fun.

Then there was the trach tube. It was one of the hardest things to deal with since it was always uncomfortable and clogged up so often. Whenever that happened, I had a tough time breathing, and the gag reflex brought me close to vomiting more than once. The trach required constant cleaning and would become an endless source of trouble.

In the midst of all this, we began the CT scans and x-ray process. Getting out of bed was a painful challenge, one that required Erica's help as well as the nursing staff's. I couldn't sit up for any length of time. I hadn't walked since before I climbed aboard the helo in Iraq. I'd never been this weak and unsteady.

One day, Erica and an orderly wheeled me down to a lab to have a three-dimensional CAT scan done on my head. The scan would help the docs determine the extent of the damage to my face. When we arrived, Erica positioned my wheelchair in front of the imaging system. A camera was supposed to rotate around me, snapping photographs as it moved. The trip down to the lab had left me dizzy and groggy; that condition, on top of the ethereal, disconnected feeling I always had on the pain meds, left me barely able to keep my head up by the time we got there.

A tech came into the imaging room, glanced at me, and said, "Stand up, please."

Stand up?

The offhand order stunned my wife. She tried to explain my condition to the man. He didn't care. According to him, there was no other way to do the process. I wanted to ask him how they used the system with warriors who had lost their legs, but I didn't have the energy.

Erica slid her shoulder under my right arm and lifted me out of the wheelchair. Unsteadily, I found myself on my feet for the first time since walking to the helo. I sagged against her for support, but the tech saw that and demanded, "Face forward, please."

I shifted to face the camera. That's when I saw a mirror in front of me, built into the framework of the machine. Erica noticed this at the same time I did. In the reflection, I saw her face register pure anguish.

Then I saw my own.

Except I was staring at a stranger. There was no resemblance to the man I once was in this mirror. The face was bloated and red. Tubes came out of what was left of my nose. Black and blue stitches intersected across my face. My blue eyes were bloodshot and looked tiny in my swollen face. The shock almost made my knees buckle, but Erica was there to catch me.

The tech started the machine and the camera whirred around me. The process only took a few minutes, and then we were released to head back to the room. As Erica pushed my wheelchair, I heard her crying softly.

A doctor noticed Erica crying and asked what was wrong.

"I didn't want my husband to see himself until he was ready. Now you've taken that away from us."

Back in the hospital room, we remained together in downcast silence. I ached everywhere from the physical ordeal of the test. I could see Erica was aching as well. I think heartache is far less endurable than physical misery, and I felt for her. I'd put her through so much, and she'd been battling for me without a second thought. I couldn't believe I ever doubted her commitment to me.

Right then, a thought occurred to me. I took up the pen and pad and wrote:

Where were you and how did you find out?

Erica looked at me and sighed. Bad memory, no doubt. Part of me was sorry I asked, especially after the morning's events. But then I saw that she needed to tell me. We'd been sharing my burden, and it was time for me to pick up some of hers too.

"I had been out running errands all morning as the kids were in school. I picked up Mackenzie and Angelica from preschool along with one of their friends. When we got home, the kids wanted to go for a bike ride and have a picnic so I packed a lunch."

A typical day.

"I was in the kitchen, and I saw the caller ID blinking *US GOVT, US GOVT*," she continued. "I checked. Somebody had called every five minutes for the last four hours. I assumed it was you, so I held off on taking the kids out to see if you'd call back."

The phone rang a few minutes later.

"I picked up thinking it was you, eager to hear your voice. Then I heard, 'Erica, it's Gil . . .'"

She stopped for a minute and collected herself. "The call dropped. Right then, I knew something bad had happened, so I put the kids on the couch and turned a movie on so I could wait for Gil to call back."

I'm sorry I put you through this, babe.

"The phone rang again. I answered it, heard Gil's voice, but the line went dead just like the first time. By then, I was getting frantic. The kids ignored the movie and were bouncing off the walls. They kept asking to leave on our picnic. All I could think about was what Gil was trying to tell me. Were you dead? What had happened?"

I could see the torment of those uncertain minutes register on her face as she relived the memory. Now I really was sorry for asking. But I needed to know. I needed to know what my life had done to hers.

"I tried to remind myself that if you were dead, there'd be no phone call. The contact team would be at my door. But what if they were calling because they had come by earlier and I wasn't home? What if they were on the way now? I started to panic, Jay. I'm sorry. I did. I had to go outside, away from the kids, to pull myself together."

While Erica was outside, she had held on to the phone with a death grip so firm it threatened to break it.

The phone rang again. Erica answered and heard Gil say, "I'm sorry the call keeps dropping. I have to tell you, your husband is the luckiest man I know. Jay was shot in a firefight last night, twice in the arm and once in the face. He doesn't have much of a nose left. His jaw is damaged, so he is wired shut, and he is trached. He is unable to talk. Once he is out of surgery and stable and if all goes according to plan, he will back in the States by Sunday night."

What did you tell the kids?

"I felt weak as his words sunk in. I couldn't believe you'd been shot in the face, and I had no idea how you could have been and not suffered brain damage. I stood there, thinking about that, and watched through the front door as the kids ran around inside."

A few last moments of normalcy.

"I walked back into the house and told them you'd been shot in the arm. I couldn't tell them about the facial wound, Jay. I didn't know what that meant to us yet, and I was struggling so badly with it myself. I was so afraid you'd come home and not be yourself. But when you wrote from Germany, I knew your brain, with all its bad jokes, was fine."

Well, babe, fine is relative on that front.

She read the note and laughed. Then she took my hand. "Jay, our world turned upside down. I had no idea what was coming next, but I did know I had to get a plan in place so the house and kids could be taken care of. I needed to get to you. That's all that mattered."

I felt the comfort of her hand and once again felt that stab of guilt for ever doubting her.

Never again. I will never put you through anything like that again.

Later that morning, two NCOs stepped into the room to introduce themselves. Sergeant Major Dan Thompson and Sergeant First Class Marty Thompson were both wounded warriors who worked as liaisons between the patients and the medical staff as part of the Special Operations Command Care Coalition. Their job was to ensure our wounded men received the best possible care while their families received the best possible support.

Erica and I dubbed them the Thompson Twins, and they soon proved to be a godsend for us. They helped arrange housing for our family when they came to visit; they took on some of the bureaucratic battles we faced; and Sergeant Major Thompson gave us a vital piece of advice.

"Be careful with the doctors," he warned us. "Most are talented professionals and are truly looking out for your best interests. But some don't play well with others, and I've seen that cause problems. Don't ever forget: you and Erica are ultimately in charge of your care. So always ask questions, and do not be afraid to get a second opinion."

Over the next few days, the revolving door into my room continued. Family. Docs. Nurses. Orderlies. Visitors. They came and went, usually waking me up as they did. At one point, another doctor introduced herself as the oral maxillofacial surgeon assigned to my case. She explained to us that her team's job was to reconstruct my face. Her name was Dr. Mallard, but she had such an electric presence in the room that in my head, I nicknamed her Dr. Lightning Bolt.

With energetic bluntness, she laid out the extent of my wounds. The machine-gun bullet entered just in front of my right ear. It shattered my jaw, vaporized my right orbital floor, destroyed my cheek, and exited through my nose. I'd suffered nerve damage as well. Virtually nothing was left of my cheekbone or the ocular floor bones on the right side of my face. She and her team were amazed I didn't suffer greater eye damage, so that was a blessing.

My nose was almost completely destroyed and would need a full reconstruction. They would need to repair my shattered jaw, implant a titanium plate to replace the ocular floor, and would have to repair the damage to the rest of my facial bones on the right side. After that, the plastic surgeons could do their work.

I still was under the impression that they could fix me right up and get me back into the teams. Now I was not so sure.

So how many weeks are we looking at here, Doc?

"Weeks?" she said, surprised. "No, Jay. We're talking years. A few years at least."

Years?

It didn't even sink in at first.

"There will be progressive surgeries. Each one will need to fully heal before we can move on to the next one."

She went on to explain that there was no road map for the extent and nature of my wounds. My case was highly complex and would require extensive bone and skin grafts in the years ahead.

After she left, I struggled to keep my spirits up. This was news I did not want to hear.

The next morning, I was wheeled into pre-op for the first of many surgeries to come. At Bethesda, the staff allows family to be with their wounded warrior in pre-op all the way to the OR doors, so Erica stayed right beside me. This first stateside surgery would be a long one, ten or twelve hours. The docs would operate in teams, first on my arm, then on my face.

The surgical staff prepped me as Erica held my hand. Then it was time. The nurses pushed me for the OR. Erica walked with me and spoke reassuringly. Hers was the last image I had before the doors opened and I was trundled inside. Then the anesthesiologist went to work.

Where's my rifle?

Panic grips me. The firefight rages. The enemy is close. And I am unarmed. Tracers streak past, machine guns bark. I hear voices in the night.

Where's my M4?

I get on all fours, sweeping my hands along the ground, searching for my weapon. The seconds pass without the feel of it in my gloved grip.

What happened? I have to find my rifle!

Frenzied now, I thrash about in the dark, night vision long gone, the scene strobed by orange muzzle flashes.

"Jay! Jay!"

Erica?

With a jolt, I find myself in post-op, half out of bed with Erica and a nurse trying to restrain me. Doctors and more nurses rush over to help out until I'm surrounded by people. I catch sight of Erica, who looks completely freaked out. I relax slowly, and they ease me back into the bed. Covered in sweat and in pain, confused, and drug-impaired, I lay there dwelling on how vivid and lifelike the nightmare was. The docs explain that this sometimes happens as a reaction to the anesthetic they used. They assure us they won't use that specific one again.

————

Despite the incident in post-op, the surgeries went well. Doc Valaik came in to debrief me on my arm. The damage was far more severe than first thought. I'd been hit by two bullets, one in the lower biceps, the other in the forearm. I'd suffered nerve damage and had no use of my left hand. Part of my humerus bone was gone, including a section of the head that fits into the elbow capsule. My elbow itself was also almost totally destroyed. Doc Valaik told me the team had considered amputation because the wounds were so severe. Ultimately, they decided they could save it.

Thank God.

Doc Valaik told us that he'd been in touch with specialists around the country about my case. He assured us he would do everything he could to repair the arm. Of that, I had no doubt.

I hovered in that space between consciousness and sleep for a long while that night, thinking about everything that had happened. I walked through the firefight, one decision at a time, feeling waves of guilt over the outcome. Had I done everything right? Could I have done something else? I'd posed that question repeatedly to Tony, Brad, and Rob while in Germany. They'd assured me we'd followed our tactics. The enemy simply got the drop on us. Still, on nights like this one, my thoughts wandered between the firefight and the reality I faced now because of it.

I had thought the docs could patch me right up and send me back into the fray. Now I wondered if I would ever look normal again. My right eye didn't even close. Those first weeks home, I literally slept with one eye open. Erica had to put drops in it every few hours for me to keep it from drying out and suffering further damage.

I'll be a scarred human.

Maybe, but I'll be a live one.

For that, I had to be grateful to God and all those who ensured my survival.

That night, I realized I now faced a medical version of BUD/S. To survive it, I had to use the same determination that got me through that ordeal: I would take it one evolution at a time. My face was a mess. My eyes were messed up. I was trached and wired. I was eating through a stomach tube. But if I could get my arm fixed, everything else would fall into place. As long as I had my arms functioning again, I could rejoin the team. My face—well, I didn't need to look like a movie star to be an operator. According to my buddies, I was never that good-looking anyway.

In the days that followed, I could feel my spirits sag. I tried hard to confront each challenge with humor but it all seemed so overwhelming now.

The next week passed in a whirlwind. More tests, more shots. People came and went. Erica was the only constant. The days blended together, each one filled with new challenges, pain, and the constant battle to keep our spirits up.

Music became another weapon with which to combat the medical Groundhog Day. Erica retrieved my iPod and its dock out of my Iraq gear, set it up in the room, and played it nonstop. We owned thousands of songs arranged in dozens of playlists. One by one, those tunes filled the days and nights. They added a meager bit of familiarity to the otherwise foreign world of life in a hospital bed.

One afternoon, two family members came to visit us. Erica took the opportunity to step out and grab lunch for herself. I talked with them for a bit, which quickly fatigued me. I started to drift off before I even realized it. While I was dozing I heard them whispering to each other. I only got fragments of the conversation, but it was enough. They were full of pity for me. Their words had that *woe-is-us* sort of quality that warriors despise. I felt a pulse of rage well up inside of me, but I remained silent. At one point, I ventured a look. They thought I was asleep, and as they whispered, they hovered over the bed, eyes full of sorrow.

As if it isn't hard enough to keep my own spirits up. I have to deal with this?

When Erica returned and my relatives departed, I wrote down all that happened. Recounting it sent me into a fury again. I tore off the sheet of paper and handed it to her. Then I thought for a minute and added:

Never again.

Never again would someone feel sorry for me. I fought for my country, and I'll fight to regain my health so I will ultimately be able to return to our nation's battlefields. I was not here for sympathy. I was here to recover, to be a leader, and to set an example of mental fortitude. It would be all too easy to give into despair, but I refused. There were men and women in this complex who were far more badly wounded than I was. Missing limbs, burned, suffering brain trauma or eyesight loss. I would be grateful for what I had, determined to succeed in the days ahead, and I would use the principles I learned over the last two years to guide me forward.

I wrote a note to all my visitors that I asked Erica to hang up on the door. A day later someone else came into my room and began to feel sorry for me. Obviously they missed the eight-by-eleven piece of white paper on the door. When that person mercifully left me alone, I asked Erica to find some poster paper. She disappeared out into the hallway and returned a few minutes later carrying an eleven-by-seventeen-inch sheet of neon orange paper. With a black Sharpie, I transcribed the note onto it.

ATTENTION
TO ALL WHO ENTER HERE

If you are coming into this room with sorrow or to feel sorry for my wounds, go elsewhere. The wounds I received, I got in a job I love, doing it for people I love, supporting the freedom of a country I deeply love. I am incredibly tough and will make a full recovery. What is full? That is the absolute utmost physically my body has the ability to recover. Then I will push that about 20% further through sheer mental tenacity. This room you are about to enter is a room of fun, optimism and intense rapid re-growth. If you are not prepared for that, go elsewhere.

From: The Management

Chapter 27

Bethesda
Mid-October, 2007

*O*ne evolution at a time.

 I was standing in the hallway beside my door. The bright orange sign hung next to me. A few days ago, a SEAL had pinned his Trident to it. I regarded it for a moment as I readied myself for the next hurdle. Today, I was seeing the kids. I'd been at the hospital a month. Though I had not undergone plastic surgery yet, I couldn't put this reunion off any longer. My heart needed to see them.

 Still, I did not want their first sight of their dad to be one where I was trapped in a hospital bed like an invalid. Every day since the first round of surgeries,

I had tried to do a little bit more. At first, just staying awake took a supreme effort. But gradually, I worked to break free of the bed's grip. Two steps forward, one step back was the routine. But I refused to slow the pace.

Little by little, I regained a measure of mobility. At first, all I could do was sit up in bed. Walking across the room seemed like scaling Everest. But I did it. Since then I'd taken short walks around the hospital, always pulling an IV tree with me for fluids and pain meds. Now I wished the kids would not have to see me attached to that thing, but I had no choice. At least I didn't have the tubes coming out of what was left of my nose.

Though I hadn't had any plastic surgery, the swelling was down and the wounds to my face had been cleaned up and closed by Dr. Lightning Bolt's team. A new round of surgeries on my face would start later in the fall, designed to lay the groundwork for further reconstructive procedures. Eventually, the plastic surgeons would have their turn, but I was resigned to the fact that such steps were at least a year away. I couldn't stay away from the kids for a year. Not after all the other time I'd missed since my Afghanistan deployment.

I took a wobbly step down the hall, right hand holding on to the IV tree with its four wheeled feet. My left arm was in a sling with large black metal rods protruding from my skin screwed into the shattered bones of my arm. It was called an external fixator and was a common sight among wounded warriors hit by high-velocity gunshots or blast injuries.

The kids were with Erica and my mom, waiting for me in a family area farther down the ward. It seemed like miles when every step required such concentrated effort. To stay on my feet, I moved with deliberation, calculating each movement carefully to ensure I didn't lose my balance. A month ago, I was running through the night to take down enemy-held compounds. Now, walking was a challenge.

Life turns on a dime.

If anything, the fragility this gift God gave us has been drilled into me. How could I not have learned that lesson when going to the bathroom alone was a significant victory?

I reached the doorway to the family area and paused a minute to collect myself. I needed this day. I dreaded this day.

Mackenzie didn't even know me when I came home from Afghanistan. What is she going to think now?

I shuffled into the room. Phoenix, Angelica, and Mackenzie were all there with Erica, her dad, Craig, and my mom. As I appeared, they turned to me and stared. I saw Phoenix's and Angelica's dark eyes, large and full of trepidation—they both had Erica's eyes—and Mackenzie's blue eyes brimmed with uncertainty, her face framed by the golden hair she inherited from her mother.

I moved to them, greeting them as warmly as I could manage. Phoenix and Angelica hesitated as they saw my arm, the metal rods, the IV tree, then my face. I paused and held my breath, not wanting to push or spook them. Then, slowly, Phoenix took a step toward me. Angelica followed her big brother. The gulf between us now was only a few feet, but it seemed like I was gazing at my old life, and they were gazing at their new one. The chasm between the two was far greater than the physical space separating us.

Mackenzie broke the spell of that moment. She flew from her mother's arms and careened into me with utter exuberance. Before I could react, she'd already wrapped herself around my leg, hugging me fiercely. I put my good hand on her and pulled her close. A heartbeat later, Phoenix and Angelica joined us. They took care not to bump my left arm or get tangled in my IV lines. Gingerly, we shared our first group hug in months.

Erica had gone out and bought all three of the kids gifts that I could give them. She handed me the bag and

I pulled out a doll baby and doctor's kit for Mackenzie, dolls for Angelica, and a red Nintendo DS for Phoenix.

I handed them out, and their joy lifted my spirits immeasurably. As they played with their new toys, it dawned on me that something significant had just happened. Their uncertainty had been replaced with acceptance that while Daddy may look funny, he was still the same Daddy who loved them and brought them goodies. By the end of our reunion, they had warmed up to me again, and I felt their open and honest love in a way that sustained me through the days that followed.

And tough days they were.

Dr. Lightning Bolt and her OMFS (oral and maxillofacial surgery) team had begun to worry me. While Doc Valaik had been open and inclusive from the outset, we received the opposite treatment from Dr. Lightning Bolt and her staff. Erica and I continued to ask questions, which they either couldn't or didn't want to answer. They continued to dissuade us from consulting with any of the other specialists. In meetings with Dr. Lightning Bolt, Erica and I repeatedly asked when we'd be in touch with the eye specialists, the plastic surgeons, and anyone else needed to reconstruct my face. The bluntness that had been her hallmark faded before those questions. Instead, she grew evasive, which only generated tension between us. The whole thing only served to make Erica and me very suspicious.

Several more surgeries followed that month in order to start that process. To repair my arm and finally close the wounds, the docs told me I needed skin grafts. They took a ten-by-six-inch strip of skin off my thigh using a tiny cheese-grater-like instrument. I woke up in agony, the wound on my thigh from the graft hurting worse than my face and arm. To get the graft site to heal quickly, the medical staff at Bethesda covered it with cheesecloth they stapled to my skin and then put a heat lamp on it. Every little movement made the new growth of skin crack or break, sending waves of pain up my body that the meds did little to diminish.

The days passed at Bethesda with interminable slowness. The routine never changed, just the levels of pain. Erica and I gradually learned which nurses to trust and depend on, and which ones were just punching the clock. I had several fantastic active-duty nurses who went above and beyond to take care of me. The opposite of these top runners were the contract civilians. With few exceptions, they were universally despised by the patients. The Thompson Twins helped guide us through the complexities of the medical system. The process was not a clean one, and it was especially difficult with a complex case like mine. Not only was there no road map for recovery, but there were multiple disciplines working on my care. My body was broken into medical areas of responsibility. Everyone focused on his or her own piece, and some of the departments refused to work with one another.

With the SEAL Team's help, we decided to go outside Bethesda for second opinions related to work on my face. Every wounded warrior had that right, but so often the younger soldiers and marines didn't realize it. They never questioned their care, merely doing what they had been taught to do from day one as young warriors: accept and obey the words of their senior leaders and officers, which is what every doctor was to them. I believe because of this blind acceptance, sometimes their care suffered. I hated seeing that.

Six weeks after I arrived at Bethesda, I was discharged to continue my recovery at home. I knew I would have many more hospital stays before and after surgery in the months ahead, but for now I looked forward to being in my own bed. My jaw was still wired, I had a stomach tube, and the trach tube was still in my throat. At least the trach had been capped. The first day the docs did that, I lasted about forty-five minutes. Breathing through a trach, when it was clean of obstructions, was far easier than breathing through clenched teeth. Those first forty-five minutes felt like I'd run a marathon, each breath becoming increasingly difficult. The next morning, my competitive instinct kicked in, and I vowed to last an hour. I ended up going all day with it capped, which convinced the docs I would be okay at home.

The best part of all that was I no longer needed the notepad. With the trach capped, I could talk again, albeit through a wired jaw. After over a month of writing to communicate basic things, I at last had the ability to speak again. It came as a huge relief.

Those first days at home became surreal blurs. I still couldn't move around much, and after my wounds and all the surgeries, the pain was intense. I spent most of my waking hours either in bed or in a chair propped in front of the television. I wore an eye patch now, so I watched Ohio State football games with my good left eye. The kids wanted to get me a parrot.

Erica was there for me 24/7. She was my best nurse, and at times a saint. She cleaned my wounds and my trach and fed me through the stomach tube. In order to give me my meds, she had to grind them up with a mortar and pestle. She and the kids became the one bright spot I clung to during those difficult months. Mackenzie, who was once so standoffish, grew into a complete daddy's girl. When I lay in bed, she often crawled under the covers to snuggle with me. When I was in the living room in my chair or on the couch, she was never far. She had this innocent acceptance of me and my condition that helped give me strength to deal with it. One night, I sat down to help Phoenix with his homework. As we worked through it together, I noticed he was deep in thought when he suddenly looked up and said, "Dad, you'd be a legend if you'd been blown up and walked away from that."

"Well, you know, buddy, I did get shot up by a machine gun and I managed to walk away from that. A lot of people think that's pretty impressive," I replied.

Phoenix thought this over, then shrugged. "Yeah, maybe. But you'd be a legend if you'd been blown up too."

Wow, tough crowd.

Little by little, I started to feel more like myself. Being home with the family, in their care and love, made all the difference. After losing almost fifty pounds, my weight loss stopped. Though I didn't gain ground, at least it stabilized. Each day, I worked hard to spend more time out of bed and less time in the chair. It took every bit of my will at times to do so, but the self-discipline paid off. In time, I was able to take walks again and even started doing basic exercises.

A few days before we had left Bethesda, an OMFS intern talked to me about the nasal reconstruction process and mentioned a doctor in Chicago who specialized in this complex surgery. His name was Dr. Burget, and he was considered to be one of the world's authorities on complete nasal reconstruction. One Sunday after I was home, I decided I was going to find him and call him. After some Internet research, I found his number and called him at home. He listened as I explained what had happened to me. When I finished, he told me to fly out and see him.

Erica and I booked a flight in mid-November. Bundled up to stay warm, my face partially covered with the eye patch and orange tubes coming out of my nose area for support, we headed to the airport, eager to learn if Dr. Burget could help us.

The airport was a nightmare. I walked slowly through the concourse on unsteady feet, growing increasingly glum and uncomfortable. Throngs of travelers streamed past me, weaving around Erica and me as they hurried on their way. With a start, I realized that I'd been scanning the crowd for threats as my anxiety grew. I later found out this is not uncommon with returning war on terror veterans. Most of us come home to discover we hate being around large groups of people.

That sense of unease was bad enough. But then I saw people staring at me. A furtive glance stolen here and there. Kids bored holes in me with their curious eyes. Others—adults—made no pretense to hide their gaze. These were the people I fought for, the ones I defended when that al-Qaida machine gunner stole my old life. This was one of the first times I'd been outside the cocoon of the military or my house since I'd come home. I was not used to this and had no defense to it.

They think I'm a freak.

My humor vanished. I grew bitter. Who were they to stare? What had they given for their country? I spent most of the trip in silence, pulled totally within myself.

The next day in Chicago, Erica and I met with Dr. Burget. He looked over my nose and studied my patient file and the imagery taken at Bethesda. When finished, he said he could help, but he leveled with me. Complete reconstructions like my nose required were incredibly difficult to perform. Without the cartilage, bone, and skin remaining, I would need more grafts. My body would essentially become a reservoir of spare parts, not just for my nose, but for my face and arm as well. When he finished laying out the complexity of my case, he told me that he and his partner, Dr. Robert Walton, could do the reconstruct together. He would do the external shaping, while Dr. Walton would rebuild the inner structure.

We left Dr. Burget's office to meet with Dr. Walton. As Dr. Walton felt my nose and looked at the CAT scans he commented, "You need to understand, you'll look worse before you look better." Then he assured me, "But you will look better."

It was good to know we had a game plan for my nose now. But we had a long way to go before we could get to that part of the journey. Before the nose reconstruction could begin, the right side of my face had to be reconstructed. Dr. Lightning Bolt had scheduled another surgery for December as part of that process. As I told Dr. Walton about that, and about the misgivings Erica and I had about some of the things we had encountered, he told us about another OMFS surgeon named Dr. Eduardo Rodriguez, who was considered the best in his field. He worked out of Johns Hopkins and Baltimore Shock Trauma. The latter had become nationally known for its pioneering treatment of gunshot wounds. Apparently the inner-city gang wars there had given the specialists a lot of practice.

Later that afternoon, we said good-bye to Dr. Walton and drove to O'Hare International determined to meet with Dr. Rodriguez when we returned home. We talked about it as we made our way through the ticket line, then through security. I was full of hope after what Dr. Burget and Dr. Walton had told us, and my mood showed it. Erica and I laughed and kept things light between discussions about how to move forward.

We finished at the security checkpoint and pulled our shoes back on as people flowed around us. I started to get that uneasy sensation again. My eyes scanned the crowd, watching for any potential threats.

Relax. Not my job right now. Or right here.

I took Erica's hand and together we walked for our departure gate. That's when I saw it happen again. The sidelong looks. The double takes poorly concealed. Surprise and in some cases horror registered on the faces around me.

Into the land of stares and gawks.

I hated this.

One prissy-looking woman striding toward me suddenly looked my way. Her face registered shock and for some reason she didn't tear her eyes away when I locked mine to hers.

Enough. I shouted, "BOO!"

She just about jumped out of her skin. She melted away into the throng, completely undone by that.

Erica was not happy with me. "Jay, was that really necessary?"

"Yes. Yes, it was."

"Let's just go."

Erica was right. I needed to lighten up. The rest of the trip, I attempted to make small talk with those around us, only to discover that most folks assumed I'd been in a car wreck or some sort of accident. We'd been at war for six years, and not a single person considered that these grievous wounds could have been inflicted on the battlefields as we fought to preserve their freedom.

Iraq, Afghanistan—they barely touched those here at home enjoying the prosperity and peace of a successful nation not ravaged by war. This wasn't the full national effort of World War II; the onus of this war fell on the strong but narrow shoulders of the volunteers who chose to defend the nation. And their families. The small talk I tried to make ended up affecting me deeply. What value was the sacrifice so many of my brothers had made if the people for whom they gave their last full measure were not even aware of their devotion? It was a troubling question, one that I dwelled on many times in the months ahead.

After a short stay at home, we went to see Dr. Rodriguez. The minute we entered his office in Baltimore, Erica and I both knew we'd found the right surgeon to work on my face. Lining the shelves in his office were rows of acrylic skulls crafted from the three-dimensional imaging I went through earlier at Bethesda. The skulls lining his walls matched the model I carried with me to discuss my case. From the ones on the shelf behind this surgeon, it was clear he'd dealt with cases at least as difficult as mine.

Dr. Rodriguez explained how he could help. Using bone grafts and microvascular surgical techniques, he would take a long piece of my fibula bone and blood vessels from my leg and use the material to reconstruct my jaw and the damage to the right side of my face. After the surgery, I would need to be immobilized for several days so as to not damage the microvascular stitches connecting the blood vessels in the bone and skin grafts to the surgical site. He had performed this type of procedure many times, including on wounded warriors. He showed me the acrylic skull and photos of a US Army Special Forces veteran whose case was similar to mine. By the time we finished with the consult, Erica and I knew this was the way forward.

We canceled the surgery scheduled with Dr. Lightning Bolt—her OMFS staff could not compete with the experience level of the global specialists we now had on board. Sergeant Major Thompson's warning had served us very well.

Dr. Rodriguez operated on me two days before Christmas. During pre-op, our nurse ran through a series of questions detailing my medical history. I answered each one without hesitating. By this point, I could rattle off my history using medical terms like any four-year medical student and I'd been through this drill so many times now it was almost annoying. I looked for ways to liven it up.

She finished her questions by asking me, "Who's this with you?"

I glanced up at Erica and said, "Dunno. Met her on the way over here. Invited her to come along."

The nurse stared at me, then looked up at Erica, who was feigning annoyance.

"I am his wife," Erica said directly.

"You are?"

"Yes."

The nurse gave me a sour expression, like I was a bad husband and she disapproved. Unfazed, I added, "Did I mention I got shot in the head?"

Erica rolled her eyes and walked out.

Instead of coming out of the surgery and seeing Erica in post-op, the medical team put me in an induced coma for the next seventy-two hours to ensure the microvascular work healed. I lay in stasis throughout Christmas Day. The stress and tension my condition placed on Erica was made worse by the restrictions imposed on visitors and family in a civilian hospital. She'd gotten used to being with me in pre-op and post-op and going to the OR door. Not this time. She saw me for the first time after the surgery in the ICU. Erica missed Christmas with the kids as she stayed by my side, watching over me through every minute of the medically induced coma.

When the docs brought me out of the coma, I couldn't see out of my right eye. The fear of being blinded compounded the pain, most of which radiated from my right eye. It turned out the new orbital floor was placed slightly too high, which put pressure on my already damaged eyeball and muscles. I'd need another surgery to correct that.

One of the bright spots was the bone and skin graft. Doc Rodriguez removed ten inches of my right fibula bone, along with the vascularized skin from my lower leg. He used that material to rebuild the right side of my face, and that part of the surgery was a complete success. Although where he removed the bone was incredibly painful, the graft site from my thigh caused me almost no discomfort. When I awoke in the ICU, I discovered they'd covered the graft site with a material that looked like clear, thick cellophane. Called Tegaderm, it was the latest technological breakthrough in treating burns and grafts. Later, when I talked to Dr. Rodriguez about it and the procedure I had at Bethesda, he shook his head in surprise. The cheesecloth and heat lamp system was years out of date. He hadn't used it in ages. That night, I wondered how many wounded warriors had gone through all that pain because the military medical system hadn't caught up with current medical technology.

The recovery from this surgery was a grueling one. Light made my eyes hurt. I developed migraine headaches that no amount of pain meds could control. Because of the bone graft, I was confined to a wheelchair for eight weeks while my fibula healed. I was unable to go up or down the stairs, which made using the bedroom impossible for me. I watched a lot of football and movies, all the while sinking into a bigger and bigger funk. At some point, I turned on a film called *We Own the Night* about the Russian mafia in 1980s Brooklyn—my kind of action flick. I enjoyed it until Mark Wahlberg's character got shot in the face. The scene made me cringe. But later in the film, after he supposedly recovers, Wahlberg's character looked perfectly normal.

This is the Hollywood version of my wounds?

I stared at Mark's unblemished face. My body's been torn apart—first by the al-Qaida machine gunner, now by surgeons who have scavenged spare parts from my legs to rebuild me. The reality sank in: I would never look normal again. I dwelled and spun further downward, wondering if I'd ever really recover and be able to operate again with my brothers.

As down as I was, God gave me an ace—three really. Mackenzie, Angelica, and Phoenix accepted all these trials in stride. They became my saving grace. As I struggled, they adapted and showed me the way. As I plunged deeper into this sense of hopelessness, they had abiding faith. One evening, Mackenzie decided to play doctor in the living room beside my recliner while Angelica watched television nearby. Mackenzie pulled out a variety of toy medical devices and began arranging them as I looked on, trying not to laugh. Then she stood up and gave me a thermometer.

"Daddy, need take your temp'ature."

"Aahhhhh," I said through clenched teeth, pretending to open my mouth. She held it up to my lips and still-wired jaw and left it there for a bit. When she finished, she took the thermometer and regarded it solemnly.

I asked, "Am I sick, Doctor?"

Angelica, who hadn't said a word, chimed in, "No, silly, you just got shot."

The laughter felt cathartic. Whatever the future looked like, I would never take a minute with them for granted again.

Chapter 28

Virginia Beach
January 2008

I n January, Erica and I discovered that our sign on the
door at Bethesda had gone viral. A friend called to
tell us that a former undersecretary of defense had written an article about the sign and my wounds on his blog.
The news dumbfounded the both of us. I'd written it
in a moment of resolve and pain to set the ground rules
for those who passed through the revolving door to my
Bethesda hospital room during those first crazy weeks of
my recovery. How it got picked up and spread across the
Net was something that took some digging to uncover.

The previous October, one of the many visitors we
had at Bethesda was the father of a firefighter and

police officer killed in New York after the 9/11 attacks. John Vigiano was a former marine who'd been a legendary firefighter himself. Since the war began he had made a point of visiting wounded warriors whenever he had the opportunity. During a trip down to Maryland, he read the sign on my door and wanted to meet its author. He came in with all the positive energy Erica and I hoped we'd see from our guests, and his visit lifted my spirits. I could tell right away we were destined to be good friends, and we remained in touch after he left.

When he returned home, he wrote about Erica and me on his blog and posted a photograph of our sign. Once up, it was posted and reposted far and wide without either Erica or me having a clue. I'd put it on the door as my mission statement. It was also a warning, though. I refused to deal with pity or sadness or sympathy. People wanted to make a big deal out of the sign and the person who wrote it. The truth was, almost all wounded warriors had this same attitude; I just captured it in writing.

One night, I pulled out my laptop to conduct a Google search. Hundreds of pages came up in response. The sign was mentioned on chat boards, on wounded warrior sites, milblogs, and by the media. In most of them, I was known only as "LT J" the SEAL. The outpouring of support astonished me, and I shared some of the sites with Erica. As we read them together, scenes at the airport and elsewhere around town when people would gawk and stare popped into my mind. I think I'd lost a little faith that anyone cared about America's warriors after those encounters. Now, as I read the outpourings of support online, I couldn't help but reevaluate those thoughts. It felt like a restoration of faith.

As I continued my recovery from the December surgery, Erica and I went to see Dr. Valaik at Bethesda. He greeted us warmly and took us into his office.

"I think we've gone as far as we can for you, Jay," he said. "I could try to do more, but I believe there are better doctors out there who can take you further than I can. I've been contacting specialists around the country about your arm, and I think there is one who might be able to help you."

Dr. Valaik had displayed the highest level of professional integrity. While many doctors would have continued to handle my case themselves, he was more concerned with my care and final results than with his own pride. He was humble enough to recognize there might be another doctor who could get me a better outcome. If only more doctors could reach this level, the system would not be so difficult to negotiate.

Dr. Valaik's former mentor, Dr. Andy Eglseder, was at Baltimore Shock Trauma as well. What a blessing this proved to be. I had another surgery on my face scheduled there for March, and if we could double stack it with one on my arm, it would get me back to the teams that much quicker.

Dr. Eglseder met with us at the end of January. After a thorough examination, he gave us his brutally honest opinion.

"Look, your arm is a wreck. It is already fused in place with a tremendous amount of bone growth, and that will make things far more difficult for us."

The biggest issue, he explained, was the elbow capsule. It was so damaged that every doc who saw my x-rays wondered how my elbow didn't dislocate all the time. Knee replacements were common these days, but nobody had perfected an artificial elbow joint that could survive real-world use, especially in a young, active patient. Repairing the elbow capsule would be the only recourse for me until that technology advanced.

The doctors we had met with before were usually willing to try to help until they saw my x-rays. Once that lighted screen flicked on and they saw the damage, they told me glumly there was nothing they could do. But this time, Dr. Eglseder gave us some hope. "There are no guarantees here, but I think we can improve your range of motion. Worst case, we re-fuse your arm and you're back where you are now."

He asked me a series of questions, culminating with, "Right now, what do you wear in bed, when you are sleeping?"

I knew he meant what sort of arm brace I was using.

"A pink bunny costume."

His nurse broke out laughing. Dr. E. blinked, his expression inscrutible. Not even a smile cracked his face.

Wow. Tough crowd.

Sense of humor or not, Dr. E. offered me the best chance of getting back to operational status. Erica and I talked it over briefly, then told him we were in, all the way. As we left Baltimore, I silently thanked Dr. Valaik for opening this door for me.

The next few weeks saw us travel up to Baltimore from Virginia Beach for the presurgical workups with both Dr. E. and Dr. Rodriguez. Each time Erica and I drove up there, the team sent one of the new guys to escort us. It was part of Naval Special Warfare's commitment to taking care of its wounded warriors, and the additional help was much appreciated.

During one of the appointments with Dr. Rodriguez, we had a Thor-sized new guy named Jim with us as our escort. The exam room was so tiny that the only place for Jim to stand was beside the door. When Dr. Rodriguez entered, he opened the door almost into Jim's face. As he greeted us, he seemed to sense a presence behind him. Glancing around the door, he saw Jim and froze.

"Who are you?" the doc asked.

"I'm Jay's bodyguard and the care better be good!" Jim replied in a deep baritone voice.

The doc looked over at me, then back to Jim.

"Better not make any mistakes, Doc," Jim intoned.

Erica and I started laughing. Doctor R. relaxed as he realized it was a joke. A moment later, he joined in.

Such lighthearted moments helped us deal with the heavy grind of what was really going on here. Little by little, modern medicine was putting me back together. That process taxed every emotion and tested every bit of our resolve, patience, and endurance. There were times of despair, times of hope, times of extreme frustration. The humor kept us centered on an even keel and gave our spirits a needed boost.

We needed every funny moment we could create when I returned for the double-stack surgeries at Baltimore Shock Trauma in March. As I checked into the hospital prior to the procedures, the intake nurse asked me, "What happened to you?"

"I got shot."

She seemed unsurprised. "Oh? What gang were you with?"

Did she really just ask me that?

"Um, do I look like I am in a gang?" I asked.

She glanced up at me. "I dunno."

"I got shot overseas defending the freedom of gang-bangers to shoot one another all they want here at home."

She had no response to that.

Later, as I was being prepped for surgery, another nurse went over my medical history with me. By now, I knew the answers before they even asked the questions.

Gesturing to Erica, the nurse asked, "And who is this? Your girlfriend? Wife?"

I looked up at my bride and said, "I found her on the street corner last night. Great night. Can she come to the surgery with me?"

The nurse's jaw dropped. She searched for a response, but nothing came out.

Erica, mock annoyance in her voice, said to me, "What is wrong with you? Why do you always do this?"

It had sort of become our thing. I'd done this before every surgery.

The nurse just stared.

"Oh, yeah! I'm married to you!" Erica said.

Without another word, the nurse shook her head and returned to her paperwork.

Dr. E. and his team used some of the HO growth in my arm as reconstruction material for my elbow. They rebuilt the capsule area as best they could, then Dr. Rodriguez and his team took over for the second half of this double stack. They realigned my jaw, reconstructed my eye orbit, and shifted the position of the orbital floor to relieve the pain I was in after the Christmas surgery.

The operations succeeded beyond all expectations. With intensive physical therapy I was told I would begin to get motion back in my arm. The pain in my eye gradually receded, though I would need further surgery on it later in the spring. The greatest part was that Dr. Rodriguez was happy with the progress of my jaw and removed the trach. I had worn it for seven months and two days.

To return to the teams, I needed a fuller range of movement with my lower arm. Despite all the progress, I still had a critical blind spot—at least critical for operating in the field. I couldn't bend my elbow enough to touch my own face, nor could I touch anywhere from the top of my head to my stomach. If this doesn't make sense, hold your arm at a ninety-degree bend in front of you and you will quickly see that without the ability to bend your elbow beyond ninety degrees it is very difficult to touch or grab things in the center of your body or face. This meant in a firefight, I wouldn't be able to pull magazines out of my gear or manipulate weapons with my left hand. I needed just ten degrees more movement for me to pull my arm to my body. Searching for that ten became my obsession.

That spring, my life settled into a constant series of medical appointments and physical therapy. One after another, they all blended together. The visits to Portsmouth and Bethesda comforted me in some ways since I was back within the military community. Out in the civilian facilities, I was the disfigured guy with the eye patch and messed-up arm, not a wounded warrior. No special treatment there. Though sometimes bitterness got the better of me, I tried to use humor as a defense as much as I could.

In one doctor's office that spring, I sat waiting for my name to be called while a little girl stared at me from across the room. She didn't look away when I faced her. Instead, she grew more curious.

Part of me flared at first. Then I calmed down.

She's only a kid.

"Hi," I said.

Her mother's face was set in stone, and she consciously refused to look at me.

The little girl piped up, "Hiya! Are you a pirate?"

"Why, yes, I am!"

She regarded me suspiciously.

"If you're a pirate, where's your crew?"

Good one.

"I left them at the ship," I said.

She seemed to accept that.

"What's the name of your ship?" she asked.

"The Black Pearl."

"What happened to your face?"

"Bad guys shot me in the face," I replied.

She looked me over for a minute and then said, "They got you in the arm with a sword, didn't they?"

"Yes. Yes, they did."

The two of us laughed heartily while her mother resolutely ignored us.

Later that spring, Erica and I went out to eat at a local Outback Steakhouse to celebrate the unwiring of my jaw. It had been almost seven months since I'd been able to chew food. I was still underweight and confined to a wheelchair because of the grafts, but we both needed a night out. In this journey, we didn't miss a reason to celebrate.

We sat and talked, just like old times. The kids, the future, the stuff we'd been through—it all flowed as we enjoyed our night out. Erica had a couple glasses of wine, which lightened the mood even more. After months of eating through straws and tubes, I didn't want to push my stomach too far, though my brain craved a massive, juicy steak. I ended up playing it safe and ordered clam chowder. As we ate, I started to feel fatigued and queasy. My energy and endurance needed some serious work. But I knew they'd return as I continued to heal.

We finished up, and Erica pushed my wheelchair to the parking lot. Suddenly, she happily started spinning me in circles, and we were laughing like two kids again. At least, we were until I threw up all the clam chowder. That sort of ruined the moment. Erica felt worse than I did. She apologized over and over as I voided my stomach right there in the parking lot until nothing was left of my first meal.

One step forward . . .

I flew to Chicago almost once a month now in preparation for my first surgery with Dr. Walton, which he'd scheduled for July. The airports and their crowds continued to be a torment. Little kids pointed at me and called to their mothers to look at me too. People refused to talk to me. They'd act ashamed or embarrassed, or they set expressions of pity on their faces.

Internally, I raged at them.

And these are the people I sacrificed for?

Coming back from Chicago on one trip, I just broke. Everyone who stared at me I treated to a sudden "BOO!" By the end of the trip, though, I realized I needed to do something different, or the bitterness would eat me alive.

I gave it some thought, then came up with an idea. I went online and designed a couple of T-shirts. The first said: STOP STARING, I GOT SHOT BY A MACHINE GUN. IT WOULD HAVE KILLED YOU. I put an American flag on the back and called it Wounded Wear. I sported it on my next Chicago airport run, wanting people to know that I was no pity case. I was a warrior who sacrificed for their freedom.

Amazingly, it worked. Through life, we all encounter embittering moments. Most of the time, we have no control of these, which is one of the reasons they cause such soul damage. But how we handle the bitterness is up to us. For too long that spring, I let it eat away at the good parts of me. The T-shirt offered a new avenue to release it that was constructive.

I felt so much better when we returned home that I decided to print a few more. One said, SHOT FOR YOUR FREEDOM. JUST SAY THANK YOU. Once again, I put the American flag and Wounded Wear on the back. One day, I put it on and went down to visit with the team, and a friend commented on it.

"That's an awesome idea. You should do something with that."

I began to think about it and realized there were probably a lot of wounded warriors who have felt this way in public. I talked to Erica about starting a nonprofit organization that would give these shirts to wounded warriors to help them rediscover the hero within, while raising national awareness of the sacrifice they had made for freedom. We loved the idea, and together, we started Wounded Wear in February of 2009. It gave us something positive to focus our energy on during my recovery.

At the same time, I took the first cautious steps toward integrating back into civilian society. I started to make grocery store runs and handled small errands. It helped to be out of the wheelchair at last, which I'd been confined to for months. That was huge progress for me, and regaining that mobility boosted my morale immeasurably. Still, I knew it would always be tough for me to be around crowds.

The pain from the skin and bone grafts eventually subsided. I detoxed off the pain meds earlier in the spring—no easy task. Withdrawal was an absolutely hellish experience. But I got through it, and I was feeling very good about my progress. I could see the goal line of full duty ahead. I'd blast through every obstacle to cross it and recapture my old life anew.

Chapter 29

The White House
October 18, 2008

I'd prepped Phoenix for this moment for weeks, teaching him how to shake hands properly. Firm grip, make eye contact. Nine years old, Phoenix would meet the president and greet him like a man.

Now we walked into a small staff room located next to the Oval Office, and the experience was almost as surreal as combat. The walls. The carpet. The deep sense of history. As Americans, we've seen the inside of this place in countless movies and television shows. But only a very few get to actually be inside it.

Lieutenant Commander Hale Michaels came up to us outside the Oval Office. After our deployment, Hale was selected to be a White House fellow. He greeted Erica and me warmly. For a moment, we talked shop, catching up on who was doing what, and what was going on back at the teams. A year ago, I was trying to win Hale over. Now I was joking with him before we met the president. The world turned on a dime.

Hale saw I had brought my sign on the door and he offered to take it into the office for me. I handed it to him, as a White House aide appeared to ask if we were ready to step into the Oval Office. We were seconds from meeting the president. Erica held my hand. The kids hung close, more than a little taken by their surroundings. They remained on their best behavior though, and I couldn't have been more proud of them.

The aide led us into a hallway, then through a door into the Oval Office. As we entered it, President George W. Bush came out from behind the Resolute desk and walked over to welcome us. The room exuded grandness and power, but the man who occupied the office was down-to-earth and accessible.

Chatting away amiably, President Bush introduced himself to my family with genuine warmth. I watched Phoenix like a hawk as he shook the president's hand and felt a surge of pride as he did so just as I taught him. The girls, young as they were, didn't grasp the magnitude of the moment. They'd been given little goodie

bags by the White House staff. They were full of pic-
tures, M&Ms, and kaleidoscopes, and they promptly
sat down on the Presidential seal embroidered in the
carpet to explore the contents.

"I heard about your sign on the door," the president
said to me as we shook hands.

Hale Michaels stepped forward and produced the
sign.

"Mr. President, I would be honored if you would sign
it," I said. "I want it to be hung in the wounded ward
at Bethesda to motivate and inspire other wounded
warriors."

"Of course," he said.

An aide handed him a pen, and he signed it. As I
watched him, movement at the edge of my eye line distracted me. I glanced over to see the girls had dumped
their goodie bags out on the floor right atop the seal.
Part of me just slow rolled in parental anguish.

*My girls are playing on the Presidential seal in the
Oval Office.*

President Bush finished autographing the sign.
When he handed it back, he saw the girls. My heart just
about stopped. But then, a wide, warm grin crossed his
face and for a moment, we all watched my two little
towheads play innocently at the center of American
power.

At length, the president asked me about my wounds. I explained to him what had happened in the firefight before telling him a little bit about my recovery.

I was scheduled for more reconstructive surgeries through the fall and spring of 2009. My arm still did not have the range of motion I needed to rejoin the teams. Erica and I were searching for another specialist who could give me those precious ten extra degrees of movement. It would happen, I was confident of that.

Hale stepped in at that point and related to President Bush several of our other combat missions, including the big June firefight. When he talked of the eleven women and children we got off target safely, the president looked me in the eyes and said, "Thank you for you and your team doing that, Jay."

I admired President Bush. The press had made him out to be a mental lightweight, but one minute with the man and you knew he possessed a powerful intellect. Charismatic, genuine, and good-humored, he did not act like a man with the weight of the world on his shoulders. Our visit came in the middle of a developing financial crisis here at home, and yet he seemed relaxed and unhurried with us.

So many leaders follow the polls. They twist in the political winds and shift their positions to mirror the majority view of their constituency merely for the purpose of retaining votes and staying in power. I admired President Bush because he bucked that trend. He followed his convictions, had done what he believed was right for the future of our great nation. History will be the judge of that.

The previous month, I'd met Karl Rove at a dinner in DC. He had arranged this visit and meeting for us. I was here with one purpose: to ask the president to personally award the Silver Star to Al and Rob. The Silver Star was America's third-highest medal for valor in combat. Both were to receive it for their actions on September 13, 2007. I owed my life to Al.

I asked the president if he would present the Silver Stars to my brothers.

"If my schedule permits, I would be honored to do that," he replied.

My family spent thirty-five minutes in the Oval Office with our president. Never once did he look at his watch.

One of his aides entered the Oval Office and said, "Mr. President, it's time to go."

Erica and I told the girls to pack up. Angelica suddenly stood up and marched over to President Bush. She violated all sense of personal space. In fact, if she had gotten any closer to the president, she would have been standing on top of his shoes.

She held her bag up to him and calmly said, "There's no kaleidoscope in my bag."

George W. Bush looked my daughter in the eye and replied, "Well, we will have to rectify that immediately."

He glanced up at an aide, who vanished through a door. In seconds, my daughter was holding her own White House kaleidoscope. Seriously, it could not have happened faster if ninjas had dropped out of the ceiling to deliver one to her.

We walked with him to the White House lawn, where *Marine One* was waiting to whisk him away to his next appointment. Before we said good-bye, he gave me two presidential coins and a pair of White House cuff links. Later, I gave one of the coins to Al.

Meeting the president was one of the inspirational moments of my life. It came at a time when my recovery had hit several roadblocks, and I needed all the inspiration possible to keep pushing forward.

Fortunately, inspiration abounded all around me. The kids and Erica were constant sources. At times, when all I wanted to do was lie in bed, or stay indoors away from people, I saw them and I knew I needed to be their example. I did not ever want to fail them. Once I was a here-and-gone-again father who parachuted in and out of their lives as my career required. Now, aside from the trips to Chicago and Baltimore, I had been home more the past year than any other time since I had graduated from college.

Throughout my stays at Bethesda and in the other hospitals, I had done my best to set the example for other wounded warriors. No pity parties, no moments of doubt: just a relentlessly optimistic focus on driving through to a full recovery. In truth, I had many moments of doubt. At times, I despaired that there was no end in sight to the healing process. Whenever those dark feelings assailed me, I dealt with them alone or away from the hospital. I had to be the example, to lead always, or I would not make it through this nightmare. Well, that's what I thought anyway. Then I went to Mike Monsoor's Medal of Honor ceremony at the White House that April. Mike was a fellow SEAL who had jumped on a hand grenade thrown onto a rooftop he and two teammates were on during a firefight in Ramadi. He shielded his brothers with his own body and paid the ultimate price for that devotion.

It was deeply moving to be there to see Mike's family receive his posthumous Medal of Honor. But while I was there, I met another SEAL named Ryan Job. He'd been a part of Team Three and had served with legendary sniper Chris Kyle in Iraq during the 2006 campaign. Ryan had been a Mark 48 machine gunner for the team, and during a firefight that spring, a bullet had struck his weapon, then hit him in the face, destroying his right eye. He survived and reached Bethesda much as I would a year later, but nerve damage cost him his vision in his left eye. The prospect of spending the rest of his life blind had to have been terrifying, though he never showed it. Instead, he announced that if he had to be blind, he would be the "best damn blind man there was."

Between surgeries to reconstruct his face, Ryan squeezed more out of life than just about anyone I'd ever met. He learned to hunt again and shot an elk. He hiked. He climbed. He finished his bachelor's degree (he'd dropped out of the University of Washington after three years to join the navy) and landed a good job at General Dynamics.

After the ceremony, there was a reception at the White House. Ryan and I got to know each other a bit. We discussed our wounds and surgery stories. He'd gone through much of the reconstructive work I still had ahead, and he gave me insight into the road I had yet to travel.

After the ceremony I climbed back aboard the bus and ended up sitting next to Ryan and his lovely wife, Kelly. Kelly had been one of Ryan's nurses and his amazingly positive attitude and sense of humor won her over. They married shortly after Ryan retired, and together they moved out to Phoenix, Arizona. Ryan had a beautiful Seeing Eye dog, a black female rottweiler. Erica and I had a rottweiler also, Athena, whom I had bought years ago to protect the house when I was gone. Ryan and I talked about our dogs and joked about being fellow slow movers. When the bus finally arrived back at the hotel, I knew I had a new friend I could share information with that most of my friends could never relate to. We exchanged numbers and agreed to stay in touch.

Ryan and I bumped into each other on multiple occasions over the next several months. On one of the occasions, Ryan had come out to the East Coast SEAL Teams for a wounded warrior benevolent organization conference. Multiple nonprofit organizations were on hand to offer their support to the SEAL Teams and explain what they had to offer. Ryan and I hung out for the majority of the day and later that evening headed to a reception with all the organizations and the SEAL admiral. As we made small talk and met different people, I, Ryan, and another SEAL who had been shot in the eye were joking around and came up with the idea for a club for SEALs who had been shot in the head. It was a very small club. We decided to call the club S.H.I.T.h.— SEALs Hit in the Head. We then unanimously voted on our motto: THIS CLUB SUCKS!

We laughed our asses off and enjoyed being able to share our unique experiences.

Ryan's full-scale desire to live so fully served as inspiration for me.

Inspiration came from other sources as well. After our White House visit, I had the Sign on the Door framed with motivational words and returned it to Bethesda, where it was dedicated in a ceremony and hung on the wall on the fifth floor. It still hangs there to this day. Wounded warriors read it as they arrive at Bethesda to begin their own journeys, and even today some seek me out to thank me. The notes they have sent I value a great deal. They remind me that though I may be out of action, I can still have a positive impact on the lives of our warriors.

In the months that followed, I knew I was in for the long game. The slog through surgeries and setbacks continued. Doctors Walton and Burget worked to reconstruct my nose. But with each measure of progress, I took big hits as infections set in and destroyed much of the work they'd done. Each reconstructive surgery required at least one graft. By the summer of 2009, I was starting to run low on available patches of skin. My body was roped with scars from surgical sites and over a dozen grafts. Part of the problem was that

I had a number of tattoos on areas of my body that would otherwise be prime graft sites. Nobody ever thinks about skin grafts when they get inked, but for warriors it is a concern, especially with the men and women who suffer burns in vehicular explosions.

As we faced the setbacks, the bureaucracy surrounding my care and its cost never failed to wreak havoc. At times, dealing with the paperwork and logistics zoomed from the frustrating to the sublime. The low point came when I received a letter from Tricare, the military's insurance provider, informing me that since I was involved in a "third party accident," they were entitled to recoup three hundred and fourteen dollars from the third party for a CAT scan I had received, and the letter asked me to identify whom the third party was.

My surgeries total almost a million and a half dollars, and Tricare wants three hundred and fourteen bucks?

I sat down in front of our computer and relished my reply.

To whom it may concern:
In response to your "Mandatory Third Party Liability" letter. Due to the nature of Naval Special Warfare operations and under the directive of the Special Operations Command in accordance with direction by the Joint Chiefs of Staff and the

Secretary of Defense I cannot divulge the names of the Al QAIDA in Iraq individuals who were directly responsible for my injuries because that information is classified. I will admit that the individuals directly responsible would have a hard time paying or being contacted due to being blown into thousands of small pieces from the multiple fire missions my team called in upon them after my injuries. Probably of little importance though; after five months of combat operations and dealing with these individuals I am of the opinion they probably do not have insurance. This is unfortunate though because I would like to seek punitive damages. The only good Point of Contact I have for the AL QAIDA organization is a man that went by the name of Osama Bin Laden. He is credited as the head of said organization. If you could contact him you may be able to recover the $314.00 you would not pay. Would you please inform him when you speak to him, there are thousands of civilians and military members waiting to seek punitive damages against him. Additionally, if you could carbon copy the entire United States Government as to his location, it would be greatly appreciated. You may not know, but we have been looking for him for the past seven years.

I would have paid serious cash money to watch a videotape of the insurance adjuster who first read that letter.

Two months later, we got another third party liability letter identical to the first one, making the same demand. Apparently, they didn't have any luck finding Osama Bin Laden. He never did pay that $314.

Every month or two, I still flew to Chicago. Either we were working up for the next surgery, or I was getting examined post-op. The grind wore both Erica and me down, and the setbacks seemed ever sharper and more disheartening. One of the worst moments came after Dr. Walton took skin from my right forearm to continue the reconstruction of my nose. Right away, I developed another infection. Every effort was made to save the tissue, but in the end, Doc Walton had to cut it all out. Once again, I was left with a hole in my face. The failure devastated me. Worse, I knew that we didn't have many more attempts left. Every failure made a good outcome less likely, and the places from which skin could be taken from my body for the grafts were fewer and fewer. Still, there was only one way to go. Forward.

Chapter 30

My nose was infected again, and Ryan Job was dead.

I was in Chicago, alone. Erica had remained at home— the one time she didn't come with me on one of these trips. Right then, I needed her strength and optimism more than ever to sustain me. The latest surgery here in Chicago to reconstruct my nose seemed to be a success at first. Then I had flown home and started to suspect something was wrong. The reconstructed area had grown tender and red. It had started to ooze and smell as if it were infected. So I had returned to Chicago to have Dr. Burget check me over to make sure I was okay.

He gave me a quick examination and told me not to worry. "Go home, let the infection run its course."

My gut had screamed this was more serious than that. I had taken a cab back to O'Hare, but once I arrived there, I had phoned Erica and explained the situation. She had convinced me to call Doc Walton. He told me to come see him immediately so I jumped into another cab over to his office, where he swabbed the reconstruction site. I had three simultaneous infections, including staph. They'd already done damage, and part of the cartilage had grown spongy. Doc Walton had sent me straight from his office to the hospital, which was where I was when the news about Ryan Job had reached me.

The next day, I was scheduled to have surgery to install an antibiotic IV drip into my nose. For eleven days, I would have to lie as still as possible and pray for the best. If I lost this battle, I didn't know where they would get skin and cartilage from me for the next attempt. Due to the scarcity of available spare parts, I was approaching the end game of the reconstruction effort.

My room overlooked Lake Michigan, and I spent that day staring out the window at the people on the beach and the runners on the boardwalk. Someday I vowed I would be back in full health and I would run there too.

What I'd give to be out there right now.

How would this all end? The outcome seemed so uncertain. Would I ever look close to normal again?

My bleak mood drove me to thoughts of Ryan Job. My warrior brother whose spirit inspired me and countless others had gone in for another round of facial reconstruction surgery at a Phoenix hospital. He made it through the surgery just fine. In post-op, a nurse accidentally gave him ten times the amount of morphine he was supposed to have. The man who survived losing an eye in Iraq and countless surgeries on his road to recovery ended up being killed by a careless civilian nurse. To come that far and die that way was the cruelest of fates. It reminded me that every day was a gift. All wounded warriors spend hours under surgeons' knives in risky procedures. One slip, one careless act, and our lives can be taken away in a heartbeat. We lived on the razor's edge in Iraq. Here at home, we live and die by the surgeon's scalpel.

It was almost too much to bear.

I hadn't known Ryan incredibly well. I wouldn't call him a close friend. We talked on the phone occasionally. We shared a common experience and discussed our notes on recovery, and we shared a twisted sense of humor. But above all, I respected his spirit and relentless energy to recapture all he could out of life. He made the most of every moment and achieved things that most people with their eyesight intact never would.

In 2008, he climbed Mount Rainier. When I heard about that I was blown away. In the climbing community, the fourteen-thousand-foot volcanic mountain in Washington State is considered one of the most difficult to summit in all North America. It has deadly crevices, narrow ledges, and glacial ice. It is as technical a climb as you can find. Mount Rainier claims on average three lives a year of those who aspire to its summit. And Ryan made it to the top two years after that bullet robbed him of his vision.

He and Kelly were getting ready to have a daughter together. Ryan had started a new life, found a fresh path to blaze, and had built something from the ruins. He really was being "the best damn blind man out there." Then, with the snap of the cosmic fingers, it was all stolen from him.

I watched the spring afternoon on Lake Michigan. Sailboats tacked and jibed. People played onshore or just lounged in the warm sun's rays. And I was here, wondering if Ryan's fate could be my own.

In two and a half years, I'd had over thirty surgeries. There had been mistakes made, but none of them crippling or fatal. I'd seen them as setbacks and driven on without a second thought. Now I wondered what percentages I was playing. The risk of something going wrong with general anesthesia was cumulative. The more you have, the more chances increased that you would have a reaction to it at some point. I'd been under for well over a hundred and fifty hours already, with more to come. Who was to say that my next surgery wouldn't end with me flatlining on the table as the surgical team struggled vainly to revive me?

Who's to say the next infection wouldn't spread? Staph infections kill people all the time. I had one now, and I'd been concerned for my reconstructed nose. But what if?

What if I never saw my children again? After coming home through the fires of Iraq, how would they go forward if I left them now after all they had given to me?

I closed my eyes and tried to relax. I missed Erica. She was my rock. I would never make it through this without her.

The surgery didn't kill me, but the recovery was the worst yet. I spent the next eleven days in the hospital with an IV antibiotic drip in my nose. I could barely move, and my spirits plummeted. Fortunately, a group of Chicago firefighters and police officers took it upon themselves to boost my morale. They brought me movies to watch and books to read. After I went through the procedure, they even busted me out for a quick drink at a local watering hole—just like when I busted Jeff out of Bethesda. That earned Dr. Walton's wrath, but it was worth it. I was going stir-crazy.

The stay in the hospital saved most of my reconstructed nose. I would need more cartilage, which Doc Walton decided to take from behind my ear. The skin needed would have to come from my left damaged arm; there was just no other place to get it.

I had a falling-out with Dr. Burget and decided to have Dr. Walton finish the work alone. After the next reconstructive surgery, with the recommendation of a navy diver friend, I underwent hyperbaric treatments at Norfolk Naval Shipyard. The pure oxygen atmosphere helped ensure that this time, infection did not set in. The *Acinetobacter* bacteria I was exposed to in Iraq had probably been the root of my other infection issues. It made wounded soldiers more prone to other kinds of bacterial attack for years after they contracted it.

The hyperbaric treatments succeeded completely. By late summer 2010, I felt like we'd finally made it over the hump. In the months that followed, I underwent a number of procedures to sculpt the nose and finish the cosmetic aspects of the reconstruction. In 2011, a navy plastic surgeon completed the work.

After thirty-seven surgeries, I looked in the mirror and saw the new me. Four years of staring at the face of a stranger and now I couldn't believe how good I looked. I'd never be "normal," like Mark Wahlberg was at the end of that movie. I would always be "scarred so that others may live free," but I could not have been more pleased with what these many talented docs had done for me. My recovery and new look was nothing short of miraculous.

My last step back to the SEAL Teams was to find another surgeon who could give me a few more degrees of movement in my left arm. I scoured the country in search of that surgeon. I met many orthopedic specialists and, at first, they offered hope. Then, as before, they looked at my x-rays and to a man, they shook their heads sadly and said they were astonished I had the range of motion that I did have.

Finally, I found a surgeon in Florida who worked with professional athletes. He saw my x-rays and didn't flinch. He told me he could restore the range of movement I needed to return to operational status. I kept searching for a second second opinion, hoping to find somebody who thought the Florida doc could do me good. Finally, I ended up in the office of an orthopedic surgeon at Duke University who was considered to be one of the best arm and elbow specialists in the country. He reviewed my case and listened to what the other doc in Florida said he could do with another surgical attempt.

"Jay, I am going to be frank with you. If you were my son, I wouldn't let you do this. What you have now is the best possible outcome. If you proceed and have another surgery, you'll probably lose some of the range of motion you have now. Worse, you'll set yourself up for a lifetime of chronic pain."

The drive home was a quiet one for me as I deliberated whether or not to roll the dice one last time. By the time I turned off the freeway for Virginia Beach, I knew it was not worth the risk. My days as an operator were over.

Part of me always suspected this might happen; now it was confirmed. I had no epiphanies during that drive about what to do now as that dream to kick in doors again slipped away. What would I do? How would I support my family? I didn't have any answers. But I knew one thing: I'd live as Ryan Job had, honor his memory, and never take another day for granted.

Later that summer of 2010, I received an invitation from a fantastic nonprofit organization called Camp Patriot. Camp Patriot took wounded warriors on outdoor adventures. They had taken Ryan Job up Mount Rainier and invited me to climb it in his honor. I'd just undergone another surgery, and I was not in anywhere near the physical shape I used to be in. In fact, I was not sure I was in any kind of shape to scale a fourteen-thousand-foot volcano. Didn't matter. Ryan did it blind. I would find a path to the top too.

I kissed Erica and the kids good-bye and flew west to meet the team. They were all wounded warriors like me who had gathered to pay homage to our fallen brother and his indefatigable spirit. Kevin Ivory was a marine corpsman who was wounded in an IED blast. Despite being hit in the leg and knee, he rushed to save a fellow marine. He passed out from blood loss as he did so. Samuel Bryant, a fellow SEAL, was hit in the head with grenade shrapnel in Iraq. He suffered from frequent headaches and memory loss. He had to learn to talk again, a process that took over a year. The last member of our team was Chief Dave Michaels, the SEAL who after being hit twenty-seven times still overcame the enemy and walked to the medevac helo. I was honored to be climbing with him.

Dave was quite the character, loud and boisterous and full of energy. During one television interview before the climb, a reporter asked me how I ended up as part of the team.

Dave, a few steps behind me off camera, blurted out, "It's because he got shot in the fucking FACE!" The reporter cringed as the rest of us burst out laughing.

I kidded Dave later that he had lost his personal filter in that firefight.

We began our ascent across the snowfields toward base camp. With a measured pace, it could be done in less than a day. The climb was long but the technical parts didn't begin until we got above our base camp. Early on, I felt the strain already. I had arrived in Washington with a cold. The exertion took its toll on me. The germs set in and with my resistance down, I developed a full-blown case of bronchitis.

As dusk approached, we closed on the base camp that would serve as our launch point for the final climb to the summit. When we paused for a break, I looked out over a vista like none I had ever seen. We were above the clouds, the Cascade Mountains stretched to the north and south—all the peaks below us. The sun falling on the western horizon cast a crimson glow across the scene. God's grace is always evident if you're willing to look.

By the time we reached base camp, I was utterly spent. I flopped down in my tent and fell into a deep sleep. We spent the next day at camp to get acclimated for the journey ahead. We were already at eleven thousand feet there, only three thousand more to go. But the bronchitis was kicking my teeth in. I couldn't stop coughing, and by late morning I was hacking up bloody chunks of mucus.

Ryan's death reminded me nothing is guaranteed in life. It can be taken away in a heartbeat. The life you've built with everything you've got can come apart in an instant from circumstances far beyond your control. You either adapt and overcome, or you become a casualty of those twists of fate.

I refused to be a casualty.

Several of the guides questioned if I could make it to the top. I told them where to go. There was no way I would come this far only to give up and let Ryan down now. I would have rather died than not summit in his honor. I just needed to tap those reservoirs of strength that had carried me through my own life's many challenges. Boot camp. BUD/S. Overcoming my own immaturity and mistakes. Ranger School. Being wounded. All had prepared me for this final ascent.

At midnight, we began.

We roped ourselves together and moved forward, headlamps illuminating the way. We took what was known as the Disappointment Cleaver route to the peak. The way ahead was the most rugged stretch of terrain I'd ever seen. We eased our way forward up the slope, working our way around gorges and sheets of brittle ice and crevices that dropped vertically for thousands of feet. I thought of Ryan doing this without his eyesight, and I marveled at him and this achievement.

At this altitude, the oxygen levels decrease significantly. The lack of oxygen tires you out and makes moving an effort. Exert too much and you can pass out from anoxia.

I kept going even as I coughed and hacked and shivered from a raging fever. The way upward was even tougher now.

I wanted to live my old life again. I wanted to be operational. Life doesn't always end up the way we planned, but what you do with the adversity thrown in your path will always be yours to control.

The snow grew deeper, the ice slick and treacherous. We moved with slow deliberation, careful where we put each step. It was impossible to get my breath at this altitude through the coughing fits, but I drove on.

Come dawn, the morning sun revealed the summit, snow shining in the new day's light.

I staggered along, lightheaded and bone weary until we reached the peak. The celebration was short lived for me. I sank into the snow and with the last bit of energy I had, I pulled from my backpack two items. One was a navy SEAL flag. I unfolded it, and someone snapped a photo of me, Dave, and Sam holding it.

I didn't have the strength to enjoy the view. I glanced around and couldn't even muster a sense of awe at the incredible sights around me. Nature's splendor played out from horizon to horizon. So few had the will to take on a challenge like this, let alone the skill or resolve to complete it. Ryan had all those things and more. In the end he was unable to witness its splendor. Yet he lived more fully than most with sight ever try.

I sat in the snow and tucked my flag away, leaving only one small item in my hands. I released my fist and looked down at it.

My Trident. I carried it in Ryan's honor.

Someday, I would take it to Ryan's daughter and tell her what her father meant to me. She never had the chance to meet her dad; he died while Kelly, his wife, was pregnant with her.

I held the Trident in my hand and had a friend take a picture of it. This golden emblem had driven my life. I focused on it. I coveted it. I became enamored by it. I almost lost it and then earned it back before I sacrificed my body for it. Only then did I finally understand what it truly represented. It carried the spirit of warrior poets like Mike Murphy, Mike Monsoor, and Chris Kyle. It carried the spirit of my friends Ryan Job, Adam Brown, Mike McGreevy, Kevin Houston, and the seventy-nine other men who have made the ultimate sacrifice for freedom and the brotherhood since 9/11.

The wind picked up and whistled around us. The others in our party stared out at the majestic view. I closed my eyes and turned within. I didn't know why God spared me. But I did know I would find a way into the future where I would use each day to honor my brothers who had not made it home.

How that would look was undefined in my mind. Ryan created a new life for himself from the ashes of his old one. I had to do the same. And on that slope, I finally accepted that my old mission of kicking down doors had truly come to an end.

What next?

Wounded Wear was growing, and I had found meaning in its purpose. Maybe this mission would become my new normal.

At fourteen thousand feet, as near to God as I had ever climbed, I drifted off to sleep. All too soon, though, my brother warriors awoke me. We needed to begin our descent. I wrapped the Trident up and placed it in my backpack. I may not have known exactly what the future would hold, but I did know one thing for sure. The way home was clear.

Epilogue

Virginia Beach
Spring 2013

I lie awake next to Erica, my eyes boring holes in the darkness of our suburban bedroom. The clock beside us on the nightstand reads 4:30. In her sleep, Erica presses close against me for warmth, and the feel of her brings a sense of comfort in an otherwise difficult moment. I run my hand gently over her shoulder. She stirs, but does not wake. My rock, my Spartan wife. She never once has failed me even through the worst life could throw at us.

What would have happened if I had not had her waiting for me when I came home from Iraq? If she had served me papers as I lay in the bed at Bethesda, as so many other wounded warriors have experienced, I'm not sure if I would have survived the trials I faced. Without Erica, my new life would never have taken root and flourished. I'd be nothing more than a statistic: a survivor of combat and the enemy, only to be killed by my many wounds back here at home.

The clock ticks off another minute. Sleep is elusive. I have been here for hours, watching each minute come and go in the dim blue glow of those digital numbers. I can't help it. Some nights are like this—not as many as there once were, but still enough to make me realize that no matter how far along in the healing process, the wounds will always run deep.

My chest feels tight; my mind refuses to shut off. It replays things I have no wish to experience again. Sometimes it is the crack of a bullet just missing my head. Sometimes it is the tortured screams of our dying enemy. There are times when I have no sympathy and feel a vengeful thrill as I hear his final earthly words. In other moments, my sense of humanity returns and fills me with immense sorrow as I recognize all the death I have experienced at such a young age.

These are the invisible wounds of war. Every warrior who has faced the fires of armed conflict carries some of it home from battle. Some struggle more than others, but we all face a new fight at home. Long after Iraq and Afghanistan are distant memories in our national consciousness, we who fought America's enemies will battle on in this invisible and intimate war.

I am one of the fortunate ones. My inner demons plague me only occasionally now. When they rise from the depths of my memories, they do so in the darkest hours of the night. And so, I lie there, my mind battling them back, taking heart from the things that have redrawn the landscape of my life and given me renewed purpose.

My family and Wounded Wear are the twin foundations of my new life. Every day, I find myself learning new things about the kids. I watch them develop and succeed. We have celebrated those successes, consoled them in their setbacks. I have found meaning in helping guide them to their own path. Where a few years ago, my weekends were filled with kicking in doors and bringing down bad guys, now I'm more likely to be out on the soccer field, cheering my kids on. The GoPro cameras so many of us wore on our helmets, I now have strapped to goalposts. I want to be able to relive and share all of my children's scoring moments.

I check the clock. Two more minutes have glowed and passed. The night will not end. I need sleep, as today is sure to be crazy busy. One of Wounded Wear's biggest events is set to start this morning. We call it Jumping for a Purpose.

Without Wounded Wear, I'd have a hard time beating back the demons. I've been to over fifty funerals of fellow SEALs, almost all of whom I knew on some personal level. Some I called friends—a word I never take lightly. I've hammered my Trident into too many coffins not to wonder why God spared me when so many other better men have died in our country's name.

Wounded Wear became the answer to that question. Born from anger after all the stares I had received in airports, the organization grew into something far more significant, thanks to Erica's steady and creative hand. We started with a few T-shirts that we shared with fellow wounded warriors that bore slogans like SCARRED SO THAT OTHERS MAY LIVE FREE. Since then we've turned Wounded Wear into a professional, nonprofit organization with national reach. Our mission is to help wounded warriors, their families, and the families of the fallen. We help them rediscover the hero within them through the clothing we produce, the clothing modifications we make for those who have lost limbs, and through our empowering events. Our goal is to transform their dedication, service, and experiences into a national dialogue, one that generates respect and honor for these incredible men and women. At the same time, we hope to empower them and show them that their wounds do not have to control their lives. They are the masters of that.

Tyler Southern, one of Wounded Wear's first wounded warrior hires, embodies that spirit. Though he lost both legs, an arm, and two fingers to an IED in Afghanistan, his humor and indomitable nature have inspired everyone who has met him. In every moment, he embraces life and knows only one speed: full throttle. In the years that I have known him, I've never seen him let his wounds dictate what he can and cannot do. He has struggled every day—even the basics of life so many take for granted have become daunting mountains for him to climb—yet he has never lost his composure or good humor.

We were at a concert together a few months back, and some drunk tripped over his prosthetic legs with such sudden force that it flipped Tyler sideways. As he fell, his other prosthetic limb smacked the drunk in the chops, and he went down hard too. Tyler hit the concrete so violently I thought for sure he was hurt. Nope. He rolled over, got his prosthetic legs back under him, and got right back up, and the only thing he talked about was how great it felt to bust that idiot in the jaw.

His wife, Ashley, comes to every event with Tyler, and their story never ceases to have an effect on those who meet them. They'd known each other in high school but had never dated, though Tyler harbored a secret crush on her. When he came home from Afghanistan and was lying in a Bethesda hospital bed, Ashley wrote him an emotional letter of how hard it hit her when she learned of Tyler's grievous injuries. He had his mother read that letter over and over for days. Later, when he returned home, Ashley came to see him, and the two connected in a way few couples I've seen have. They married about a year later.

Tyler just told me the other day that Ashley's expecting. I've never seen him so excited. Hell, I'm excited for him. The world better stand by for the child of Tyler Southern, for he or she will take this world by storm.

I look at the clock. Ten more minutes have passed. Might as well get up. I slip out of bed, careful to not wake Erica. After five years of surgeries and recovery, I have become a shadow of the man I once was physically.

Time to change that.

No excuses. Tyler has never made any. Neither has Michael Schlitz, a US Army Ranger I have gotten to know through Wounded Wear. He'll be skydiving with us today at our Jumping for a Purpose event. During his last Iraq tour, Mike's vehicle was hit by the particularly insidious type of IED called an EFP, which I mentioned earlier. Basically, these Iranian-built weapons spray molten metal and shrapnel through even the heaviest armor we can produce. When the EFP struck Mike's rig, it took both his arms off below the elbow and burned over ninety-five percent of his body. Mike was the only one in the vehicle to survive.

He never made any excuses. Today, he will show thousands of our guests that indomitable will to conquer life as he, a slightly banged-up man, leaps from a perfectly good airplane.

I thought of him as I struggled to put on my Wounded Wear Sprawl workout shorts. The arthritis in my left arm and elbow throbbed with pain. It always does until I can get the blood flowing a bit. The cool night air often makes it ache, and this spring morning had a chill to it. I know I will never be able to do some of the things I used to do. When those bullets struck me, they forever changed my physical capabilities. But like Tyler and Mike have shown, that will never be an excuse to stop trying. Settling will never be an option. If we are to thrive, wounded warriors must always strive to find their new hundred percent, then push beyond it to expand the boundaries of our lives. That will always be a part of my new sense of normal.

I pause by the door and see Erica one last time. It never ceases to amaze me how peaceful she looks in repose. Even in sound sleep, her radiance shines through. How many women would have kissed me that night at Bethesda when my nose was gone and the tubes were sticking out in all directions?

We'll get through this together, babe.

Only her.

Professions of loyalty mean nothing until tested by life's challenges and circumstances. I have found that words are cheap, and the most heartfelt professions of devotion mean nothing if not followed through. We never talk about our love or relationship much, but we have always shown each other how we felt. Together, we conquered our challenges, and through those fires was forged an even deeper bond.

In the hallway now, I walk quietly past the kids' rooms. Their doors are open, and I can hear their soft breathing in the darkness. It causes me to stop and listen for a minute. The sound makes me smile, and I feel the night's demons recede. Years ago, I would not have even noticed this gift. Now I feel gratitude. God gave me these moments and denied them to so many of my brothers. I will never take them for granted again.

I walk downstairs and find myself in the front room, where I always put my shoes on. I glance up from tying their laces and catch sight of the wooden Trident hanging behind my bar.

Erica gave it to me years ago after we were first married. Two feet wide, crafted by hand from rich, dark South American wood, the level of detail the artist devoted to it has never ceased to inspire comments from visitors to our home. In a few months I will retire from the navy with almost twenty-one years of service to our nation. As I look at the Trident I think of how that emblem and what it represents to me has changed over the years.

As a kid, I saw it as a symbol of fierce action and adventure, of valorous American battles, worn by the best warriors history has ever seen. Today, I see the Trident much differently. I still believe it represents everything that is right with America and one of our most elite warrior classes, but I no longer see ferocity. I see restraint. I no longer see it heavily armed to ruthlessly attack America's enemies. I see it as a protector, ready to defend our people and our way of life when called upon. To wear the Trident means you have a clear understanding of what it is to lead other men into battle who also wear this insignia, always recognizing that some of them may not make it home.

Above all else, when I look at the Trident now, I see a tempered sorrow. When I was younger, all I wanted to do was have that emblem adorn my chest. Now I have witnessed it adorn dozens of caskets for my teammates, and I truly believe it humbly recognizes this tremendous responsibility to honor these men who chose this path so much greater than themselves.

If you look at any other official US insignia featuring the American eagle, the eagle holds his head high with pride. The US Navy SEAL Trident is the only emblem in the US military to bow its head. When I was younger, I was too young and immature to even see it, much less understand it. Now I fully understand. I have physically felt the pain of loss as I tacked my Trident into my brothers' caskets. These were all men I knew. Men who, like me, strived for excellence and sometimes fell short. Who willingly entered the lion's den night after night and sometimes did not come back out.

The Trident to me now is the symbol of ultimate sacrifice.

I set off on my morning run through the still and silent streets of our neighborhood. In a few months,

I'll be a civilian for the first time in my adult life. I know I will miss Naval Special Warfare, and I know that once I do leave, I will feel severed from the brotherhood. That will be the toughest transition to make.

But I will follow my new plan. I used to kick in doors and take down bad guys; now I plan to kick down the doors to people's minds. I will go forward with that as my new mission. Wounded Wear will always be part of that, but I have also begun speaking around the country, relaying the hard lessons I have learned from my mistakes and immaturity: lessons in leadership, communication, teamwork, and overcoming adversity. I speak about these lessons, and the responsibilities that are vested in these roles. In the years ahead, I will speak of my experiences as cautionary tales; I wish somebody had shared those lessons with me when I was younger. Maybe my road would have been easier.

I want to speak to motivate, to inspire and educate, and to talk about the gift of life. About never taking it for granted. I've had opportunities to do so, and I've found meaning and purpose in talking to my fellow Americans about this gift and the sacrifice and devotion that have sustained our nation through even its darkest hours.

Above all, in the years ahead, I'll do everything I can to show our nation that the American Dream still burns bright. We veterans have always believed in it, have defended it, and have given our lives for the ideals it represents. In return, we ask only that our country-men and -women listen to our experiences and appreciate what we have sacrificed so that all Americans can be given a chance at that dream. Hard work, tenacity, and a will to overcome—those are the keys to success. With them, you can accomplish greatness here in the United States of America.

Every wounded warrior and family of the fallen questions what he or she has given up at some point in their recovery.

Was my sacrifice worth it? Do my fellow Americans recognize what I have lost so they can live in peace and freedom?

In the years ahead, I intend to motivate as many people as I can to answer those questions for our wounded and fallen warriors. The Vietnam generation suffered terri-bly because so much of the country rejected their devo-tion and suffering. The Korean veterans were ignored, and they spent their postwar decades forgotten in the shadows of the Greatest Generation.

Neither mistake can ever be allowed to happen again. That has become my vision, my mission. God granted me a second chance at life, and this will be how I use it.

Every day, I will do my best to honor my brothers who came home. And especially the ones who did not.

The sun blooms full over America's eastern shore. I run toward it, knowing no matter how long and dark the night is, the sun, eventually, always will rise. Tomorrow always will come. It may not be the tomorrow you wanted or hoped for, but it will come. It is up to you to be ready for it, to shape it and make it what it will be. You can't change the past but you control your future as long as you're willing to . . .

OVERCOME

There is nothing in life that cannot be overcome if you're genuinely willing to try and never quit.

LIVE GREATLY

Lift up those around you, always give back, climb a mountain, jump from a perfectly good airplane, and never pass up life's opportunities.

LOVE DEEPLY

In the end the only thing you will have left are the relationships you forged and sustained in life.

STAY HUMBLE

Pride has destroyed more men than all wars combined.

LEAD ALWAYS

True leaders lead at all times regardless of the situation they are in and who's watching.

If you follow these principles, when your hour is called, you can go, knowing you had . . .

NO REGRETS
Long Live the Brotherhood.
JCR

Acknowledgments

J ason Redman:
   This book would not have been possible without
the support of my friends, family, and colleagues.

First and foremost, I want to thank my Spartan
wife and best friend, Erica. You have been beside me
through everything life has thrown at us and never
batted an eye. My story is as much yours as it is mine,
and I am thankful you encouraged me to write this
since I got the opportunity to tell the world how amazing you truly are.

To my incredible children: my man cub, Phoenix;
my angel, Angelica; and my princess, Mackenzie—your
love brought me home and sustained me through some
of the darkest hours of deployments, being wounded,
and my recovery. I hope this book lets you know how

much I love you and how grateful I am that God gave me a second chance to watch you grow up.

To my father, Roger Redman, thank you for telling me about the SEAL Teams and setting the example with your love of country and military service. Thank you also for teaching me how to be a godly man. I did not always walk this path and still struggle from time to time, but you have always set the example as an honorable, godly man. Thank you for raising me that way.

To my mother, Colette Redman, thank you for always supporting me and my dreams. You never dissuaded me from my heroic visions, even though I am sure it was tough to stomach the thought of your son risking his life in a dangerous career. I don't know if I would be a SEAL today if you had not encouraged me to come to Florida my senior year when I was in danger of losing my way. You helped ignite that fire by driving me to the UDT/SEAL museum and never stopped encouraging me to train harder and never back down as I aspired to achieve my dreams.

I want to thank my stepmom, Betsy Redman, for helping to raise me and putting up with my obnoxious behavior as an unruly teenager. Having grown up on a farm, you showed me how to work hard, and the benefits of physical labor. Although I didn't realize it at the time, I enjoyed the time we spent together and have no doubt the work we did in the woods and fields of North Carolina helped prepare me for the hard work and physical labor of the military.

I wish to express thanks to my brothers and sisters, Selby, David, and Renee. Selby and David, both of you went on to be a part of the warrior class also, and I am immensely proud of both of you carrying on the family tradition. Renee, thanks for always supporting and caring about me, and always calling to check on me.

To my swim buddy and best friend, Gremlin. You are the epitome of loyalty and true friendship, never judging me for mistakes I made or allowing my head to get too big with my successes. You are not mentioned in this book for the world couldn't handle the fraternity pledging, fights when you were the only one to get arrested, Halloween nights evading the police, and attempts to find my truck at Red Lobster. You once said, "I'm the only reason you ever got commissioned." There is no doubt some truth in that, my friend, and I thank you for it.

I want to thank my other two best friends, Bison neck man and the Matador. We grew up as enlisted SEALs together and became officers together, making mistakes and learning what it was to lead men of this caliber. Both of you stood by me in some of my darkest times, and I thank both of you for your loyalty and dedication. Both of you continue to excel in the path we all set out to accomplish. I look forward to a time in the near future when you are both commanding officers.

I wish to thank the following people for helping me become a SEAL: Ricky Scott and Henry Horne. Ricky, with your passion for all things Special Operations, you eagerly shared everything you had with me, which helped shape my future. And Henry, I don't know where you are out there, but I would not be a SEAL today if you had not believed in that skinny kid who kept coming into the recruiting office. Thanks for your military service and friendship.

Erica and I are forever grateful to the following people who helped keep our family together by taking care of the kids after I was wounded and providing world-class support while we traveled across the country putting Humpty Dumpty back together: Erica's mom, Debbie, who made the trip to Virginia Beach on a regular basis to take care of the kids; my mom, Colette, and Erica's dad, Craig, for all the time they spent at our home keeping the kids and Erica's zoo on schedule and adhering to a sense of normalcy for the almost four years Erica and I traveled back and forth; and my favorite aunt Patty and cousin Sara who were always there for Erica and me through the entire recovery and still are today.

We also want to recognize an amazing American patriot, John Vigiano, of the New York Fire Department—and all the amazing support the New York Fire Fighters have given to us and our children over the years—as well as the Chicago Fire Department, specifically Tommy and Jimmy Gorman, Pat Maloney, Pat McCauley, and Art Aranda. Thanks for everything you guys did to take care of Erica and me during all the time we spent in Chicago.

I wish to thank everyone in the SEAL Teams whom I had the honor to work alongside and who helped grow me into the man I am today. To Captain Vince Peterson—you are one of the greatest leaders I ever had the honor to work with. Thanks for always setting the example and saving my career when I was too dumb to do it myself.

To the men of One Troop: J.P.—thanks for giving me a chance when you knew the baggage I carried coming back from Afghanistan. You were a great mentor, leader, and friend. Al and Pat—thanks for being great friends throughout the workup and deployment, and, Al—thanks for running forward to drag me out when I moved too slow. To the rest of the men of One Troop: Thanks for giving me a second chance. You were the greatest task unit and platoon I ever worked with in my entire career, and I was honored to live, train, and fight alongside all of you.

To Commander George Walsh: Thanks for giving me a second chance and believing in me.

And to all the members of the US Navy and SEAL Teams I worked alongside my entire career—the operators, the sled dogs, the pipe hitters, and the knuckle draggers. To the door kickers, the long gunners, and the silverbacks. To the goat locker, the cake eaters, the head shed, the pencil pushers, the paper shufflers, and the desk jockeys. To the spooks, the intel weenies, the secret squirrels, and the analysts. To the hackers, the computer geeks, the frequency hoppers, the communicators, and the store keepers. To the pecker checkers, the bubble heads, the glass bedders, and the sear filers. To the building sheriff, the grease monkeys, the wrench turners, the builders, and the hammer swingers. Thanks for everything.

I wish to express profound thanks and recognize the tremendous medical care provided by all of National Naval Medical Center Bethesda, the SEAL Teams Medical and Rehab Departments, Baltimore Shock Trauma, Johns Hopkins, and St. Joseph's Hospital. Specifically I'm grateful to all the doctors, nurses, corpsmen, therapists, and staff who began the long process of putting Humpty Dumpty back together again. Personal thanks and recognition to: Dr. Dan Valaik, Dr. Thomas Gwinn, Dr. Thomas Hines, Dr. Robert Walton, Dr. Eduardo Rodriguez, Dr. Andy Eglseder, Dr. Ashley Schroeder, and Dr. Alan Lim. Thanks to all my amazing nurses of 5 East: Brandi Epperson, Julie Zelman, Anna Karlowizit, and Crystal Bathon.

To the amazing support of the Care Coalition: Jim Lorraine, Korrina Donald, Dan Thompson, Marty Thompson, and Brandon Soleau. You took phenomenal care of Erica and me and made incredibly complex and trying situations easy to deal with while knocking down red tape like it didn't exist.

Last to thank on my medical team is Stu Bender—thanks for getting me back in shape and pushing me to the edge.

I'd like to recognize my creative writing teacher from Boca High, Mrs. Martin, who created a lifetime love of writing and poetry. Mrs. Martin, I probably never would have started writing about this journey I walked if it hadn't been for your class.

I want to recognize my staff and all the volunteers as well as the dedicated patriotic Americans who have helped support Wounded Wear and given me a new mission in life. I'd specifically like to thank those individuals who were there from the beginning: Joe and Danita Jacobs, Paul Ekoniak, and Jimmy and Kristina Halleran. Thanks to all of you for helping to fulfill my mission.

I want to recognize my newfound friend, fellow warrior, and author Sean Parnell. Sean, you have been a tremendous resource for all things related to this process and have helped me as I walked this uncharted path that you had already traveled. We share a mutual passion now to support wounded warriors and preserve American values and the American Dream, and I look forward to working together with you in the future.

Thanks to my agent, Jim Hornfischer, for believing in my humble story and helping me navigate these uncharted waters.

To David Highfill and the amazing staff at William Morrow. Thanks for taking a chance with my journey. Thanks for the guidance, the edits that helped smooth our story, and for all the support William Morrow has put behind the publication.

Last but not least, to my new friend and talented co-author John Bruning. John, *The Trident* is a story of my learning to lead and overcoming adversity. You have been through your fair share of adversity as we wrote this and I know at times it took everything in you to drive forward. We make a great team, as you took my story and crafted it into words that successfully captured the complicated issues from my relationship with Erica to what it is to be a part of this brotherhood of warriors. As we say in the navy to highlight a job well done, Bravo Zulu, my friend.

John Bruning:

Jay and Erica, you have been such an inspiration to me that it is hard to articulate the ways in which your example has changed my own life. When we first met, and I heard the story of how Erica responded to seeing you there in the hospital bed at Bethesda, Jay, I knew I wanted to help give voice to your life and experiences. That moment was pivotal to me when we first talked. It highlighted the true nature of this book: it is a love story above all else. After the hell of Katrina and my experiences in Afghanistan, I've learned that love like what you and Erica have is a woefully short commodity in this world. Your story is one of devotion and inspiration, not violence and hate. More than anything, I wanted to write *that* story with you both. Thank you for letting me take part in this journey.

To David Highfill: your presence, experience, guiding hand, patience, and support have been vital these past months. Working with you has been a tremendous pleasure, one of the highlights of my professional life. I am looking forward to the time when we can sit down in New York and finally meet face-to-face. I am grateful for all you have done for me and my family.

Jessica Williams and the rest of the team at Morrow—you are all consummate, dedicated pros. It has been a joy to work with you.

To Jennifer, when I've gone to ground to write during these frenzied last twenty-four months, you've always shouldered more of the burden here in Independence. Thank you for giving me the freedom to operate with your willingness to step up and carry the load so I could concentrate on writing. That logistical support has been essential throughout my career, and you've never received enough credit for that. Thank you for all you've done, and thank you for being such a tremendous, loving mother to our children. They are outstanding human beings thanks to your guidance and example.

While writing this book, my daughter, Renee, underwent neurosurgery at Oregon Health Sciences University to have a cyst in her brain removed. Jay sent Renee a laminated color copy of the Sign on the Door, along with several photographs and morale-boosting goodies. Renee kept that sign up in the ICU throughout her recovery. As a result of Jay's incredible kindness and consideration, Renee took an abiding interest in *The Trident* and the writing process. Many times, I sat down with her and my son, Eddie, and read the latest chapters and listened to their reactions. Ed and Renee, you're part of this crazy process of mine now. Thank you for all the love, support, devotion, and morale-boosting moments you have given me over the rough road we've walked together these past eighteen months. Know that you two are essential to me, and I have been amazed and so full of pride as you've gone forward down your own life paths, already so full of achievement and success. I love you with all I've got, even if I sometimes forget to tell you.

Ed, I look forward to more California road trips with you in the months ahead as I slow my pace to be with you and Renee more. The Reno air races need to become another yearly ritual, as Chino will for sure. You've got WWII aviation in your blood, and being named after a P-40 pilot and battlefield surgeon turned out to suit who you have become perfectly. Both men would be full of pride for how you've chosen to lead your life.

When Allison Serventi Morgan and I met at Redwood Junior High School, Quarterflash was on Billboard's top forty and *Endless Love* was in the theaters. Allison has been my reader, my adviser, and editor (*Heart for the Fight*'s copyedits never would have been finished without her), and a collaborating writer on articles and my pictorial book, *Battle of the Atlantic.*

Your eye for detail, your dedication to the craft, and your support for me through ups and downs has been significant to me these past years. I am a better writer thanks to you and the inspiration you give me. In the latest hours of the night, you're always willing to read the day's pages despite all the million things you face in your daily grind after the sun comes up. Thank you for everything you've shared and done for me.

Jordan Morgan, your interest in SEAL operations helped propel me forward throughout this project, and more than once I paused to recall your thoughts on how *Outlaw Platoon* was written. Thank you for the inspiration, and I am looking forward to hearing your review of the *The Trident* when you finish reading it.

To Jeff Pullman, I owe you a debt of thanks. When the chaos of the world needed to be shut out, I retreated to your cabin and focused alone in the woods on every word and page. Your place was the most important geographic spot for the writing process of *The Trident,* though I wrote it in many locales including Capitola, California, and my hometown of Saratoga. Thank you for the use of such a beautiful refuge.

To Jim Hornfischer, my agent: thank you for introducing me to Jay. You have a knack for pairing me with incredible human beings, and when I look back in my dotage, I'll take great pride in the opportunities you have given me. Thanks to you, I've been able to do what I love the most. The other day, Renee came up to me and said, "Do you have any idea how cool it is to have a writer for a father?" Without you, that moment would never have been. Thanks for changing the arc of my life these past seven years. I will always be grateful.

Last, Specialist Taylor Marks, whenever we do meet again, thanks to projects like *The Trident* I'll be able to look you in the eyes and tell you I lived by your example. I never left anything in the tank; I swung for the fence with every at bat. I live for you, and carry your spirit with me as the most precious part of my heart. RIP, my 973rd brother. As long as I am alive, I will make sure you will never be forgotten.

THE NEW LUXURY IN READING

We hope you enjoyed reading
our new, comfortable print size and found it
an experience you would like to repeat.

Well – you're in luck!

HarperLuxe offers the finest in fiction and
nonfiction books in this same larger print size and
paperback format. Light and easy to read, HarperLuxe
paperbacks are for book lovers who want to see
what they are reading without the strain.

For a full listing of titles and
new releases to come, please visit our website:

www.HarperLuxe.com

SEEING IS BELIEVING!